Bryn Thomas was born in Zimbabwe, where he grew up on a farm. His wanderlust began early with camping holidays by the Indian Ocean in Mozambique and journeys to game parks in other parts of Africa.

Since graduating from Durham University with a degree in anthropology, travel on four continents has included a Saharan journey in a home-built kit-car, a solo 2500 km Andean cycling trip and 40,000km of rail travel in Asia. In 1989 his first guide, the *Trans-Siberian Handbook*, was shortlisted for the Thomas Cook Guidebook of the Year Awards. He has travelled widely on the Indian subcontinent and is co-author of Lonely Planet's *India - a travel survival kit*. He is also a co-author of *Britain - a travel survival kit*.

He first trekked in Nepal in 1983 and has since visited the Annapurna region six times.

Trekking in the Annapurna Region
First edition 1993
Second edition 1996

Publisher Trailblazer Publications
The Old Manse, Tower Rd, Hindhead, Surrey, GU26 6SU, UK
Fax (+44) 01428-607571

British Library Cataloguing in Publication Data
Thomas, Bryn
 Trekking in the Annapurna Region. -
 (Nepal Trekking Guide Series)
 I. Title II. Series
 915.49604

ISBN 1-873756-07-0

Edited by Patricia Thomas
Typesetting by Anna Jacomb-Hood
Maps and index by Jane Thomas

Photograph opposite p32 copyright © Jamie McGuinness 1996

Photographs opposite p64, p96, p97, p197 copyright © Henry Stedman 1996

Photograph opposite p225 copyright © James Powell 1993, 1996

Text and all other photographs copyright © Bryn Thomas 1993, 1996

Every effort has been made by the author and publisher to ensure that the information contained herein is as accurate and up-to-date as possible. However, the
author and publisher are unable to accept responsibility for any inconvenience,
loss or injury sustained by anyone as a result of the advice and information given
in this guide.

Set in Times and Helvetica by Trailblazer Publications, UK
Printed and bound by Technographic Design & Print, Colchester, Essex, UK

TREKKING
IN THE
ANNAPURNA
REGION

B R Y N   T H O M A S

with additional research by

H E N R Y   S T E D M A N

NEPAL TREKKING GUIDES

For Jane

Acknowledgements

It takes more than one person to compile a comprehensive and accurate guide-book. I am greatly indebted to the numerous people who have helped me with the research and execution of this project through its two editions. First, I'd like to thank my sister for the long hours spent drawing and updating the route maps (without which this guide would be incomplete) and also for compiling the index. Thanks to Henry Stedman for braving the monsoon leeches and updating the Pokhara and Annapurna Sanctuary sections and for the photographs on p64, 96-7 and 197. I'd also like to thank my mother for her thorough editing of the text and Anna Jacomb-Hood for typesetting.

Thanks to James Powell for the photograph opposite p225 and for coming along on the first research trip; Tara Winterton for the language section, for contributions to the text; and Rosemary Higgs for explaining Bagh Chal.

I'd also like to thank Jamie McGuinness for the photo opposite p32 and for information on the Tilicho Tal route, Chris Beall for much useful update information, Lilli Eriksen and Torben From (Denmark) for information on the Begnas Tal to Khudi route, Simon Cohen (UK) for the detailed ornithological information, and Liz Hamilton and Mân Um (UK) for help with the Pisang High Route.

For help and suggestions on a variety of subjects I'd like to thank Anne Tiede and Greg Whiteside (Nepal), Carol Stone and Neil Cunningham (UK), Andrew and Caroline Blatter (UK), Heather Oxley (Japan), Vijaya Shakya (Nepal), Brigu Raj Kanal (Nepal), EP Morgan (UK), Steffen Graupner (Germany), Theo Kiewert, Andi Hindle (UK), Cassie Cleeve (Australia), Peter Knowles (UK), Suzanne McMaster, Eric Shumway, Dave Donsky and Jon Moon (USA), Kevin Peakman (UK), Judy Pettigrew (Nepal), Sharon Hepburn (Nepal), Tim Webster (Australia), Eaddy Roe (USA), Dr David Nixon (New Zealand), Bhakti Hirachan, ML Pradhan and Dev Singh Gurung (Nepal), Anita Chandler at Intermediate Technology (UK), Johnnie Woods at KEEP (UK), Barry Arthur (Australia) and Hum Bahadur Gurung at ACAP (Nepal).

Thanks to the numerous people I've trekked with over the years for their ideas and suggestions, particularly Fiona (Fe) and Anna Saunders (NZ), Kerry Brady (USA), Mary Ogden (USA), Bryan and Teresa Bass (Canada), Barnaby Gibbons (UK), Anders Ekspong and Ann Thors (Sweden), Henny Boer, Carla van Klaveren and Annet Marsman (Netherlands), Sally Fraser and Fiona McPherson (UK), Rambahadur Thakuri (Nepal), Jim Blilie and Jeff Mellor (USA), Kirsten Claus (Germany); Charlie Colville, Juliet Bray and Judy McNeile (UK), Dennis Lützow (Germany) and Manmahadur (Nepal).

A request

The author and publisher have tried to ensure that this guide is as accurate and up-to-date as possible. However things change quickly in this part of the world. Prices rise, new lodges are built and trails are rerouted. If you notice any changes or omissions that should be included in the next edition of this book, please write to Bryn Thomas c/o of the publisher (address on page 2). A free copy of the new edition will be sent to persons making a significant contribution.

Front cover: On the trail between Manang and Thorung Phedi.

CONTENTS

INTRODUCTION

The history of trekking in Nepal is surprisingly short. Until 1948 the borders of this mysterious Himalayan kingdom remained firmly closed to outsiders and the race to climb Mt Everest, which had begun in the 1920s, was conducted from Tibet. As the first mountaineers entered the country reports of their exploits were widely publicised. The first peak over 8000m or 26,000ft to be climbed was Annapurna, by Frenchman Maurice Herzog in 1950. Everest was conquered by Edmund Hillary and Tenzing Norgay with a British team in 1953.

The ensuing blaze of publicity focussed world attention on Nepal and in 1955 Thomas Cook organised the first guided tour to Kathmandu. The tourists were welcomed and entertained by Boris Lissanevitch, the legendary White Russian who ran the only Western-style hotel in the country. They were met by King Mahendra who is reported to have watched in disbelief as the tourists haggled amongst each other to buy up all the curios they were shown. The King immediately recognised a source of foreign exchange of rich potential and the experiment in tourism was declared a success. An industry was born that is now the country's top foreign currency earner.

While Boris Lissanevitch is often credited with being the father of tourism in Nepal, the man who initiated the sport of trekking is Colonel Jimmy Roberts. He led a small party of American tourists on a short trek in 1964, with porters, tents and all the paraphernalia of a mountaineering expedition. This set the style for guided treks and is essentially how they are organised today. The word 'trek' is derived from the 'Vortrekkers', the Dutch pioneers who travelled across South Africa in their ox-carts.

The trekking routes themselves are nothing new, having existed as a network of paths ever since there have been people in the mountains. Some, such as the trail up the Kali Gandaki, are old trade routes leading to Tibet. For as long as there have been traders driving their pack animals along these routes there have been *bhattis*, tea-houses where they could get a meal and spend the night. Discovered by budget travellers in the 1960s, tea-house trekking is now the most popular way to trek in Nepal.

Had Robert Louis Stevenson lived today and had the opportunity to go trekking his 'To travel hopefully is a better thing than to arrive' might well have emerged as that favourite misquotation, 'It is better to travel than to arrive'. Trekking is most emphatically, are not about arriving; the interest and enjoyment is along the way. Trekking is about walking at whatever speed suits you, slow or fast, for as many or as few hours per day as give you time to enjoy the scenery and to experience something of the culture; here an ancient, Tibetan culture. There could surely be no better place to do this than among the highest mountains and deepest valleys in the world, with some of its most friendly and welcoming people.

PART 1: PLANNING YOUR TREK

With a group or on your own?

To travel properly you have to ignore external inconveniences and surrender yourself entirely to the experience. You must blend into your surroundings and accept what comes. In this way you become part of the land and that is where the reward comes.
Dame Freya Stark

The modern trekking holiday has evolved from the Himalayan mountaineering expeditions of the first half of this century. It is hardly surprising, therefore, that the two basic types of treks to choose from today reflect the styles of these early expeditions.

Most expeditions were grandiose affairs involving enormous quantities of equipment and armies of porters to carry it. The packing-list for Maurice Herzog's 1950 Annapurna Expedition ran to 50,000 items. There were, however, a few mountaineers (Eric Shipton, for example,) who preferred to travel light and live off the land, like the local traders who travelled along the many trade routes to Tibet.

Today's trekkers have the choice of joining an organised trek with accommodation in tents and everything carried by a team of porters or travelling independently, staying in *bhattis* (tea-houses or lodges) along the main routes. They may carry their own packs or employ a local porter.

TEA-HOUSE TREKKING

Carrying your own pack and eating and sleeping in village tea-houses is the cheapest way to trek. On a very tight budget it would be possible to get by on as little as £3.50/US$5 a day. A daily budget of £6.50/US$10 would be better and £10/US$15 would be difficult to spend.

Since the route up the Kali Gandaki has been an important trade route for centuries, the network of lodges is well developed in the Annapurna region but things have been changing fast on the bhatti scene recently. When the first few hippies stumbled into the lodges in Tatopani in the late 1960s, they could expect nothing more than *daal bhat* (rice and lentils) and a place by the fire to unroll their sleeping bags. There are still some basic places like these to be found but most resourceful lodge-owners have adapted their premises and services to the needs (or whims?) of the modern Western traveller. Often lavatories are still just a hole in the ground but there has been some advance in sewage disposal and some lodges have even installed flushing Western-style sit-down loos. In many places hot showers and varied menus are available. There are now some lodges that are more like small hotels than traditional tea-houses.

The pros and cons

Apart from being cheap, the advantages of tea-house trekking are that it is easy to arrange (just get a trekking permit and hit the trail), and that it allows you to stop where you want and make changes to your itinerary as you wish. Since you're using local services, more of the money you spend stays in the local economy. Staying with Nepali families gives you more of an insight into the country and its people than you might get on an organised trek, sleeping in tents.

The main drawback to tea-house trekking is that it is confined to the main routes and at the height of the season on the main trails the lodges can be quite crowded.

Guides and porters

A **guide** is really not necessary since most routes are easy to follow and local people are helpful over giving directions. A guide can, however, greatly increase cultural appreciation and interaction with local people by explaining things and acting as interpreter. On the main trails, however, most of the lodge owners speak English.

Not many independent trekkers employ a **porter**, which is a pity. If you can afford £3-5/US$5-8 a day, then it's a good idea to employ someone locally (see p85 for how to go about it). Apart from the advantage of taking a load off your back, the money you spend directly benefits the local economy. Another option is the **porter-guide**, who speaks good English and will carry a light pack but charges a little more than a porter. Nepalis are unable to understand why Westerners who earn in a year what few Nepalis could earn in a lifetime seem to prefer to carry their packs themselves. You should not feel in any way guilty about employing a porter or porter-guide – quite the reverse, in fact.

On the trail with a trekking group

A typical day on the trail with a guided trekking agency begins with a cup of tea in bed ('bed-tea'), followed by a bowl of hot water for washing. After a good breakfast (usually including porridge or muesli, and eggs), the day's trek begins.

Group members carry only a small day-pack, containing camera, documents, water-bottle and jersey. The pace is usually leisurely, allowing kitchen staff to race ahead to prepare another meal at the designated lunch spot. A couple of hour's walking follows and the group arrives at the next camp well before sun-down. This allows time for relaxing and taking in the spectacular scenery, writing up diaries or, for those with excess energy to work off, games of volley-ball or frisbee. After a large dinner most people are in bed by about nine.

GUIDED TREKKING GROUPS

The early Himalayan mountaineers would recognise and, no doubt, approve of the style of the modern guided trekking groups. Accommodation is usually in tents and food prepared in the camps, so large numbers of porters are required to transport everything.

Although levels of service vary from agency to agency, if you book a trekking holiday through an agency in your country you can usually expect a representative from the company to be always on hand from the moment you arrive at the airport.

Where to book – at home or in Nepal?

The alternatives are booking through a trekking agency in your country (addresses listed below) or, once you've arrived, with a Kathmandu- or Pokhara-based agency. Trying to make arrangements with a Nepalese agency from abroad by phone or fax can be difficult.

Booking a trek once you've arrived in Nepal is a cheaper option than signing up abroad. You will, however, need to allow at least four days to make arrangements.

If you're pressed for time, it's better to book with a travel agent at home or go tea-house trekking.

The pros and cons

Most people sign up for a guided trek because it is easy to arrange. Some, however, may be doing so because they don't realise that arranging a tea-house trek themselves is really very easy. Others join guided treks because of the higher levels of comfort and food that are offered (except with the cheapest agencies).

Although most guided treks in the Annapurna region follow the standard tea-house trekking routes some adventurous agencies offer itineraries off the beaten track, a few of which include high altitude routes and even a little mountaineering. If you're interested in climbing one of the trekking peaks (see p85) in the Annapurna region, probably the best way to do it is to join a guided trek operated by an adventure travel company. Perhaps the biggest advantage of joining a guided trek is to get away from the standard routes: easy to do since you're camping.

The main drawbacks to the guided trek are that it is more expensive than tea-house trekking; that by staying in tents rather than lodges you have less contact with village Nepalis; and, of course, you are stuck with a fixed itinerary.

In theory, trekking with an agency should be more environmentally friendly than tea-house trekking since groups are required to use kerosene rather than precious firewood. In practice, if kerosene is used at all it will only be for the group members, not for the porters. If kerosene is provided for them, they may save it to sell after the trek.

TREKKING AGENCIES

Outside Nepal there are many specialist agencies offering guided treks in the Annapurna region. Treks range from a few days to several weeks and may include sightseeing in the Kathmandu Valley, river-rafting trips, and visits to Chitwan National Park. Most agencies have a representative company in Nepal.

Trekking agencies in the UK

Most prices include return airfares from London and all accommodation in Nepal, usually in tents. A few operators have started offering guided treks with accommodation in tea-houses. Prices are £1100-£1400 for a three-week trip. It is, however, just as easy (and cheaper) to arrange these yourself in Nepal.

Prices for fully-guided treks with accommodation in tents are £1500-£1900 for 24 days including the Annapurna Circuit and around £1700 for 21 days with the Annapurna Sanctuary. Several operators now feature treks to Mustang for about £2800 for 24 days. Note that the number of days spent trekking is about five to seven fewer than the total tour length.

Adventure trekking agencies offer some interesting routes that may include some mountaineering. Some, for example, combine the Annapurna Circuit with a climb of the trekking peak, Chulu East (6200m/20,305ft) – 30 days for about £2200.

• **Classic Nepal** (☎ 01773-873497, fax 01773-590243) 33 Metro Ave, Newton, Derbyshire, DE55 5UF, features a good mix of standard routes and adventure treks including Mustang. Trekking peaks include Chulu East and Pisang Peak.
• **Encounter Overland** (☎ 0171-370 6845, fax 0171-244 9737) 267 Old Brompton Rd, London SW5 9JA, offers guided treks in the region.
• **Exodus Expeditions** (☎ 0181-675 5550, fax 0181-673 0779) 9 Weir Rd, London SW12 OLT, have a wide range of guided treks with accommodation in tents or tea-houses.
• **ExplorAsia/Abercrombie & Kent** (☎ 0171-973 0482, fax 0171-730 9376) Sloane Square House, Holbein Place, Sloane Square, London SW1W 8NS offers a large selection of standard and adventure routes.
• **Explore Worldwide** (☎ 01252-319448. fax 01252-343170) 1 Frederick St, Aldershot, Hants GU11 1LQ, offers a number of treks.
• **Foreign Window** (☎ 01584-874031, fax 0584-874983) Burway House, Ludlow, Shropshire SY8 2BN, runs the luxurious Laxmi Lodge (see p134), used by Abercrombie & Kent and Cox & Kings. Foreign Window can also arrange upmarket tailor-made treks in the area.
• **Guerba Expeditions** (☎ 01373-858956, fax 01373-858351) Wessex House, 40 Station Road, Westbury, Wilts BA13 3JN, lead small group treks off the beaten track in the Annapurna region.

• **Himalayan Kingdoms** (☎ 01179-237163, fax 01179-74493) 20 The Mall, Clifton, Bristol BS8 4DR, have several treks in the region, including Mustang. Their expeditions section (☎ 01142-763322) organises more ambitious trekking and mountaineering holidays.
• **Himalayan Quest** (☎ 01926-450835) 12 Euston Place, Leamington Spa, Warks CV32 4LY.
• **KE Adventure Travel** (☎ 017687-73966, fax 017687-74693) 32 Lake Rd, Keswick, Cumbria CA12 5DQ) offers several guided treks including the Mustang trek.
• **Ker & Downey** (☎/fax 01737-373566)18 Albemarle St, London W1X 3HA, maintain that 'adventure does not have to mean hardship' and offer short treks with accommodation in their own well-appointed lodges (Birethanti, Ghandruk and Dhampus).
• **Naturetrek** (☎ 01962-733051, fax 01962-733368) Chautara, Bighton, Nr Alresford, Hampshire SO24 9RB offer bird-watching tours in the area, covering the Kali Gandaki, Marsyandi or Mustang.
• **OTT Expeditions** (☎ 01142-588508, fax 01142-551603) 62 Nettleham Rd, Sheffield S8 8SX, is a mountaineering and adventure trekking company. They lead trekking peak expeditions in Nepal but not always in this area. They do, however, have two guided treks in the Annapurna region.
• **Sherpa Expeditions** (☎ 0181-577 2717, fax 0181-572 9788) 131a Heston Rd, Hounslow, Middx TW5 ORD, have over 20 years experience in Nepal and a wide range of guided treks.
• **World Expeditions** (☎ 01628-74174, fax 01628-74312) 7 North Rd, Maidenhead SL6 1PL feature a range of standard treks plus a 25-day trek around Dhaulagiri.
• **Other operators** offering tours in the Annapurna region include **Bales Tours** (☎ 01306-885923, fax 01306-885991) Bales House, Junction Rd, Dorking, Surrey RH4 3HB; and **Ramblers Holidays** (☎ 01707-331133, fax 01707-333276) Box 43, Welwyn Garden City, Herts AL8 6PQ.

Trekking agencies in Continental Europe
• **Austria   Okistra** (☎ 0222-347526) Turkenstrasse 4, A-1090 Wien. **Supertramp Reisen** (☎ 01222-5335136) Helferstorfer St 4, A-1010 Wien.
• **Belgium   Connections** (☎ 02-512 50 60) Kolenmarkt 13, rue Marche au Charbon, Brussel 1000 Bruxelles, with branches in Antwerpen (☎ 03-225 31 61), Gent (☎ 091-23 90 20) and Liege (☎ 041-22 04 44). **Joker Tourisme** (☎ 02-648 78 78) Boondaalsesteenweg 6, Chaussee de Boondaal 6, Brussel 1050 Bruxelles. **Divantoura** (☎ 03-233 19 16) St Jacobsmarkt 5, 2000 Antwerpen. **Roadrunner** (☎ 03-281 16 50) Belgielei 209, 2018 Antwerpen. **Divantoura** (☎ 091-23 00 69) Bagattenstraat 176, B-9000 Gent.

• **Denmark Green Tours** (☎ 33-13 27 27) Kultorvet 7, DK-1175 Kobenhavn K. **Inter-Travel** (☎ 33-15 00 77) Frederiksholms Kanal 2, DK-1220 Kobenhavn K. **Marco Polo Tours** (☎ 33-13 03 07) Borgergade 16, 1300 Kobenhavn K. **Topas Globetrotters** (☎ 86-89 36 22) Skaersbrovej 11, 8680 Ry.
• **Germany Explorer** (☎ 0211-379 064) Huttenstrasse 17, 4000 Dusseldorf 1. **SHR Reisen** (☎ 0761-210 078) Kaiser Joseph Strasse 263, D-7800 Freiburg.
• **Iceland Icelandic Student Travel** (☎ 01-615656) V/Hringbraut, IS-101 Reykjavik.
• **Ireland Maxwells Travel** (☎ 01-779 479) D'Olier Chambers, 1 Hawkins St, Dublin 2. **Funtrek** (☎ 01-733 633) 32 Batchelors Walk, O'Connell Bridge, Dublin 1.
• **Italy CTS** (☎ 06-46791) V. Genova 15, 00184 Roma.
• **Netherlands NBBS** (☎ 071-22 1414) Schipholweg 101, PO Box 360, 2300 AJ Leiden. Branches in Groningen (☎ 050-126 333), Amsterdam (☎ 020-20 5071), Utrecht (☎ 030-314 520) and Rotterdam (☎ 010-414 9822). **De Wandelwaaier** (☎ 020-622 6990) Herngracht 329, 1016AW Amsterdam. **Terra Travel** (☎ 020-275129) Singel 190H, 1016AA Amsterdam. **Royal Hansa Tours** (☎ 050-127799) Stoeldraalerstraat 11, 9712 BT Groningen.
• **Norway Terra Nova Travel** (☎ 47-2 42 14 10) Dronningens Gate 26, N-0154, Oslo 1. **Eventyrreiser A/S Adventure Travel** (☎ 22-11 31 81) Hegdehaugsvn 10, 0167 Oslo.
• **Spain Expo Mundo** (☎ 03-412 59 56) Diputacion, 238 Stco, 08007 Barcelona.
• **Sweden Aeventyrsresor** (☎ 08-654 1155) Hantverkargaten 38, PO Box 12168, S-102 24 Stockholm. **Himalayaresor** (08-605 5760) Box 17, S-123, 21 Farsta.
• **Switzerland S.S.R.** (☎ 01-242 30 00) Backerstr. 52, CH 8026, Zurich. **Suntrek Tours** (☎ 01-462 61 61) Birmensdorferstr. 187, CH-8003 Zurich. **Case Depart Voyages** (☎ 021-311 13 61) Avenue de Bethusy 4, Case Postale 107, CH-1000, Lausanne 4.

Trekking agencies in the USA
North American trekking agencies quote land-cost only but are generally of a high standard. They range from a few days in the Annapurna foothills for US$900 to US$1500-2000 for the Circuit (28 days). Treks that include some climbing cost from US$2500 to more tha US$3500. Some US companies sell cheaper 'no frills' trekking holidays for UK or Australian trekking agencies.
• **Above the Clouds Trekking** (☎ 508-799 4499, fax 797 4779) PO Box 398, Worcester, MA 01602.

• **Adventure Center** (☎ 415-654 1879, ☎ 800-227 8747, fax 654 4200) 1311 63rd St, Suite 200, Emeryville, CA 94608 – agents for Explore (UK).
• **Geeta Tours & Travels** (☎ 312-262 4959) 1245 West Jarvis Ave, Chicago IL 60626.
• **Himalayan Travel** (☎ 800-225 2380, fax 203-359 3669) 2nd Floor, 112 Prospect St, Stamford CT 06901 – agents for Sherpa Expeditions (UK).
• **InnerAsia** (☎ 415-922 0448, ☎ 800-777 8183) 2627 Lombard St, San Francisco, CA 94123.
• **Journeys** (☎ 313-665 4407, ☎ 800-255 8735, fax 665 2945) 4011 Jackson Rd, Ann Arbor, MI 48103. Also includes some family treks.
• **Ker & Downey** (☎ 713-744 5260, fax 744 5277) 13201 NW Fwy, Suite 850, Houston Texas 77040-6096. Upmarket treks, see K&D UK, p13.
• **Mountain Travel & Sobek Expeditions** (☎ 510-527 8100, ☎ 800-227 2384) 6420 Fairmount Ave, El Cerrito, CA 94530. Upmarket treks.
• **Narayan's Gateway to Nepal** (☎ 303-440 0331, fax 440 6958) 948 Pearl St, Boulder CO 80302 is run by a Nepalese family based in Colorado and Kathmandu. Study programmes are offered.
• **Overseas Adventure Travel** (☎ 800-221 0814) 349 Broadway, Cambridge MA 02139 offers a number of treks in this area.
• **Safaricentre** (☎ 310-546 4411, ☎ 800-223 6046, fax 546 3188) 3201 N Sepulveda Blvd, Manhattan Beach, CA 90266 – agents for Exodus (UK).
• **Wilderness Travel** (☎ 510-548 0420, ☎ 800-368 2794) 801 Allston Way, Berkeley, CA 94710.

Trekking agencies in Canada

•**Adventure Centre** (☎ 416-922 7584) 17 Hayden St, Toronto, Ontario M4Y 2P2.
• **Canadian Himalayan Expeditions** (☎ 800-563 8735, fax 416-360 7796) 2 Toronto St, Suite 302, Toronto, Ontario M5C 2B6. This is one of the few Canadian companies that run their own treks, rather than acting as agents for other companies.
• **Mountain Travel & Sobek Expeditions** (☎ 604-876 5511) 101 511 West 14th Ave, Vancouver BC V5Z 1P5, offers upmarket treks.
• **Market Square Tours** (☎ 800 661 3838) 54 Donald St, Winnipeg, Manitoba, R3C 1LC – agents for Exodus (UK).
• **Travel Cuts**, also agents for Exodus (UK), have offices in **Edmonton** (☎ 403-488 8487) 12304 Jasper Ave, Edmonton, Alberta, T5N 3K5, **Toronto** (☎ 416-979 8608) 187 College St, Toronto, Ontario M5T 1P7 and **Vancouver** (☎ 604-689 2887) 501 602 West Hastings St, Vancouver BC, V6B 1P2.
• **Trek Holidays**, agents for Explore (UK), have offices in **Calgary** (☎ 403-283 6115, 336 14th St NW, Calgary, Alberta T2N 1Z7), **Edmonton**

(☎ 403-439 9118, 8412 109th St, Edmonton, Alberta T6G 1E2), **Toronto** (☎ 416-922 7584) 25 Bellair St, Toronto, Ontario M4Y 2P2 and **Vancouver** (☎ 604-734 1066), 1965 West 4th Ave, Vancouver BC V6J 1M8.
• **Worldwide Adventures Inc** (☎ 416-963 9163, from USA ☎ 1-800-387 1483) 920 Yonge St, Suite 747, Toronto, Ontario M4W 3C7 – agents for World Expeditions (Australia).

Trekking agencies in Australia
• **Adventure World** has branches in **Adelaide** (☎ 231 6844, 7th floor, 45 King William St, Adelaide SA 5000), **Brisbane** (☎ 229 0599, 3rd floor, 333 Adelaide St, Brisbane Qld 4000), **Melbourne** (☎ 03-670 0125, 3rd floor, 343 Little Collins St, Melbourne Vic 3000), **Perth** (☎ 221 2300, 2nd floor, 8 Victoria Ave, Perth WA 6000) and **Sydney** (☎ 956 7766, toll free 008-221 931, 73 Walker St, North Sydney, NSW 2059).
• **Ausventure** (☎ 02-960 1677, fax 969 1463) Suite 1, 860 Military Rd, (PO Box 54) Mosman, NSW 2088. This long-established adventure travel company offers a comprehensive range of treks.
• **Back Track Adventures** (☎ 07-368 4987) 226 Given Terrace, Paddington, QLD 4064.
• **Exodus Expeditions** (☎ 02-552 6317) 81A Glebe Point Rd, Glebe, NSW 2037 – agents for Exodus (UK).
• **Outdoor Travel** (☎ 03-670 7252, fax 670 3310) 55 Hardware St, Melbourne, Vic 3000 – agents for Sherpa Expeditions (UK).
• **Peregrine Adventures** is a Nepal specialist with branches in **Melbourne** (☎ 03-663 8611, fax 663 8618, 2nd floor, 258 Lonsdale St, Melbourne, Vic 3000) and **Sydney** (☎ 02-241 1128, 5th floor, 58 Pitt St, Sydney, NSW 2000) and offers a good range of treks.
• **Peregrine Travel** (08-223 5905) 192 Rundle St, Adelaide, SA 5000.
• **Summit Travel** (☎ 09-321 1259) 1st floor, 862 Hay St, Perth WA 6000.
• **World Expeditions** (☎ 02-264 3366, fax 261 1974) 3rd floor, 441 Kent St, Sydney NSW 2000. The main competition for Peregrine. As well as range of standard treks, some climbing expeditions are offered.

Trekking agencies in New Zealand
• **Adventure World** (☎ 09-524 5118, 0800-652 954, fax 520 6629) 101 Great South Rd, Remuera, PO Box 74008, Auckland – agents for Exodus and Explore (UK).
• **Suntravel** (☎ 09-525 3074, fax 525 3065) PO Box 12-424, Penrose, Auckland – agents for Peregrine Adventures (Australia.)
• **Venture Treks** (☎ 09-379 9855, fax 770 320) PO Box 37610, 164 Parnell Rd, Auckland – agents for Sherpa Expeditions (UK).
• **Himalaya Trekking** (☎ 06-868 8595, 025-466 465), 54a Darwin Road, Gisborne.

Getting to Nepal

BY AIR

Carriers that fly into Nepal include the national airline Royal Nepal, Lufthansa, Singapore Airlines, Thai, Pakistan International, Indian Airlines, Bangladesh Biman, Aeroflot, Dragonair (Hong Kong), Druk Air (Bhutan) and China Southwest Airlines. Royal Nepal and Indian Airlines operate international flights daily, Thai five times a week, and the other airlines each average two flights a week.

Kathmandu is the only international airport in the country.

From the UK
• **Airlines and routes** The **shortest** route is on Royal Nepal's direct London-Kathmandu flight with short stops in Frankfurt and Dubai. Modern Airbuses are used and they're maintained in Europe. The flights are fully booked months in advance for the high (Oct/Nov) season. Lufthansa's in-flight service is rather more superior but their flights require a change in Frankfurt. The **cheapest** flights are with Aeroflot and Bangladesh Biman but changing planes in Moscow or Dacca will add hours to the journey time. Usually each operates only one flight a week and delays are all part of the service. Biman may require you to stay overnight in Dacca on the return journey. If so you should ensure that your ticket includes hotel accommodation or they may try to charge you at the airport.

Flying **via India** is now less popular since the number of airlines flying into Kathmandu has increased as has the price of the Delhi-Kathmandu sector (see below). In the high season, however, this may be your only option.

• **Travel agents and prices** For up-to-the-minute prices check the travel pages of the Sunday newspapers or magazines like *Time Out* since prices vary considerably according to the season. As well as phoning several travel agents, it's sometimes worth trying airlines or main agents direct: Brightsun Travel (☎ 0171-287 4949), 4 New Burlington Street, London for Royal Nepal; **Aeroflot** (0171-493 2410).

Sample return London-Kathmandu fares are currently £400-425 on Aeroflot, £370-499 on Biman, £555-£698 on Lufthansa, £525-£673 on Royal Nepal and £529-£598 on Pakistan International.

Recommended travel agents to try include: **Quest Worldwide** (☎ 0181-547 3322, 29 Castle St, Kingston, Surrey KT1 1ST) for a good price on the Aeroflot ticket; **Trailfinders** (☎ 0171-938 3366, 42-50 Earls Court

Rd, London W8 6EJ; ☎ 0161-839 6969, 58 Deansgate, Manchester M3 2FF; or ☎ 0141-353 2224, 2 McLellan Galleries, Sauchiehall St, Glasgow) offering good deals on Biman; **Travel Cuts** (☎ 0171-255 2082, 295 Regent St, London W1); **STA Travel** (☎ 0171-937 9962, 74 Old Brompton Rd, London SW7 3LQ) and **Campus Travel** (☎ 0171-730 8111 or 0131-668 3303).

From USA & Canada

The Sunday newspapers are a good source of information for cheap flights from North America. Travel agents to try include **STA Travel** (branches in many cities) and in California, **Overseas Tours** (☎ 800-323 8777, 475 El Camino Real, Rm 206, Millbrae, CA 94030) have been recommended. Most flights go via Bangkok and many require an overnight stop there. Expect to pay from about US$1200 round trip to Kathmandu from the west coast, US$1500 from the east.

In Canada try **Travel Cuts** with branches in Edmonton (☎ 403-488 8487, 12304 Jasper Ave, Edmonton, Alberta, T5N 3K5); Toronto (☎ 416-979 2406, 187 College St, Toronto, Ontario M5T 1P7) and Vancouver (☎ 604-681 9136, 501 602 West Hastings St, Vancouver BC, V6B 1P2).

From Australasia

Cheapest routes are also via Bangkok and cost A$1600-2000 return. Travel agents to try include **STA Travel** (☎ 02-212 1255, 1 Lee St, Railway Square, Sydney) and **Suntravel** (☎ 09-525 3074, PO Box 12-424, Penrose, Auckland).

From Asia

• **India** You can fly into Kathmandu from Delhi (£95/US$142) on Royal Nepal or Indian Airlines daily, from Varanasi (£48/US$71) daily and from Calcutta (£64/US$96) on Tuesday, Thursday, Friday and Saturday. Student/youth discounts of 25% are applicable. The Patna-Kathmandu flight, discontinued for several years, is now operated by Royal Nepal.
• **Tibet** The Lhasa-Kathmandu flight (£127/US$190) on China Southwest Airlines might be convenient if you're visiting Nepal via China. There are flights both ways on Tuesday, Thursday and Saturday.
• **Thailand** Prices on Bangkok-Kathmandu flights are currently around £130/US$200.
• **Singapore** The best deal from Kathmandu to Singapore is on Singapore Airlines, at £194/US$290.
• **Hong Kong** Prices are around £186/US$280 to Kathmandu.

OVERLAND

• **From the UK** The classic route to Kathmandu is, of course, the overland route. Doing it yourself is still possible (via Bulgaria, Romania and

Hungary to by-pass European hot spots around Bosnia). The UK operator, Encounter Overland (see UK trekking agencies above), offers an 11-week package in purpose-built trucks from £1650. Dragoman (☎ 01728-861133) is another overland operator.

• **From India via Sunauli/Belahiya** The most popular overland route to Nepal is via Gorakhpur and the Sunauli/Belahiya border post. On this route you could bypass Kathmandu entirely (although it's a fascinating city well worth a visit), and catch a direct bus to Pokhara from the border. Beware of ticket touts in Delhi, Varanasi and Gorakhpur who will try to sell you 'through' tickets to Kathmandu or Pokhara. Everyone has to change buses at the border anyway so there's no such thing as a 'through' ticket. Doing things yourself gives you a choice of bus from the border and is cheaper.

It's best to travel by train from Delhi to Gorakhpur ($14^1/_2$ hours, about £2.50/US$4 in 2nd class). The bus journey between Varanasi and Gorakhpur (Katchari bus station) takes $6^1/_2$ hours. Buses to Sunauli go from Gorakhpur's other bus station, near the railway station. If you want to catch the day bus to Pokhara or Kathmandu to arrive at the border in time you'll have to take the 5.00 am bus from Gorakhpur which reaches Sunauli in three hours. There are, however, many other Gorakhpur-Sunauli buses throughout the day.

Visas (US$25 for 30 days) are available at Sunauli. The border post is staffed from dawn to dusk, although you're allowed to walk through at night to stay in the cheap hotels on the Nepalese side (better than the choice on the Indian side). Don't continue into Nepal without getting your passport stamped next day or there may be serious problems when you try to get a trekking permit in Kathmandu or Pokhara.

From Sunauli, buses to Kathmandu (£1.25/US$2, taking 12 to 14 hours) leave between 5am and 9am for the day service. Night buses depart between 3.30pm and 8.30pm. The best day-bus to get is the government 'Sajha' bus but this leaves only from Bhairawa (4km from Sunauli) at 6.30am and 7.30am for Kathmandu. Buses to Pokhara (£1/US$1.50, 8 to 10 hours) leave Sunauli from 5am to 9am and 3.30pm to 8.30pm.

• **From India via Raxaul/Birganj** The overland route through crowded and polluted Raxaul/Birganj is less pleasant and involves travelling via Patna in India. The bus journey between Patna and Raxaul takes 5 hours. Visas are available at the border. There are buses from Birganj to Kathmandu (£1.25/US$2, taking 10 to 12 hours) and Pokhara (£1.25/US$2, 9 to 11 hours). Buses to Kathmandu now travel via Narayanghat and Mugling rather than the shorter (and much rougher) Tribhuvan Highway via Naubise.

• **From India via Kakabhitta** Reputed to be one of the worst bus trips on the Indian sub-continent, the Darjeeling to Kathmandu route goes via Kakabhitta. The road is often washed away during the monsoon. Buses from Kakabhitta to Kathmandu (£3.25/US$5) take 16 to 19 hours.

• **From Tibet** In the 1980s the hip way to travel between Lhasa and Kathmandu was on a mountain bike. Chinese regulations governing the movements of foreigners in Tibet have always been in a state of flux, sometimes it's tour groups only, sometimes independent travellers. In 1994-5 quite a few independent cyclists made it through until, for the 'celebrations' of 30 years of Chinese rule in Tibet, the Chinese were letting in only groups. If regulations are relaxed a regular Lhasa-Kathmandu bus service may be initiated. There are regular overland tours between Kathmandu and Lhasa, easy to organise in Kathmandu (see p112).

Budgeting

It's hardly surprising that Nepalis consider Westerners to be made of money. Just one night in a suite in the Soaltee Holiday Inn Crowne Plaza in Kathmandu (£450/US$675) would cost the average Nepali four years' wages. Alternative accommodation is, however, available from as little as £0.65/US$1, so your holiday money can go a long way if you want it to.

Costs in Kathmandu
Budget hotels tend to be rather better value in Nepal than in India and it's possible to get a very basic room for just £0.65/US$1, or £3/US$5 for a double with attached bathroom. In a more upmarket hotel a comfortable double with attached bathroom and constant hot water would be £6-12/US$10-20.

In most Kathmandu restaurants you'll pay around £2-3/US$3-5 for an evening meal. Compared to food, beer is an expensive item at £1/US$1.50 a bottle, about the same as a main dish.

Apart from the hotels and restaurants, there are other drains on your resources in Kathmandu. In Thamel, the travellers' quarter, the streets are lined with shops selling a tempting array of souvenirs from woollen sweaters to prayer wheels. There are also some excellent bookshops here.

Costs on the trek
Few lodges charge more than £0.50/US$0.75 for a night although there are now four upmarket places in the region charging £3.50/ US$5.

Since everything has to be brought in by porters, food prices depend on how far a village is from the main road. Some sample prices for food in lodges are: daal bhat £0.30-0.60/US$0.50-1; porridge, omelette or apple pie £0.30/US$0.50 each; small bar of chocolate £0.25-0.50/ US$0.40-0.80; cup of tea £0.03/US$0.04; Coke £0.20-0.55/US$0.30-0.85. A daily budget of £3.50-5/US$5-7.50 should be adequate if you quench your thirst with water you've purified yourself, tea or the occasional Coke rather than with beer, which costs £0.60-1.20/ US$1-2 in the hills. Employing a porter will add £3-5/US$5-8 to your daily costs, if arranged locally.

Economise but don't penny-pinch

Many tea-house trekkers are travellers spending several months in Asia and trying to make their money last as long as possible. On a very tight budget, it would be possible to get by on less than £2.50/ US$3.75 per day, as some travellers do. Among them, however, you will always meet the ones that seem to have lost sight of the fact that they are on holiday. Every transaction becomes an aggressive exercise in seeing just how little they can pay. I once met a couple who were trekking because it was cheaper than staying in Kathmandu and, sharing plates of daal bhat and bargaining even for their accommodation, they'd come to hate Nepal and the Nepalis. No doubt the feelings were mutual but the local people remained polite and good tempered.

If you're travelling on a very short shoestring give yourself occasional splurges and you'll find the trip much more enjoyable. Stay in dormitories and eat a basic diet for a few days then reward yourself with a private room and a slice of apple-pie or a beer. Taking along as little as £50/US$75 extra, the price of a few CDs in the West, could make all the difference to your holiday.

Your overall budget

Average daily budgets for shoestring travellers will work out at £5-10/US$7.50-15. Although this will be what you get by on for most days, you should take considerably more with you to allow for unforeseen circumstances (for doctor's fees or a flight if, for example, you are ill). You should also allow for any side trips (river-rafting or jungle safaris – see p112) which you might want to add on.

When to go

Before going on a journey, it is customary to consult an astrologer about the proper time for departure. The traveller takes some rice, one betelnut and one coin in a piece of cloth to ensure a successful journey. If, for any reason, he is unable to depart, this bundle is sent out of the house at the auspicious time determined by the astrologer.
Kesar Lall *Nepalese Customs and Manners*

The Annapurna region is one of the few trekking areas in Nepal where year-round trekking is not only possible but also enjoyable. The northern part of the region receives little of the monsoon rain since it's shielded by the Annapurnas and other ranges.

Mountain-viewing is a prime reason for going trekking, so it's not surprising that the most popular trekking seasons correspond to when the Himalaya are at their clearest and most dramatic and the weather is neither too cold nor too wet. These seasons are reflected in the following figures showing the numbers of tourists passing through Chomrong for the Annapurna Sanctuary (mid-1994 to mid-1995):

July (34)	November (2188)	March (1166)
August (131)	December (856)	April (1648)
September (572)	January (232)	May (940)
October (2423)	February (319)	June (150)

SEASONS
While Nepal has four seasons corresponding to the winter, spring, summer and autumn of Europe or North America the pattern of rainfall is very different. About 70% of the total annual rainfall occurs in the monsoon season, between June and September.

October and November
The post-monsoon season is the most popular time to go trekking. The atmosphere has been flushed clean by the rains leaving the mountains stunningly clear and the weather is still warm. Above 3000m/9843ft, however, the temperature will usually drop below freezing at night. The drawback is the fact that from mid-October until the end of November the trails are very crowded and lodges fill up early in the afternoon.

December to March
Early December is quieter than November, though cold at higher altitude. From mid-December to late February is the coldest time. The Thorung

La, the 5400m/17,769ft pass on the Circuit, may be closed by snowfalls for days at a time between January and March. If you plan to attempt a crossing in this season, ensure you are in a group of at least five people with adequate supplies in case you get stranded, and take local advice. Each year somebody dies up here either because they get caught in a storm or because they were overcome by the effects of the altitude (see p225) and were unable to descend on their own. The lodges in the Annapurna Sanctuary stay open as long as the path up is not blocked by

AVERAGE TEMPERATURES

Kathmandu (1336m/4383ft)

Month	Jan	Feb	Mar	Apr	May	Jun	Jul	Aug	Sep	Oct	Nov	Dec
min °C	-3	-2	2	5	9	11	18	13	12	7	2	-2
max °C	22	27	30	33	37	33	33	32	32	32	27	25
min °F	27	28	36	41	48	52	64	55	54	45	36	28
max °F	72	81	86	91	99	91	91	90	90	90	81	77

Pokhara (833m/2733ft)

Month	Jan	Feb	Mar	Apr	May	Jun	Jul	Aug	Sep	Oct	Nov	Dec
min °C	3	2	7	9	12	15	20	19	15	11	6	3
max °C	23	28	32	35	37	33	33	33	34	31	28	25
min °F	37	36	45	48	54	59	68	66	59	52	43	37
max °F	73	82	90	95	99	91	91	91	93	88	82	77

Gorkha (1200m/3937ft)

Month	Jan	Feb	Mar	Apr	May	Jun	Jul	Aug	Sep	Oct	Nov	Dec
min °C	3	4	7	10	11	14	17	15	12	9	8	5
max °C	22	26	32	34	34	34	33	32	31	29	28	24
min °F	37	39	45	50	52	57	63	59	54	48	46	41
max °F	72	79	90	93	93	93	91	90	88	84	82	75

Jomsom (2800m/9186ft)

Month	Jan	Feb	Mar	Apr	May	Jun	Jul	Aug	Sep	Oct	Nov	Dec
min °C	-4	-2	2	3	5	10	12	11	9	3	0	-3
max °C	13	14	14	22	25	27	27	27	25	22	16	14
min °F	25	27	36	37	41	50	54	52	48	37	32	27
max °F	55	57	57	72	77	81	81	81	77	72	61	57

Chame (2670m/8760ft)

Month	Jan	Feb	Mar	Apr	May	Jun	Jul	Aug	Sep	Oct	Nov	Dec
min °C	-4	-1	1	5	5	8	7	7	7	5	0	-5
max °C	10	14	15	22	22	23	23	22	20	19	15	12
min °F	25	30	34	41	41	46	45	45	45	41	32	23
max °F	50	57	59	72	72	73	73	72	68	66	59	54

As a rule of thumb, temperature decreases by 2°C or 3.5°F for every 300m or 1000ft of altitude gained. The highest places where you are likely to spend the night on a teahouse trek are at Thorung Phedi (4450m/14,600ft) on the Circuit and at Annapurna Base Camp (4130m/13,550ft) in the Sanctuary. In November at these altitudes you can expect temperatures at night to fall to minus 10°C or below.

snow. Avalanche danger is greatest on this route in the spring. Information about conditions is available in Chomrong. Between mid-March and mid-April is the best time to see the rhododendrons flowering in the forests around Ghorepani. The display is spectacular, whole hillsides aflame with the scarlet, pink or white blooms.

April and May

This is the second most popular trekking season and an ideal time to do the Annapurna Circuit. The high passes are usually free of snow and the mountain views are still clear in April although by May they're becoming increasingly hazy and may be obscured by the odd afternoon cloud. As the heat builds up on the plains with the approach of the monsoon, trekking at lower altitudes becomes uncomfortable.

June to September

The monsoon reaches the Annapurna region in mid-June and continues into September.

Trekkers have been put off coming to Nepal at this time by reports of torrential downpours, landslides and plagues of leeches. This is certainly true of the lower altitudes – the Pokhara area boasts the highest rainfall in the country and the rhododendron forests around Ghorepani are infested with leeches – but the higher, northern region is very different. Geographically, this area could really be included in Tibet; it lies in rain-shadow, protected by the mountains from the force of the monsoon. Monthly precipitation figures (rainfall) at the height of the monsoon average 800mm in Pokhara but only 50mm in Jomsom and 60mm in Marpha.

Trekking in this season has a number of things to recommend it. You meet few other trekkers on the trails and as the only foreigner in the lodge you're given special attention by the lodge-owners. There is an abundance of flowers and plant life, revitalised by the rains. This is the time of pilgrimage and festival. The annual horse race in Muktinath usually takes place in August and draws people from all over Mustang and Manang.

If you can afford to fly to Jomsom, you can avoid the lower altitudes and the monsoon. Flights to Ongre (Manang), however, are suspended during the monsoon. See p237 for some itineraries.

Senior trekking

In our fifties, we were proud to discover from the police checkposts that we were the oldest couple trekking independently. For really enjoyable senior trekking we suggest:
   1. Don't carry anything. Employ a porter or a porter-guide.
   2. Walk with a stick and take your time.
   3. Make frequent stops – a real 'tea-house' trek!

Lilli Eriksen and Torben From (Denmark)

Route options

The popularity of the Annapurna region with trekkers is entirely understandable. Amongst some of the most dramatic scenery in the world there are trekking routes to suit all seasons and levels of fitness.

The main trekking routes in the Annapurna region follow the two major river valleys (the Kali Gandaki and the Marsyandi) and the trail into the Annapurna Sanctuary via Ghandruk and Chomrong. As well as these main routes there are many alternative trails and short cuts offering trekkers numerous possibilities. The options are even greater for those with camping equipment who can explore some of the rarely-trekked high altitude routes.

Planning your route
Most people are constrained by time. A common mistake when route-planning is to try to pack in too much. Your trek, which should be a holiday and escape from the rigid schedules of work or study, then becomes a race against time. It's far better not to trek every day but have some rest days, not only to allow yourself to become acclimatised if you're walking at altitude but also to appreciate fully the places you're passing through.

Don't forget to allow for at least two nights in Kathmandu or Pokhara to collect your trekking permit and get ready for your trek, plus extra days if you're flying to or out of Jomsom or Ongde (Manang) in case planes are delayed.

THE ANNAPURNA CIRCUIT (16-21 DAYS)

This is the region's classic long-distance trek for which you'll need an absolute minimum of 16 days. Three weeks would be safer and more enjoyable. The route follows two river valleys, crossing between them over the Thorung La, at 5416m/17,769ft the highest pass on this trek. The best seasons for doing the trek are October to December and mid-March to May.

Clockwise or anti-clockwise?
Most people do the Circuit in an anti-clockwise direction because there's only limited accommodation (and then only during the trekking season) between Muktinath (about 1600m or 5300ft below the pass on the western side) and Thorung Phedi (about 966m or 3170ft below the pass on the eastern side). Crossing between the two is a long day whichever way you

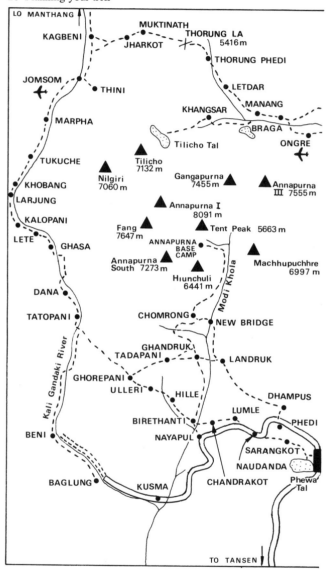

The Annapurna Region

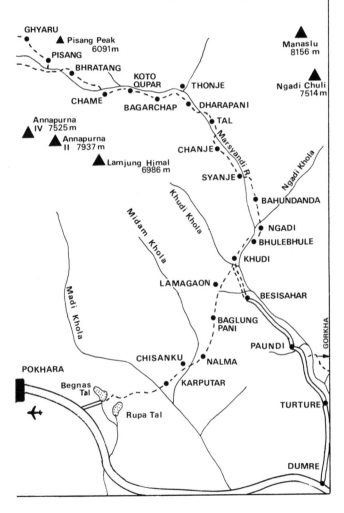

come but less strenuous from east to west. One advantage of doing the trek clockwise is that you'll be travelling against the flow, rather than with the same people each day. Outside the main seasons, though, this is a positive disadvantage on the dangerous pass. Safety in numbers.

The route
The traditional start of the trek is Dumre, a five-hour bus ride from Kathmandu along the road to Pokhara, although it's possible to walk from Begnas Tal (near Pokhara) to Khudi, adding another three days to the circuit. Few trekkers pass this way as the lodges are fairly basic and there are some steep climbs early on in the trek but the views are superb. See p230. The other alternative to Dumre is to walk from Gorkha (see p225). Most people still go via Dumre, from where trucks and buses run up the rough track to the roadhead at Besisahar. Trekkers follow the Marsyandi River up to the Manang Valley and Manang town, where they spend a day or two acclimatising before continuing to cross the Thorung La.

Muktinath, the first village west of the pass, is in a side valley leading to the Kali Gandaki River valley. The temples here have attracted both Buddhist and Hindu pilgrims for hundreds of years. Passing through the region's capital at Jomsom, trekkers follow the valley to Tatopani where most climb up the ridge to Ghorepani. It's possible to avoid the climb (although you will miss the superb view from Poon Hill) by continuing along the river to the roadhead at Baglung. The lodges along this route are fairly basic, though.

From Ghorepani the alternatives are to descend to Birethanti (you can catch a ride on a bus or truck to Pokhara from the road nearby) or cross the rhododendron forests to Ghandruk (and Chomrong for the Sanctuary) reaching Pokhara via Landruk and Dhampus.

Pros and cons
Varying in altitude between 445m/1460ft and 5416m/17,769ft, this is a strenuous trek passing through a tremendous range of ecological zones from sub-tropical to alpine. It is also culturally diverse and you'll meet Hindu Gurung and Magar people in the south, Buddhist Manangbhot and Thakali in the north.

The fact that it's a long trek is another plus since it takes a few days to get into the rhythmn of trekking. As it's a circuit, there's no need to backtrack.

THE ANNAPURNA SANCTUARY (9-12 days)

For those with less time the trek into the natural amphitheatre amongst the Annapurnas, known as the Sanctuary, offers stunning mountain views.

The trek requires a minimum of nine days but it's well worth allowing extra time so as to be able to explore the areas around the Base Camp and to take alternative routes back to Pokhara. In the winter the route into the Sanctuary may be blocked by snowfalls but as long as trekkers are getting through, a few lodges stay open; as they do during the monsoon. A maximum altitude of 4130m/13,550ft is reached on this trek.

The route
From Pokhara, trekkers take a bus or truck for the half-hour journey along the new road as far as Phedi and trek to Chomrong via Dhampus, Landruk and New Bridge. Chomrong is the gateway to the Sanctuary and has some excellent trekkers' lodges and superb views of the Annapurnas and Machhapuchhre. Between Chomrong and Annapurna Base Camp (4130m/13,550ft) in the Sanctuary are a string of lodges purely for the benefit of trekkers; there is little permanent habitation above Chomrong.

To leave the Sanctuary you must return to Chomrong along the same path, after which there are a number of options. If time is short continue through Ghandruk to Birethanti. From the road nearby you can return to Pokhara. With more time you can cross to Ghorepani from Chomrong, climb Poon Hill for the magnificent sunrise panorama and then either continue north up the Kali Gandaki to Jomsom or turn south to Birethanti and Pokhara.

Pros and cons
The dramatic mountain scenery is the reason for doing this trek. Standing in the middle of the Sanctuary, surrounded by towering snowy peaks, ranging from 6000m to 8000m (20,000ft to 26,000ft), is a truly awe-inspiring experience.

Against this, though, you get neither the cultural nor the environmental diversity of the Circuit or a trek to Muktinath. In fact, above Chomrong there is very little of cultural interest since all accommodation is purely for trekkers but the views once you reach Base Camp are compensation enough.

THE JOMSOM TREK (12-16 days)

This popular trek follows the old trade route along the Kali Gandaki River, part of the Circuit trek described above. The fact that this has been a trade route for hundreds of years means that the system of tea-houses is very well-developed. The friendly Thakali people who inhabit the area in the northern half of this trek are renowned for being accommodating hosts, ready to turn their hands to anything to satisfy the culinary tastes of their guests.

Jomsom has an airfield with daily flights by plane or helicopter to Pokhara and Kathmandu so, if you can afford it, you can cut several days off this trek and save backtracking. Be prepared for delays, though: flights do not operate when it is cloudy or windy.

The route

From Pokhara, you take a bus, truck or taxi to Nayapul, near Birethanti. Don't let the hard climb which follows to Ghorepani put you off this trek as it's otherwise very easy. You descend from Ghorepani to the Kali Gandaki at Tatopani, famous for its hot springs by the river. The trail follows the Kali Gandaki into the Buddhist villages of the north via the world's deepest valley between the 8000m+ peaks of Dhaulagiri and Annapurna I.

The surroundings change dramatically, the country becomes much drier and the river bed widens. There are some very pleasant places to stay here. Marpha, the Thakali village surrounded by apple orchards and just south of Jomsom, must be the cleanest village in the whole of the Annapurna region. From Jomsom, Kagbeni is a half day's walk north and is as far up the Kali Gandaki as you can go without a costly permit for Lo Manthang (see p32). From Kagbeni most trekkers walk up the side valley to Muktinath. Allow an extra 3-4 days for the return trip from Jomsom.

Pros and cons

The cultural diversity, good views, excellent tea-house accommodation and the fact that, apart from the climb up to Ghorepani, this is an easy trek all contribute to the popularity of this route. Its main drawback, in fact, is that it can be relatively crowded in October, November, March and April.

If you're not flying back from Jomsom, on the return journey you can avoid backtracking the whole way by continuing along the Kali Gandaki from Tatopani as described in the Circuit trek above.

SHORT TREKS (3-9 days)

There are a number of short treks that can be undertaken from Pokhara any time between late September and May. Since they cover low to middle altitudes they can be followed even in January or February, at the height of winter. During the monsoon, however, these trails receive the full force of the rains and since they pass through perfect leech habitat (rhododendron forest) they are not much fun at this time of the year.

Luxury tea-house trekking

The building of four upmarket lodge-hotels, in Birethanti (Laxmi Lodge), just outside Birethanti (the Sanctuary Lodge), in Ghandruk (Himalaya Lodge) and in Dhampus (Basanta Lodge) means that this little circuit from Pokhara can be now be made with the comforts of tiled bathrooms with lashings of hot water, comfortable beds with clean sheets and cosy sitting-rooms equipped not only with roaring fires but also with copies of the *Tatler* and *Hello* magazine. Laxmi Lodge is usually reserved for clients of Foreign Window (see p12, and in Kathmandu ☎ 471630) and the other lodges for clients of Ker & Downey (see p13 and p15, ☎ 416751 in Kathmandu). Outside the high season, however, passing trekkers can rent rooms (about £5/US$7.50) when the trekking companies are not using the lodges.

The routes

• **Ghandruk Circuit (4-5 days)** For this popular short trek, take a bus, truck or taxi to Nayapul, a short walk from Birethanti. The route follows the Modi Kola and climbs to the prosperous Gurung town of Ghandruk. To reach Landruk across the valley a steep descent is required. Return to Pokhara via Dhampus and a bus, truck or taxi from Phedi. There's no shortage of accommodation (including the luxury lodges above) on this short trek and some good views towards the Annapurnas, particularly from Dhampus, Landruk and Ghandruk.

• **Poon Hill (3-4 days)** This view-point just above Ghorepani is a popular place to catch the sunrise panorama, with good views of Dhaulagiri (8167m/26,794ft) and the Annapurnas. In spring the rhododendrons are spectacular. It takes two days to reach Ghorepani from Pokhara, via Birethanti, and a day to return the same way.

• **Ghorepani-Ghandruk Circuit (6-7 days)** This trek combines the above two short treks, going via Birethanti to Ghorepani, then through the rhododendron forests to Tadapani and Ghandruk. You can return to Pokhara via Birethanti (saving a day) or via Dhampus.

• **Chomrong extension (+2 days)** If you can afford another couple of days, it's well worth continuing to Chomrong from Ghandruk for even closer views of the Annapurnas. The lodges in upper Chomrong turn out some of the best trekkers' meals in the region.

• **Return flights to Jomsom or Ongre/Manang (min 4 days)**
Flying in and out is one way to spend as much time as possible in these interesting northern areas. There are numerous day walks in both these valleys but the altitude would preclude anything too energetic for the first day or so. With several airlines now offering flights up here the area is developing fast and standards in some of the lodges are high.

SIDE TRIPS

Dhaulagiri Ice-fall (1 day from Larjung)
This day-trip up to the high altitude yak pastures (3800m/12,467ft) by the icefall below Dhaulagiri can be made from Larjung on the Kali Gandaki. There are superb views across the deep valley to the Annapurnas. See p150.

Tilicho Tal – tents required (3-4 days from Khangsar)

The trip up to this high altitude lake (5000m/16,404ft) and back to Khangsar, near Manang, may be completed in three days but only if you're very well acclimatised.

The army camp between the lake and Jomsom means that individual trekkers are not allowed to continue down from Tilicho Tal to the Kali Gandaki Valley but permission has recently been granted to some groups. It's a spectacular but much tougher alternative to the route over the Thorung La. See p216.

OTHER OPTIONS AROUND THE ANNAPURNA REGION

The Mustang Trek (14-18 days – groups only)

Tantalisingly sealed off from foreign trekkers until 1992, the upper reaches of the Kali Gandaki River above Kagbeni are now open for business – but at a price. Government restrictions have imposed not only a US$700 (£466) entry fee (for the first ten days, US$70 per day thereafter) but have also stipulated that only organised groups arranged through a trekking agency and complete with guide, porters and policeman will be allowed in. There can, however, be as few as just one member in the 'group'.

Most groups fly from Kathmandu to Jomsom before trekking through Kagbeni into north Mustang. The barren landscape is similar to that around Kagbeni. High winds race up the valley for much of the day weathering the sandstone into weird shapes. The trek passes through villages, each of which, like Kagbeni, has a crumbling castle and a Buddhist temple, to Lo Manthang, the region's capital. The return route is back the same way.

Only 1000 permits are issued each year and the attraction of being one of the first foreign trekkers to venture into Mustang fills the spaces available on organised treks. The drawback is the high cost and the fact that you can't do this as a tea-house trek. The less adventurous may find the wind annoying since driving sand permeates everything.

The Royal Trek

So-called because Prince Charles trekked this way in the 1980s, the Royal Trek is a 4-day, low altitude circuit from Pokhara east to Begnas Tal with night stops at Kalikathan, Shaklung, and Chisopani. Tea-house accommodation is basic; most people who do this walk are with guided trekking groups.

(**Opposite**) There's an austere beauty to the arid landscape of the upper Kali Gandaki. This is the world's deepest valley and at one point you stand 3½ miles (5½ km) below the summits of Dhaulagiri (8167m/26,794ft) and Annapurna I (8091m/26,545ft). (Photo: Jamie McGuinness).

Dhampus Pass

The return trip from Tukuche or Marpha to the top of this 5182m/
17,001ft pass takes 3-4 days. The panoramic views are spectacular. Take
camping equipment and a guide from Tukuche or Marpha.

Around Dhaulagiri

Via Dhampus Pass and the Hidden Valley and French Col, it's possible to
trek right around Dhaulagiri. This is, however, a much tougher proposi-
tion than the Annapurna Circuit, a true wilderness experience that passes
through stunning alpine terrain and links with the Kali Gandaki Valley at
Marpha and Beni. Guides, tents, ice axes and crampons are all required.
Several trekking companies advertise this trek.

Around Manaslu

Starting from Gorkha or Dhading, it's possible to trek around Manaslu in
about three weeks, joining the Annapurna Circuit at Thonje, between
Bagarchap and Tal. The area was opened, to group treks only, in 1991.
Permits cost US$90 per week in the main trekking seasons and the
restrictions applicable to the Mustang Trek (see p32) also apply here.

North Annapurna Base Camp

This trip to the Base Camp of the French expedition that conquered
Annapurna in 1950 takes 5-6 days from Lete. The views across the valley to Dhaulagiri are magnificent. Camping equipment is required. A
guide is recommended as the trail is difficult to follow.

Trekking peaks

Around the Annapurna Sanctuary are four peaks that may be climbed
with trekking peak permits. They are Mardi Himal (5588m/18,333ft),
Hiunchuli (6441m/21,132ft), Tent Peak (5663m/18,579ft) and Fluted
Peak (6501m/21,329ft). Accessible from the Manang Valley are three
other trekking peaks: Pisang Peak (6092m/19,987ft), Chulu East
(6558m/21,516ft) and Chulu West (6420m/21,063ft). For further information see *The Trekking Peaks of Nepal* by Bill O'Connor.

(Opposite) Top: DHC-6 Twin Otter STOL (Short Take Off and Landing) aircraft are
used on the landing strips in the mountains. In the Annapurna region there are services
to Pokhara, Jomsom and Ongre/Manang. **Bottom:** Mule caravans are still used to
transport goods up the valley between Pokhara and Lo Manthang.

What to take

The basic essentials
How much you take obviously depends on the type of trek you'll be doing, how high you'll be going and the season but, nevertheless, almost everyone seems to take far too much.

The key to sensible packing is to take just what you'll need to make yourself comfortable enough to enjoy the trek. What constitute the bare necessities varies from person to person and assessing your own needs is the difficult bit.

Independent minimalists on a short low altitude trek (Pokhara to Poon Hill to Ghandruk to Pokhara, for example) get away early or late in the season with just a day-pack containing water bottle and change of clothes. Travelling this light would be impossible in winter and would not be recommended in the main trekking seasons when lodges may not have enough quilts to go round. Most people, however, consider a sleeping-bag and a little more than just a change of clothes essential on a tea-house trek. If you're on an organised trek, companies usually provide a list of things you should bring.

In Kathmandu and Pokhara it's possible to rent down jackets, backpacks and sleeping-bags. These can also be bought there, new and second-hand but don't believe all the labels – some of the ruck-sacks are fakes, although perfectly serviceable. Some climbing equipment is also available.

What to pack it all in
Deciding what to pack your belongings in depends on your style of trekking but most people will find it comes down to three containers –

Pack in plastic
There's nothing more miserable after a day in the rain than a night in a damp sleeping-bag. With your gear packed into plastic bags this is entirely preventable. I once met a meticulous organiser who had packed everything into colour coded plastic bags labelled 'bedroom' (sleeping bag), 'dressing-room' (clothes), 'bathroom' (washing-kit/medical) and 'canteen' (trail snacks) – just slightly over the top but she did always seem to know where everything was and it all stayed perfectly dry.

A heavy gauge plastic bag to line the pack-back will protect against dust (on the road from Kathmandu or Dumre) and the odd shower of rain. It's also worth having a second strong bag to help protect your pack from nimble-fingered baggage-handlers on the flight out to Nepal. Most check-in counters are able to supply a roll of strong tape to secure it.

backpack/large hold-all, small day-pack and a hold-all to leave in Pokhara or Kathmandu. If you'll be carrying your pack yourself or arranging your own porter then it's worth buying a good quality, internal frame **back-pack**. Get one bigger than you think you'll need so you don't have to compress everything into it.

If you're on an organised trek a hold-all is as good as a backpack, since it'll probably be tied to the back of a mule or put in a porter's *doko* (basket). If the hold-all does not have a lock, sew on a small hoop at the zip end so a padlock can be attached. This is enough to discourage light fingers.

A **small day-pack** is vital for valuables (cameras etc) that you would not want to leave in your room when you come down to eat in your lodge. During the day it can be packed into the top of your backpack. On an organised trek a day-pack is essential for carrying your camera, water-bottle and anything else you may need while walking.

Most people find it useful to leave a **hold-all** at their hotel in Kathmandu or Pokhara, containing a change of clothes and other things they don't need while trekking. Hotel owners are usually happy to store things free of charge as long as you come back to stay with them after your trek.

Sleeping-bag

A good-quality bag is essential since, although some lodges do have quilts, they're usually in short supply in the high season, and they're often of dubious cleanliness.

A down-filled bag is preferable to a synthetic one because it is lighter and can be rolled up tighter so it takes up less space in your pack. If you're trekking off-season between mid-May and early September a light sleeping-bag (one or two season) is sufficient; a thick bag would be too warm.

Some people like to bring a sleeping-bag liner, made from a folded sheet sewn up on two sides. This is easily washed and helps keep the bag clean; it also makes it warmer.

Unless you're planning to spend some nights outside you won't need a sleeping-mat or insulating-pad. It's true that the mattresses on the beds in the lodges are often not quite the 'Supa Dunlopilow Spong' advertised outside but you'll be tired enough not to notice this.

Footwear and foot care

Overtaken on the trail by Nepalis in flip-flops (thongs) or even barefoot, trekkers may feel overdressed in big hiking-boots but for soft Western soles good footwear is vital. The condition of your feet will have a direct effect on your enjoyment of the trek. What you need is a pair of boots that will support your feet properly and keep them dry and blister-free. If you're buying new boots do so well before your leave to allow time to wear them in. Walking with blisters is no fun, and may become so uncomfortable that you are forced to give up your trek.

• **Choosing boots** Many people get by in just a pair of trainers but this is not recommended, especially if you're carrying your own pack.. Apart from the chance of twisting your ankle, trainers cannot keep your feet warm and dry in snow. Crossing the Thorung La with the possibility of sudden snowstorms, there's the risk of frostbite which could result in the amputation of toes.

Choose a boot that offers **good ankle support**, especially impotant if you're carrying your own pack. They needn't be heavy; there's a wide range of modern boots. A leather boot treated to make it water-resistant is better than a Gore-tex or Sympatex boot. Ensure that there is enough room around the toes for steep descents.

• **Socks** In middle- or heavy-weight boots, wearing thin silk socks under thicker boot-socks can help prevent blisters. With close-fitting modern light-weight boots this is not necessary as long as you wear good quality hiking socks.

• **Foot care** It's important to keep your feet as dry as possible since this also helps stop blisters forming. Since your feet will sweat as you walk you should take off your boots and socks during your lunch break and let them dry in the sun.

Wash your feet and change your socks regularly. See p243 for information about how to deal with blisters.

• **Extra footwear** A pair of trainers as backup to your boots is a luury you'll probably only wish to indulge in if someone else is carrying your pack. A pair of **flip-flops** (thongs) is well worth taking, however. They're light and you can wear them while your boots are drying off in the middle of the day, for washing in and even in the evening with a pair of socks if necessary, though this looks pretty daft. Some people bring down booties for evenings at high altitude. Who cares what you look like as long as you're warm?!

Clothes

Since most treks in the Annapurna region take you through a widerange of altitudes, you need to have clothes to cope with a corresponding range of temperatures. On the day you cross the Thorung La on the Circuit trek, for example, in November the temperature could fall as low as -10°C/14°F during the night at Thorung Phedi and reach +15-20°C/59-68°F by the time you reach Muktinath the next day.

The accepted principle of wearing a number of thin layers of clothing rather than one thick one applies as much in the Himalaya as in the

Yorkshire Dales. Air is trapped between the layers helping to insulate you from the cold and as you warm up the layers can be shed one by one.

• **Jacket** A good thick jacket, preferably down, is essential in the autumn, winter and spring. Although you won't need it during the day when the sun's shining, the temperature plummets as soon as the sun sets. On very cold nights you may even need to wear it inside your sleeping-bag.

• **Jersey/fleece top** One or other is essential. The thick Tibetan sweaters sold in Kathmandu and Pokhara are warm but very bulky.

• **Trousers/pants & skirts** Cotton trousers are sold in the tourist shops in Kathmandu and Pokhara and these are ideal for trekking. Poly-cotton travellers' clothing of the sort sold by Rohan is also good since it dries quickly but it's expensive. Thick trousers, jeans especially, are not a good idea as they restrict movement and are difficult to dry. If it's cold you can wear a couple of pairs of light trousers or some thermal underwear.

Long skirts are better than trousers for women because they are more culturally acceptable and also useful as a screen if there are no bushes to crouch behind.

• **Windproof/down trousers/pants** Windproof over-trousers are useful at altitude and take up little space in a pack. In winter down trousers are worth considering.

• **Shirts/blouses** Light cotton shirts with long sleeves and collars are best. Many people take T-shirts and end up with burnt necks in the fierce sun. I take two or three shirts, and a T-shirt to wear at night or under a shirt during the day if it's cold.

• **Underwear** Three changes of whatever you usually wear is fine. In the winter thermal underwear or thick tights are essential and, if you feel the cold, worth bringing in the autumn and early spring seasons, too.

• **Socks** If there's enough room in your boots to wear thick socks over thin, then bring two pairs of thick and two or three pairs of thin. Otherwise three pairs of thick socks is enough.

• **Hat** A sun-hat with a wide brim is important protection against the heat during the day. A woolly hat or balaclava is essential in winter and at altitude and useful on cold evenings in the trekking seasons.

• **Gloves or mittens** Cheap woollen gloves are available in the tourist shops in Kathmandu and Pokhara and are essential during winter and the trekking seasons.

• **Swimsuit** This is useful for hot springs and for swimming. Both sexes should also wear a T-shirt if the bathing-spot is in a public place although for women it's better to do as local women do and wear a sarong.

• **Towel** This can be difficult to dry so bring only a small one. A tea-towel works well enough and can be pegged to your pack to dry as you trek. One trekker recommends taking a large chamois cloth, as used for cleaning car windows.

• **Rain/wind gear** Don't worry about trying to equip yourself with fully waterproof clothing. Even during the monsoon it rarely rains for more than a few hours and people simply dash into the nearest tea-house to wait for it to pass. A plastic cycling poncho or tailored pack-cover will keep your back-pack dry but Nepalis use the big heavy-gauge plastic bags available in most village shops.

Some people recommend buying one of the big black umbrellas available in Nepal. As well as keeping off the occasional shower, a sturdy umbrella can also be used as a walking-stick and sunshade.

If you're going to be spending some time at altitude a wind-cheater is useful protection against cold winds. Most people on the Circuit trek get by with just a thick jacket, though.

Watch what you wear

Foreigners should take care over what they wear in Nepal as it can have a profound effect on the way Nepalis relate to them.

For Nepali men, shorts are generally a sign of the low status labourer, so you'll probably see only porters wearing them among the Nepalis. On the more popular tourist routes it's generally acceptable for Western men to wear shorts, although you'll be accorded higher status in a pair of long trousers. Far more serious than the long trousers vs shorts issue for men is shirtlessness. Men should always wear a shirt.

Nepali women never show more than their ankles. I once wore a plain cotton skirt that came to just below my knees and they all thought I'd forgotten to put my skirt on, and that this was just my petticoat! However, along the more popular routes Nepalis have got used to seeing Western women in shorts (as long as possible, no short shorts) but you'll probably not notice until you wear a skirt that the reception they give you is much warmer.   **Tara Winterton** (Nepal)

Toiletries

A well-equipped washbag doesn't have to be bulky. Take only the balms and lotions you really need to be comfortable but in the smallest (plastic) bottles available. Bring a bar of **soap** in a plastic soap container. You won't be washing your hair much so a few of the **sachets of shampoo** sold in Kathmandu and Pokhara are better than a big bottle. The smallest tube of **toothpaste** is fine for a trek. **Tampons** are available only in Kathmandu or Pokhara so are better brought from home. Likewise, don't expect to be able to obtain in Nepal the brand of **condom/contraceptive pill** you may be using.

Loo paper is available along tea-house trekking routes, though expensive. If you can't face the water-and-hand method then keep a **lighter** in the same bag as your loo paper to burn it after use. Some people recommend bringing **'Wet Ones'** (pre-moistened towelettes).

If you want to sleep in Kathmandu, **ear-plugs** are recommended as defence against the barking dogs. **Sun-screen** is essential protection against the powerful sun at altitude. **Lip balm** is useful in the dry atmosphere of the Kali Gandaki Valley.

Medical kit

There's no need to drag around a vast chest of medicines that you don't really know how to use. Self-diagnosis is not recommended unless you're off the beaten track and have no alternative. If you're doing a standard tea-house trek, basic health facilities are available in some of the villages. At Manang the Himalayan Rescue Association has a health post staffed by Western volunteer doctors during the trekking season. The problems that most commonly affect trekkers are discussed in the health section (see p238).

Take along **paracetamol** for headaches and **aspirin** for inflammation of the joints; both can be used as general painkillers. The only drugs you really need to take on a tea-house trek are best purchased in Kathmandu or Pokhara (no prescriptions necessary): **Diamox** (10 tablets) for altitude sickness – if you're doing the Circuit or Sanctuary treks, **Tinidazole/Tiniba** (10 tablets) for giardia, and **Norfloxacin** for diarrhoea. See the health section for dosages.

Plasters/bandaids and **antiseptic cream** are needed for dealing with cuts. If you get blisters **Second Skin**, the gelatin film, is the best cure. In the UK, it's available only in climbing/hiking shops. Bring a **bandage** for sprains. **Knee supports** can be a real boon for the long descent over the Thorung La or down from the Sanctuary. **Throat lozenges** and **Lemsip** can be useful as colds and sore throats are not uncommon.

For lower altitudes, Kathmandu and Pokhara, **insect repellent** is recommended. To be really effective it should contain at least 30% diethyltoluamide (deet). Jungle Formula contains 40% and is widely available in the West; JJ Pickles is 100% deet but harder to find. If you're taking **antimalarials** (see p47) don't forget these. Most brands leave a foul taste in the mouth and are best taken immediately after you've cleaned your teeth as the toothpaste masks the taste. Since they can also cause nausea, take them last thing at night.

All travellers to third world countries should have an **anti-Aids kit** containing sterilised syringes, needles and suture materials that might be needed in an emergency. These kits are sold by travel clinics and at some pharmacies in the West. If you're going on a long low-budget trek **multivitamin tablets** may be a good idea.

You must not drink untreated water in Nepal so bring some form of **water purification kit**. See p239 for details. Bottled mineral water is available but you can't always be sure it is pure. The plastic bottles in which it is supplied are creating a serious litter problem.

General items

A good pair of **sun-glasses** is necessary in summer as well as in winter when the sun on the snow is particularly bright. Note that snow reflects up to 75% of ultra violet light. If you wear **contact lenses** note that some people have problems with the soft variety – check with your optician. Don't forget your **cleaning solution** which should be kept in your sleeping-bag at night if there is a chance of its freezing. A **torch/flashlight** is essential. Best is a head-torch but a small pocket torch will do. Candles are provided in lodges so you don't need to bring these with you but you will need **matches** or a **lighter**.

Other items that may be useful: a **penknife** (Swiss Army knife is best), **clothes-washing liquid** (biodegradable; see also p84), a few **clothes pegs**, **sewing-kit**, **games** such as Travel Scrabble, pocket chess or a pack of cards and a **camera** (see p42) with adequate supplies of **film**. Leave the walkman behind and listen to the sounds of the river, the forest insects and the thundering avalanches.

Some trekkers find a walking stick helps take the weight off knees during steep descents. Rather than pillage the dwindling forests for a suitable stick bring a **ski pole** with you or use a strong umbrella.

A litre-capacity **water-bottle** is essential. The blue Swiss-made aluminium ones are best since, filled with boiling water, they can double as a hot water bottle. They need to be covered with a sock, though, or you'll burn yourself. Since it's been boiled, the water can then be drunk in the morning. You should do this only when it's very cold since boiling water for drinking, rather than purifying it with iodine, wastes valuable firewood.

Old clothes needed by Kathmandu charities

If you have a little space in your luggage there are a couple of worthy local charities that would be very grateful for some old clothes.

Kumbeshwar Technical School in Patan was set up to cater specifically for the very low caste groups. It incorporates a small orphanage, a primary school and a technical school where carpet weaving and carpentry are taught. High quality sweaters are on sale in the showroom here. The principal is Karuna Khadgi (☎ 536483).

Child Workers in Nepal (CWIN) is a charity working for the rights of children and the abolition of child bonded labour (16% of children in the country are bonded labourers). They also run a 'Common Room' to support the 1000 children who live on the streets of Kathmandu. Clothes are always needed; children's clothes are best but they can alter adults' clothes. They can also make use of any medicines you may have left after your trek. CWIN is near the Soaltee Holiday Inn in Kalamati. It's run by Gauri Pradan (☎ 271658).

Most people keep a **diary** while they trek. Overdosing on fresh air and exercise seems to concentrate the mind; writing comes easily providing a record of your trek that will give pleasure long after you've left Nepal.

Ideas for gifts
• **For Nepalis** Don't load up with sweets and ball-point pens to answer the children's begging calls. Although playing Father Christmas may make you feel good it can have detrimental effects upon the recipients, decreasing their self-worth and leading to a picture in the child's mind of all things good coming from and being to do with the West, rather than from their own country.

There will be occasions, however, when you wish you had something to give. Obviously what you take with you will need to be small and light: a few ball-point pens, even some small toys (simple things purchased in Kathmandu may never have been seen by hill children), postcards of your country's more famous sights.

• **For Westerners** If you have expatriate friends working in Nepal there are several things they might appreciate. In the last few years, however, numerous foreign goods and foodstuffs (French wine, cheese, chocolate etc) have become available, although they are quite expensive. Find out if there's anything they particularly need (replacement part for an appliance, for example) before you arrive. A recent 'want' list from a Kathmandu expatriate included real English bacon, dental floss, Bendicks Bittermints, and assorted baby gear. Herbal teas go down well, as do good bottles of wine and other luxury items. Glossy Western magazines and the Sunday papers are also well received.

Provisions
Since the tea-houses in the Annapurna region are probably the best in Nepal a varied enough diet is available and it's not necessary to bring any food. You may, however, wish to take a few 'comfort foods' with you such as **Marmite, Bovril or Vegemite** (decanted from their heavy glass jars). Marmite is, however, now obtainable in Kathmandu; and Mars Bars are available along all the major trails in Nepal. **Kendal Mint Cake** is worth bringing with you; it gives you a good boost on long climbs. You can get **Peanut butter** in the lodges but many people bring their own to put on cream crackers sold in village shops. You can also buy little boxes of **glucose powder** (an instant energy restorer) at these shops.

Most trekkers treat the water they drink with iodine. The unpleaant taste that this leaves can be neutralised with vitamin C tablets or masked with **fruit drink powder**. These must not be added until the iodine has purified the water. Some people even lug small bottles of **champagne or wine** to the top of the Thorung La for a celebratory drink. At 5416m (17,769ft) the effects are certainly interesting!

Money

In banks, you get a better rate for **travellers' cheques** than for cash and your money is obviously far safer in this form. Bring cheques from a well known company such as Thomas Cook or American Express. The better-known currencies are all accepted but New Zealand dollars seem to be difficult to change.

The major **credit cards** are accepted in many hotels, restaurants and shops in Kathmandu and Pokhara. You can get instant cash advances on cards at some banks which may be useful in an emergency.

Black market exchange rates are about 5-10% above bank rates. Large denomination **US$ bills** are best but you won't be helping Nepal's balance of payments by changing money this way.

A **money-belt/pouch** is a useful way to carry your money safely while you're travelling around Nepal. Most people find them too hot to wear while trekking, though, and put them into the top of their pack on the trail.

Photographic equipment

Most travellers will want to bring a camera with them. Kodak, Fuji, Agfa and Konica print film is widely available in Nepal and some brands of transparency film are stocked. It's better to bring your own film with you; then you know it hasn't spent several days in the sun in transit. Bring more film than you think you'll need – 100ASA is best as the light is bright. Try to avoid letting your film go through the X-ray machines in airports in Asia even if the notices tell you it's perfectly safe.

A spare set of batteries is essential, especially if you're trekking in the cold. If they go dead in the cold, however, they can be rejuvenated by warming them up in your hand or pocket.

> **Panorama cameras**
> One of the problems with photographing mountains is that the printed result can be disappointing. With a standard lens you can't show the powerful sweep of mountains that are visible in many parts of the Annapurna region; with a wide-angle lens you may get all the mountains in the picture but they will be mere dots. I'd recommend one of the lightweight disposable makes of 'panorama' or stretch' camera (Kodak, for example) which produce long prints (approximately $3^1/2$"x10"/100mmx250mm). The lens and shutter speed are fixed so good light is essential but that's rarely a problem in Nepal. They are expensive (about £9 in the UK with developing a further £9) but worth it as the results can be breathtaking – all four Annapurnas in one stunning photo!
> **Heather Oxley** (Japan)

RECOMMENDED READING

Background reading will make your trip all the more enjoyable and much has been published on Nepal and the Annapurna region. The best place to buy books on Nepal is Kathmandu where there are several excellent bookstores. There are also many second-hand bookshops and book exchanges in Kathmandu and Pokhara.

Guidebooks

Lonely Planet's *Nepal – a travel survival kit* is the best general guide to Nepal with good coverage of the whole country. There's also the *Rough Guide to Nepal* and Moon Publications' *Nepal Handbook*. Photography in the APA's *Nepal Insight Guide* is excellent.. For treks other than those covered in this book the best general trekking guide to the whole of Nepal is *Trekking in Nepal* by Stephen Bezruchka, now in its sixth edition. This American doctor has been visiting Nepal since 1969. Lonely Planet's *Trekking in the Nepal Himalaya* gives useful overviews of the main treks in Nepal. For those attempting trekking peaks Bill O'Connor's *Trekking Peaks of Nepal* has all the details.

Flora and fauna

ACAP publishes *A Popular Guide to the Birds and Mammals of the Annapurna Conservation Area* by Carol Inskipp, an excellent little guide available in Nepal. *Himalayan Flowers and Trees* by Dorothy Mierow and Tirtha Bahadur Shrestha has numerous photographs to help identification of plants. Ornithologists should try to get hold of a copy of *Birds of Nepal* by RL Fleming though this is now out of print. There's also *A Birdwatcher's Guide to Nepal* by Carol Inskipp, the Collins *Handguide to the Birds of the Indian Subcontinent* and S. Ali's *Field Guide to the Birds of the Eastern Himalayas* (OUP).

Other books

Maurice Herzog's *Annapurna – Conquest of the First 8000-metre Peak* is a classic and, unlike some mountaineering adventures, very readable; the French expedition made an attempt on Dhaulagiri before conquering Annapurna. Chris Bonington's *Annapurna South Face* describes the technically more difficult climb of the face of Annapurna that you can see from the Sanctuary.

The Snow Leopard by Peter Matthiessen charts the author's journey from Pokhara to Dolpo with naturalist George Schaller. It's more a journey of self-discovery as far as the author is concerned.

In Kathmandu you may be able to buy the reprint of Giuseppe Tucci's *Journey to Mustang*, an account of the expedition made in 1952. Even if you're not going all the way to Lo Manthang it's interesting for the descriptions of Kathmandu, Pokhara and the lower Kali Gandaki. *Mustang – a lost Tibetan Kingdom* is Michel Peissel's account of the journey made in the 1960's. His biography of Boris Lissanevitch, *Tiger for Breakfast*, gives an good idea of what the country was like when the first tourists arrived and explains how a former dancer with Diaghilev's Ballet

Russe came to be running Nepal's first international hotel.

HW Tilman, the mountaineer who led the 1938 attempt on Everest, was one of the first Westerners to travel in the Annapurna region. His very readable *Nepal Himalaya* is reprinted in *The Seven Mountain Travel Books*.

David Snellgrove's *Himalayan Pilgrimage* is an interesting account of travel in this area in the mid 1950s. For his research into Buddhism, the author visited virtually every monastery and temple in the region.

Dervla Murphy's *The Waiting Land – A Spell in Nepal* is an interesting description of what Pokhara was like in the mid 1960s, before it was linked to the outside world by a road. The author was working with Tibetan refugees here.

In *Nepali Aama: Portrait of a Nepalese Hill Woman*, Broughton Coburn translates the life story of the elderly Gurung woman who was his landlady when he lived in Danda, a village south of Pokhara. They make a pilgrimage to Muktinath together. It's a charming book, full of universal truths and excellent photographs.

Charlie Pye-Smith's *Travels in Nepal – The Sequestered Kingdom* is both an entertaining travelogue and an analysis of the success (and often failure) of aid programmes in the country. It includes an account of a trek from Jomsom to Pokhara.

MAPS

The best map is *Annapurna* (1:100,000), recently published by Schneider, known for their accurate maps of the Everest region. It's sometimes available in Kathmandu, for about £10/US$15: better to buy a copy from a travel bookshop in your own country. In London, Stanfords (☎ 0171-836 1321) can supply the map by mail order.

Locally-produced maps are available in Kathmandu for under £1/US$1.50. They're marketed under a variety of names, *Pokhara to Jomsom Manang (Round Annapurna Himal),* for example, and inaccurate even though they may be headed 'New Improved Latest Edition' (plus next year's date!). Most people make do with one of these maps and in conjunction with the route maps in this book, they're good enough. More expensive is the *Annapurna Conservation Area Map*, a full-colour map with contours, or Nepa Maps' ('For Extreme and Soft Trekking') *Annapurna*. All these maps are at the same scale: 1:125,000.

The *Annapurna Sattrek Map, Nepal*, published by Cartoconsult, Austria, is an enhanced satellite image map. It gives the best idea of the extent of the valleys and mountains but at a scale of 1:250,000 is not much use for trekking.

Health precautions and inoculations

There is always a greater risk of getting ill when travelling to a country where levels of hygiene are far below those in the West. These risks can, however, be considerably lessened by ensuring you're in reasonable physical shape when you arrive; by being aware of the dangers and by taking the relevant precautions (see p238). Check carefully that your inoculations are still valid.

WHO SHOULD AVOID HIGH ALTITUDE TREKS?

Most people of all ages with a reasonable level of fitness will have no difficulties trekking but the altitude on some treks in this area will create problems for certain groups. People with chest or heart diseases or high blood pressure should get the advice of a doctor who may recommend that they do not ascend above a certain altitude.

Children are more susceptible to altitude sickness than adults so should not be taken above 3000m or 10,000ft. Young adults (in their teens or early twenties) are also more susceptible and extra days should be allowed for acclimatisation.

If you are on any special medication you should seek the advice of your doctor before trekking to altitude. The greatest danger to these people (asthma sufferers and those with diabetes, for example) is losing their medication but with due care this needn't be a problem.

PRE-TREK PREPARATIONS

Getting fit – before or during your trek?

Although most people hit the trail without any training it makes sense to do some preparation, especially if you usually lead a sedentary existence. Ideally you should start about three months before you go and do something to emulate what you'll be doing in Nepal: walking up and down hills with a pack on your back. Any form of exercise is better than nothing. The dedicated urban-dwelling health freak will find a convenient block of flats, at least 20 storeys high, and spend several evenings a week walking up and down the stairs with a pack full of bricks. Most people don't bother, simply taking it very easy for the first few days to get fit as they trek.

Visit your dentist

Since dental care in Nepal is in its infancy you should ensure that your teeth are in order before you leave.

INOCULATIONS

No inoculations are listed as official requirements for foreigners visiting Nepal unless they are flying in from Africa or South America, in which case a yellow fever certificate is required. You would be particularly imprudent, however, not to get yourself vaccinated against several diseases listed below.

Travel clinics are usually better informed than your local doctor. Up-to-the-minute health information and an on-the-spot vaccination service is available in London at **Trailfinders** (194 Kensington High Street, ☎ 0171-938 3999). Note that in the UK few vaccinations are now available on the NHS and NHS prices for some inoculations may actually be higher than those at the travel clinics above. It can pay to shop around. You should be given a record book in which your inoculations are listed. Although it's much better to have all the required inoculations before you arrive in Nepal, most can be obtained in Kathmandu.

Note that some inoculations cannot be given at the same time and in some cases boosters may be necessary four to six weeks apart. Check the situation a couple of months before you leave to ensure you will have time for full courses if necessary.

• **Tetanus** A vaccination is vital if you've not had one in the last ten years. If you then cut yourself while travelling you won't need another.

• **Infectious hepatitis** Infectious hepatitis (or hepatitis A) is a disease of the liver that drains you of energy and can last from three weeks to a couple of months. It's spread by drinking infected water, and by using utensils or eating food that has been handled by an infected person.

Gamma globulin injections are the usual form of vaccination and give a certain amount of protection for two to six months, depending on the strength of vaccine used. To be effective for as long as possible they should be given just before departure. Havrix is the more expensive vaccine now also being offered. The full course (3 injections) is given over a 6-month period but protection lasts 10 years.

• **Meningitis** The inoculation is recommended. There have been some cases of the disease amongst Westerners in Nepal.

• **Typhoid** The disease is caught from contaminated food and water and the inoculation is recommended for travel to Nepal.

• **Japanese Encephalitis** Recommended if trekking in the monsoon.

• **Rabies** There is a minimal risk of being bitten by an animal carrying this often fatal disease and you may wish to consider the vaccination. The course of three injections is expensive (£45-72).

• **Others** Most people in the West will have been vaccinated against **diphtheria**, **tuberculosis** (TB) and **poliomyelitis** in their childhood. Check your medical records. Note that a **cholera** shot is only worth considering if you're travelling to or through an area where an epidemic has broken out; and the vaccine gives very little protection.

Malaria prophylaxis

This mosquito-borne disease that is debilitating, occasionally fatal and on the increase, occurs in Nepal only at elevations below about 1000m/ 3280ft. This, therefore, excludes Kathmandu, Pokhara and the Sanctuary and Jomsom trekking routes. The first few days of the Circuit trail from Dumre are below this elevation and there may be a very slight risk but it is higher in the Terai, the lowland area which includes Chitwan, particularly during the monsoon.

If your travels in Nepal are an extension of a holiday in India, if you're doing the Circuit between May and September or if you're also visiting Chitwan and other lowland areas you should certainly take anti-malarials. Some trekkers may want to take anti-malarials at other times of the year, too, but this is not really necessary.

The parasite (carried by the *Anopheles* mosquito) that causes malaria is resistant to chloroquine, so you may need to take two kinds of tablet, usually Chloroquine/Maloprim (two tablets once a week) and Paludrin/ Proguanil (two tablets daily). Start the course one week before you go and continue for four weeks after you leave the malarial zone. Lariam (Mefloquine), taken only weekly, is a more recent alternative to Chloroquine and Paludrine.

Whether you decide to take anti-malarials or not you must try to avoid being bitten by mosquitoes since some insects also carry **dengue fever**. There's also a chance of bites becoming infected if you scratch them. Note that if you change planes in a malarial zone (eg Delhi where the airport is infested with mosquitoes) there's a risk of contracting malaria. *Anopheles* mosquitoes operate only at night when you should cover your legs and arms, use a powerful insect repellent and a mosquito coil (available in Nepal). Once you get up into the mountains you leave the mosquitoes behind.

TRAVEL & HEALTH INSURANCE

You may not need to use it but insurance is definitely very sensible to have. Beware of credit card companies that advertise free travel insurance if you book a flight with them. You will find that you're covered only for what you've paid for on the card (your flight).

For further information on health matters see p238.

PART 2: NEPAL

Facts about the country

The country is wild and mountainous, and is little frequented by strangers, whose visits the king discourages. **Marco Polo**

GEOGRAPHICAL BACKGROUND

Sandwiched between India and China, Nepal is roughly rectangular in shape, 500 miles long by 125 miles wide (800km by 200km). With a total area of 147,181 square km it's about the same size as England and Wales combined, or Florida.

Although Nepal's geographical claim to fame is indeed the Himalaya (eight out of ten of the world's highest peaks are here) there is a tremendous range in elevation across the country. Everest, the top of the world, stands at 8848m/29028ft while the lowest place in Nepal, the town of Kechanakawal, is a mere 70m/230ft above sea-level.

Mountains, valleys and plains

Nepal conveniently divides into three distinct regions, running as east-west bands across the country:

• **Himalayan region** The world's longest range of mountains stretches almost 5000 miles (8000km) across Asia and along the top quarter of Nepal. The Nepalese section of the Himalaya includes eight of the world's fourteen Eight-thousanders (as mountaineers refer to peaks over 8000m/26,247ft).

• **Middle region** Lying between the Himalaya and the southern lowland, the middle region comprises mountains and hills, river valleys and basins, including the Kathmandu and Pokhara Valleys. It covers about half the country.

Running parallel to the Himalaya are the Mahabharat, rising to 4877m/16,000ft and the Siwaliks (or Churia) ranging from about 600m to 1500m (2000ft to 5000ft).

• **The Terai** Along the southern border with India is the lowland plain known as the Terai, covering a little under a quarter of the country. Once a dense subtropical forest, much has now been cut down to make way for settlers and provide firewood and building materials for both India and

Nepal. Some of the remaining forest areas, such as Chitwan, have been set aside as national parks. Almost 60% of the country's cultivated land is in this area, its fertility enriched by the alluvial soil washed down annually from the mountains to the Terai.

Rising peaks, deepening valleys

The Himalaya were formed by the collision of the Asian and Indian continental plates, the Indian plate forcing up the edge of Tibet on the Asian plate. This collision is still continuing today, at the rate of a few mm each year, resulting in landslides, erosion and mountains that are still rising. Quite how fast the Himalaya are growing is difficult to say since not all peaks are pushed up at the same rate. The annual growth rate is estimated at between 1mm and 3mm (up to one eighth of an inch).

These are also the youngest mountains in the world and geographers are especially interested in the fact that they don't form the watershed. This is further north on the Tibetan plateau which is why the major rivers that flow through Nepal into India's Ganges have their sources north of the Himalaya, cutting south through deep valleys. On the Jomsom trek you follow the world's deepest valley, the Kali Gandaki, and at one point you stand almost 3 miles (4.8km) below Dhaulagiri and Annapurna I. Several of these valleys form ancient trade routes with Tibet.

CLIMATE

Dramatic variations in temperature

With variations in altitude of nearly 8000m/26,247ft, climatic extremes from sub-tropical to alpine are to be expected.

In June on the Terai the temperature can rise as high as the mid-40s°C (around 110°F). Winter temperatures in the mountain towns of Jomsom and Jiri (Everest region) fall well below zero °C (32°F) each night but can rise to 20°C/68°F in the middle of the day. Trekkers start and end the day in thick jackets but can eat lunch in shirt-sleeves.

Kathmandu's climate is pleasant year round, with average temperatures ranging from 18-30°C/65-86°F during the day and 2-19°C/36-66°F at night.

Rainfall

The climate of the southern half of the country is affected not only by altitude but also by the monsoon. Up to 80% of the total annual rainfall is during this June to September season.

The monsoon, which affects the whole sub-continent, is caused by the land and sea heating up at different rates. It reaches eastern Nepal in the first week of June, and the west about ten days later. The monsoon clouds sweep up to the Himalaya which act as a barrier, denying areas to the north more than a sprinkling of rain. The wettest area in Nepal is the

Pokhara Valley with a mean annual rainfall of 4000mm. Most of this falls during the monsoon. Kathmandu's mean annual rainfall is 1400mm.

See p22 for Nepal's trekking seasons.

HISTORICAL OUTLINE

Out of the Tethys Sea
On the trek to Jomsom, you may be lucky enough to find an ammonite, a fossilised mollusc, amongst the pebbles of the wide Kali Gandaki Valley. Thousands of these fossils, over 180 million years old, have been found, clues to the submarine origins of parts of Nepal as the floor of the Tethys Sea. Around 55 million years ago the north-bound Indian continental plate drifted into the Asian plate and since then has been lifting up the southern edge of Tibet, creating the Himalaya.

The Kathmandu Valley
The first evidence of humans in Nepal dates back to about 200,000 years ago, when the Kathmandu Valley was a lake. An ancient Newari myth tells of the monk, Manjushri, draining the Valley by creating the Chobar Gorge. This he did single-handed with two slashes of his sword. Many of the world's myths and legends seem to have been triggered off by some catastrophic event that really did happen and this is no exception. Scientists have shown that about 10,000 years ago the rim of the Kathmandu Lake ruptured at Chobar, allowing the water to drain out, leaving a fertile valley.

Early history
Among the earliest known rulers of the Kathmandu Valley were the Kirati, from whom the Rai and Limbu people of eastern Nepal claim to be descended. The Kirati had their capital in Matatirtha, west of modern Kathmandu in the second half of the first millennium BC.

Other centres were springing up on the Terai at around this time. It was in one of these lowland kingdoms, Lumbini, that Prince Siddhartha Gautama, who was to become the Buddha, was born in 543BC. Buddhism developed in India and spread into surrounding parts of the sub-continent, particularly under the Indian emperor, Ashoka. Several of the stupas (Buddhist religious monuments) he built around Kathmandu in the 2nd century BC can still be seen.

The Lichhavi
The Kirati were replaced by the **Lichhavi** around 200 AD. With their capital near Pashupatinath in Kathmandu, the Lichhavi dynasty orchestrated a golden age of art and culture, fuelled by trade with states to the north and south of the Valley. Their legacy to modern Nepal is the pagoda style of architecture, extensive stone carving (some of the work at Pashupati-

nath dates from this time) and the caste system. Although Hindu, the Lichhavi were tolerant of other religions and this, too, has been passed down to the present day.

By the 9th century the Lichhavi had been overpowered by the **Thakuri**, invading from the Terai. The next 300 years are known as the Nepalese Dark Ages but, as with the European Dark Ages, art and learning continued to prosper in the monasteries and temples. The **Khasa** controlled the western area of the country including Pokhara, in an empire that stretched west as far as Kashmir.

The Malla Dynasty

This period in Nepal's history was a second Golden Age, a renaissance of art and architecture under the Malla kings (1200-1768). The palaces and temples of the Durbar Squares in Kathmandu, Patan and Bhaktapur date from this time.

The name Malla, meaning 'wrestler', is said to have been coined by King Ari Deva who was in the ring when his son, the first Malla, was born. This was, however, a title used by other kings at the time, including the Khasa.

Jayasthiti Malla (1382-95) was one of the greatest reformers in the history of the country, with a penchant for bureaucracy that led to the restructuring of Nepalese society on an orthodox Hindu framework. Thirty-six main castes, which included Buddhists as well as Hindus, were created in a system that is still observed by many Nepalis today. He unified the four main city states in the Kathmandu Valley: Kathmandu, Patan, Banepa and Bhaktapur.

Centralised control reached its peak under **Yaksha Malla** whose empire extended into India, west to the Pokhara Valley and east to Sikkim. On his death in 1482, Kathmandu, Patan, Banepa and Bhaktapur were split between his heirs. Competition between them seems to have been no bad thing as far as the rich architectural heritage from this time shows; but the feuding led to the disintegration and weakening of the Malla kingdom over the next 200 years.

The unification of Nepal

By the 18th century Nepal was again just a large collection of independent kingdoms. In the Terai and lower hills these were in the hands of Rajput princes ousted from India. The hilltop kingdom of Gorkha was the domain of the Shah dynasty to which the reigning King of Nepal belongs. In 1743 the King of Gorkha, Prithvi Narayan Shah, set off on a pilgrimage to Varanasi. He took the opportunity to restock his arsenal while there and on his return took the town of Nuwakot in 1744 to begin the slow conquest of the Kathmandu Valley. Kirtipur fell in 1764 after a siege of six months. For wounding the king's brother all the inhabitants (except musicians and children) were punished by having their noses removed.

The last of the Malla kings of Kathmandu, Jaya Prakash Malla, sought help from the British East India Company who sent a force of over 2000 soldiers. The Gorkhalis provided the British with a display of bravery they never forgot. Only a third of the British force returned and the Gorkhalis were left with a rich hoard of weapons.

In 1768, Prithvi Narayan Shah took Kathmandu without a struggle on the eve of the Indra Jatra festival (still held to mark the end of the monsoon) and became the acknowledged founder of modern Nepal.

Wars with Tibet and Britain

The territorial aspirations of the Shah dynasty led to further expansion and a number of embarrassments. In 1792, with the help of China, Tibet managed to halt Nepal's northern advance and Nepal was burdened with annual tributes to China that lasted 120 years.

In the south there was confrontation with the British East India Company, this time more successful from the point of view of the British. By the Treaty of Segauli in 1816 Nepal was forced to relinquish claims to parts of the Terai and to accept a permanent British ambassador, or Resident, in Kathmandu. So impressed were the British with the fighting skills of their enemy that they started immediately recruiting Nepalis, thus beginning a tradition of Gurkha regiments that continues in the British and Indian armies to this day.

The Kot Massacre

By the 19th century, the power of the Shahs had been weakened by internal conflict and palace intrigue. The Queen was planning to seize power from the King and was furious when one of her allies was murdered. She asked **Jung Bahadur Rana**, a young general, to avenge her. He took her at her word and arranged the murder of 55 of the top officials who had gathered for a meeting in the armoury in Durbar Square, in what became known as the 'Kot Massacre'.

The Ranas – Nepalese Borgias

Following the Kot Massacre, Jung Bahadur made himself prime minister and took most of the power away from the throne. He was wise enough to preserve the monarchy since the people believed the king to be an incarnation of the Hindu god Vishnu. The office of prime minister (and therefore the reins of power) became hereditary within the Rana family, with the monarchy mere puppets for the next 104 years.

The country's new rulers did virtually nothing to advance the lot of the Nepali peasantry, their main legacy being the bizarre collection of white-washed palaces that litter the capital. If these vast neo-classical wedding-cake buildings look out of place in the eyes of the Western tourist, they must have seemed almost extra-terrestrial to the Nepalese in the 19th century. This architectural fashion was started by Jung Bahadur after his European tour in 1850. He visited England and had an audience with Queen Victoria; his visit to the opera at Covent Garden is said to have made more of an impression on him.

Restoration of the monarchy

The policy of isolationism that had always been a characteristic of the country's rulers began to break down in the 20th century. Although the borders were effectively sealed against outsiders, more than a quarter of a million Gurkhas travelled abroad to fight in the two world wars, bringing back new ideas as well as foreign exchange.

Discontent with the Ranas was growing, not only amongst the Nepali people but also among the many members of the Rana family who did not hold positions of power. The Nepali Congress Party was formed under BP Koirala in 1946, in India, backing King Tribhuvan, virtually a prisoner in his palace in Kathmandu, as the figurehead.

On 6th November 1951 the King managed to escape to the Indian Embassy in Kathmandu, where he was granted asylum. The forces of the Nepali Congress Party attacked the country from India, gaining control of most of the Terai. An agreement was reached with the help of Indian prime minister, Nehru, and Tribhuvan returned to a hero's welcome in Kathmandu on 15 February 1951. A coalition government comprising the Nepali Congress Party and the Ranas was installed with the promise of free elections in 1952.

Panchayat system

The promised elections didn't materialise until 1959, after Tribhuvan had died. The Nepali Congress Party swept the board with almost three-quarters of the seats and BP Koirala became prime minister.

The new King Mahendra was less keen on this experiment with democracy than were his people. In 1960 he took matters into his own hands, jailing BP Koirala and dissolving parliament on allegations of corruption. In its place he installed the *panchayat* system, which he considered more appropriate to the country with its largely illiterate population. Panchayat, meaning 'council of five', involved sending locally elected representatives to a district council, which in turn elected a representative to the national assembly. Ultimate power remained with the king who chose the prime minister and cabinet.

1979 Referendum

On the death of his father in 1972, the reins of power passed to Birendra, who is still the reining monarch. The new king, educated at Eton and Harvard, began his reign with a crackdown on corruption. This had little effect and discontent grew, erupting in riots in 1979. Still convinced that the panchayat system was the most appropriate form of government for

Nepal, he held a national referendum. Fifty-five per cent of the votes called for its retention but there were widespread allegations of vote rigging.

The 1980s

During the last decade of real power for the monarchy, the prisons filled up with political dissidents. Newspapers were strictly censored and journalists imprisoned without trial. The king became increasingly distanced from the people, who, having successfully removed the Ranas 30 years before, were now being ruled by another form of autocracy. The Ranas still held many of the highest positions of power, particularly in the army. The queen, too, is a Rana.

It appeared that even the gods were displeased with the situation. In 1988, 1200 people died in a devastating earthquake in eastern Nepal and in 1989 a temple in Patan collapsed.

Rajiv Gandhi showed India's displeasure at the Nepali decision to buy arms from China by refusing to renegotiate a trade-transit treaty. He imposed a trade embargo on Nepal, virtually sealing the border. This led to fuel rationing and an increased rate of inflation.

Democracy in the 90s

The democracy movement was given added impetus in February 1990 when the Nepali Congress Party and the Nepal Communist Party campaigned together for the lifting of the ban on political parties. The leaders were arrested but there were democracy rallies and strikes across the country.

By April the movement reached a dramatic final stage. An uprising in Patan was followed on 6th April by a demonstration of over 200,000 people in front of the palace in Kathmandu. The police began by beating the people back and, when a demonstrator climbed on to the statue of King Mahendra and symbolically removed his sceptre, the shooting began. At least 100 people (and probably as many as 300) lost their lives. Their martyrdom, combined with pressure from the West, forced the king to lift the ban on political parties and appoint an interim government to oversee the change to a constitutional monarchy similar to Britain's.

'Vote for Tree'

The 1991 elections, the first for over 30 years involved a large amount of political graffiti. Since many of the voters were illiterate each party chose a symbol (tree, spade, cow, sun etc). The Nepali Congress Party (the tree) defeated the United Marxist-Leninist Party (the sun) but by only a narrow margin. The Maoist Masale Party was popular in the Pokhara area.

Given that the collapse of communist states in eastern Europe was a major catalyst for the democracy movement in Nepal, it seems surprising that communist parties had such support in these first elections. Part of this may be attributed to the fact that people think that the Nepali Congress Party is too pro-India. Nepalis have an ingrained fear of foreign domination that stems from the 1814 war with the British and accounts for the long policy of isolationism.

Broken promises

When things go wrong Nepalis shrug their shoulders and say 'Ke garne' – literally, 'What to do?'. No doubt many must have thought that once the monarch had been removed from power all would be well. They must have had the same hopes back in 1951 when they got rid of the Ranas. Three years down the democracy tracks nothing seemed to have changed. Corruption was rife at in all levels of government office (as it still is today). The promised rise in living standards never came and it was not long before the people lost confidence in their new government.

The opposition parties were quick to take advantage of this, stirring up riots in which several people were killed. The government itself was torn by internal dissent and Nepal's second general election was called 18 months early, in November 1994. The communists took power, ruling in a coalition government under the leader of the United Marxist-Leninist Party, Man Mohan Adhikari.

September 1995 – new government

Nepal's experiment with communism lasted till September 1995 when Adhikari's party lost a vote of no-confidence in parliament. A tripartite coalition government composed of the Nepal Congress Party, the right-wing Rastriya Prajatantra Party and the pro-India Nepal Sadbhavana Party, was sworn in under prime minister Sher Bahadur Deuba.

ECONOMY

Nepal is one of the world's poorest countries in terms of average per capita income. Forty-two per cent of the population earns an average of just £50/US$75 per year. The overall per capita income is only £110/US$170 per year.

It's said that in a country where over 90% of the people work as subsistence farmers outside the cash economy, per capita income figures don't mean all that much. It's certainly true that most people manage to feed their families off the land producing a surplus that is used to buy tea, sugar, salt and clothes but in many cases this is a small surplus, where it exists at all. Although very few starve to death in Nepal many people (and up to 75% of children) are undernourished. Along the comparatively affluent Annapurna trekking routes you will not see much evidence of this. Nevertheless, with a rapidly rising population putting ever increasing pressures on the environment, the situation is likely to get worse rather than better.

Agriculture
Less than 20% of Nepal is cultivatable yet it employs over 90% of the population and produces 56% of the GNP. Most farmers own their own plots of land but these are generally very small. Tenant farmers must hand over half their crops as rent.

A trek up the Kali Gandaki will take you through most of the crop regions of Nepal. Rice is grown on the Terai and up to about 2000m (6562ft), wheat and maize up to about 2500m (8202ft). Other crops include barley, millet, sugar cane, jute, oilseed, tobacco and potatoes.

There are orchards of apple, peach and apricot at about 2500m (8202ft) in the Annapurna region but, as with rice on the Terai, distribution of any surpluses produced is a problem. Whilst some of the mountain regions suffer from a shortage of food in the winter months, Nepali rice from the Terai is sold to India. Agriculture accounts for about 70% of exports.

Industry
The manufacturing industry is minute in comparison to agriculture, accounting for less than 5% of GNP. The largest industries in terms of employees are carpet-making, weaving and tile- and brick-making. On the Terai there are factories producing soap, cigarettes, beer, cloth and cement, and processing jute, grain and oilseed.

Tourism
In 1993 (the most recent year for which statistics are available), 293,567 tourists visited the country. Of these, 28.4% were Indians, 10.9% from Germany, 8% from the UK, 6.9% from the USA and 6.1% from Japan. Tourism earned the country US$72 million, accounting for 30% of Nepal's foreign exchange earnings but each year about half of this money leaves the country to pay for the foreign goods that tourists demand.

Energy resources
Over 80% of the country's fuel requirements are provided by fire-wood. Consequently forest cover has been reduced from 60% in 1951 to little more than 30% now. Deforestation is a very serious problem that can only worsen as the population rises. In 1984 a US$24 million forest development programme was begun. Although Nepal has to import all its petroleum products (most from Russia), several companies are at present prospecting for oil in the south-east.

One abundant Nepali resource that can be harnessed to provide energy is water. Several hydroelectric projects have been built but it's estimated that less than 0.5% has yet been utilised. Most of these projects, however, are large, expensive and sometimes environmentally damaging. The potential for valuable foreign currency earnings through the sale of electricity to countries like India is undeniable. Several micro-hydroelectric schemes have been successfully set up in the hills (a number in the Annapurna region) but, however it's produced, few Nepalis can afford electricity.

See p80 for advice on how to limit your environmental impact.

See p80 for advice on how to limit your environmental impact.

> **Development programmes and foreign aid**
> Nepal abounds in foreign aid programmes. Playing on his country's position between two giants, India and China, King Mahendra allowed Nepal to be wooed by almost any foreign power willing to pour money into the country. Foreign aid now amounts to over US$300 million annually, which is about 35% of foreign exchange earnings and comprises up to 45% of the government's annual budget.
>
> Development schemes of every kind have been thrust upon Nepal: everything from massive hydroelectric projects to small tree-planting schemes in villages. They vary widely in their efficacy but the more successful programmes now seem to be the small-scale ones initiated by the people themselves. With the large projects, substantial amounts of foreign aid get pocketed long before they reach the projects. Development has become very big business here with many owing their lucrative jobs to foreign agencies.
>
> One of the most successful development projects is the Annapurna Conservation Area Project (ACAP), established in 1986 to provide resource management and sustainable development in a tourist area (see p81).
>
> Charlie Pye-Smith's *Travels in Nepal* gives an excellent assessment of some of the aid programmes operating in the country in the late 1980s, including projects in the Annapurna region.

DEFENCE

Nepal is a member of the United Nations and the Colombo Plan. In 1975, King Birendra declared the country's neutrality by proclaiming Nepal a 'Zone of Peace'. India has rejected this since it contravenes a longstanding mutual aid defence treaty between the two countries.

The army comprises the royal guard, seven infantry brigades, one air squadron, and engineer, artillery, signals, transport and parachute battalions. The air force operates three transport planes and four helicopters (also used for mountain rescues). The armed forces employ 40,000 people and 27,000 in the paramilitary police force.

See p58 for information about Gurkha regiments.

EDUCATION

There have been considerable advances in education in the last 40 years but by Western standards there is still a very long way to go. The country's literacy rate stands at 27%, amongst the lowest in the world. By comparison, Bangladesh's rate is 36.6%, India's 52% and Indonesia's 84%. In Nepal, the literacy rate of men is almost three times that of women: 51% to 18%.

Primary education of a sort has been provided free by the government since 1975. It's pretty miraculous that the children manage to learn anything in the classroom since most of the learning seems to be achieved by rote chanting.

Almost half the teachers have no proper training and pupil-teacher ratios are about 40:1. There are about 1,800,000 boys and 1,000,000 girls in primary education, the disparity in numbers being caused by parents keeping their daughters away from school to help in the fields. The ratio of boys to girls in secondary education is similarly discouraging: 240,000 boys to 102,000 girls.

There are now two universities: Tribhuvan University in Kathmandu with a second campus in Pokhara, and Mahendra Sanskrit University (solely for the study of Sanskrit). In 1990, many of the 95,000 students played a major part in the democracy movement.

The Gurkhas

Forming what is probably the world's most famous fighting force, the tough Nepali hill men who fill the Gurkha battalions within the British and Indian armies are renowned for their bravery and resilience. Stories of their fearlessness have been sending shivers down the spines of every enemy they've faced since recruitment began in 1815.

During the Falklands Conflict, it is said that rumours were circulating through Argentinian ranks that the Gurkhas were not only tough fighters but that the extent of their ruthlessness included decapitation of their victims (with the famous khukri followed by ritual cannibalism! In June 1983 when it was leaked that Gurkhas would be used in an assault on an outpost near Port Stanley, the Gurkhas arrived to find that the enemy had fled.

Since Britain began recruiting the soldiers of the disbanded Gorkhali Army nearly two centuries ago (see p000) these 'Gurkhas', as they came to be known, have served in every conflict that has involved Britain or India. In World War I, 200,000 Gurkhas served; 250,000 in World War II. When India became independent in 1947 six of the ten Gurkha regiments remained with the Indian Army; the others becoming part of the British Army.

Gurkha wages, pensions and payments for associated services (eg frequent charter flights to Hong Kong for families of Gurkhas going on leave or returning from Nepal) were, until recently, the country's largest source of foreign currency. They are still a vital source of earnings, accounting for about 20% of Nepal's GNP. There are now about 100,000 Gurkhas in the Indian Army, 7500 in the British Army.

Competition for places is intense, becoming more so as Britain reduces its armed forces. In 1992 it was announced that the overall strength of the Brigade of Gurkhas would be cut to 2500 by 1997 when Hong Kong reverts to China. The four infantry battalions will be reduced to two, one based in Britain and the other in Brunei, where one battalion is already on loan to the Sultan. In September 1995, however, the Gurkhas received a reprieve. Despite a £17.5 million advertising campaign, the British Army admitted that it was having such difficulty in finding new British recruits of a sufficiently high calibre that 400 Gurkhas due to be made redundant over the next two years would be asked to stay.

HEALTH

Health care in Nepal is still in its early stages of development. Although Bir Hospital, the country's first, opened in 1890, it was not until 1960 that the Ministry of Health was established. There are now about 16,100 people for every doctor, compared to 6786 in Indonesia, 2165 in India, 581 in the UK and 419 in the US. In the entire country there are fewer than 5000 hospital beds. Most health care is through health posts staffed by local workers trained in both Western and ayurvedic medicine.

Infant mortality is approximately 88 deaths per 1000 births – a third of what it was thirty years ago but still unacceptably high compared to the 6-8 per 1000 rate in the West. Cleaner water supplies, vaccination programmes and oral rehydration powders have helped reduce this rate.

Life expectancy, at 54 years for men, 52 for women, is amongst the lowest in the world.

THE PEOPLE

In 1951 Nepal's population was just eight million people but, rising at a fast 2.3%, it's now 21.5 million.

Basic health care and cleaner water supplies have led to this disturbingly high growth rate. As has now been discovered in many Third World countries education, not just the provision of free contraceptives, is the key to controlling the population explosion in Nepal.

Ethnic patchwork

According to information from the Central Bureau of Statistics, Nepal comprises at least 35 different peoples with unique cultures and languages, although 58% of the population now describe themselves as Nepali. Most of these people are also Hindus. Brahmins and Chhetris (see p61), the higher Hindu castes, are not ethnic but cultural groups very different from the lower castes.

• **People of the Terai** After Nepalis, there are three main groups on the Terai. The **Maithili** constitute Nepal's next largest group: 11% of the total population. The **Bhojpuri** constitute 7.6% and the **Tharu**, one of the country's few indigenous groups, 3.6%.

• **Newar** The indigenous Newar make up about half the population in the Kathmandu Valley but only 3% of Nepal's overall population. The buildings in Durbar Square bear witness to a long and rich cultural history of these craftsmen and merchants. Bhaktapur, near Kathmandu, is a largely Newar city.

The Newar are Hindu and Buddhist, and many follow a mixture of the two. They have over 80 caste divisions and their own calendar (Nepal Sambat).

• **Tamang** This group of people originated from the north. Constituting 3.5% of the population, they live in the middle hills in central and eastern Nepal and work as porters and farmers.

• **Gurung & Magar** Living in the southern area of the Annapurna region, the Gurung (see p174) farm the higher slopes and the Magar the lower. Most Gurkha recruits come from these two groups.

• **Thakali** This small but prosperous ethnic group (see p152) comprises a number of villages along the Kali Gandaki. The Thakali controlled the old trade route up the river to Tibet and have a well-deserved reputation for running the best travellers' lodges in Nepal.

• **Manangbhot/Manangba** The inhabitants of the Manang Valley (see p208), in the Annapurna region, are traders with links as far away as Hong Kong. They speak a Tibeto-Burman language and are Buddhists. The Manangba are just one of the many *bhotia* (mountain people originally from Tibet) in Nepal.

• **People of the east** The **Sherpa** are the most famous of Nepal's ethnic groups. From the Solu-Khumbu (Everest) region, they've been so closely linked with mountaineering and the trekking industry that their name now stands for any Nepali who works on an organised trek, particularly porters.

The **Rai** and **Limbu**, known collectively as the **Kirat**, the descendants of Nepal's earliest inhabitants, are also from the east of the country, in the lower hills.

RELIGION

According to the new constitution, Nepal describes itself as a Hindu Constitutional Monarchy. Official statistics state that 89.5% of the population is Hindu, 5.3% Buddhist, 2.7% Muslim, 2.4% shamanist and animist, 0.1% Jain and 0.04% Christian. Since being Hindu and Nepali-speaking can confer greater employment opportunities and higher social standing, it's likely that there are more Buddhists and fewer Hindus than these figures suggest..

The long tradition of religious toleration has led to a blurring of distinctions, especially between Hinduism and Buddhism. You'll see Buddhist prayer-flags fluttering over a Hindu temple and statues of Hindu gods in Buddhist *gompas* (monasteries). In fact, many Hindu deities have their Buddhist counterparts.

Hinduism

The most complex of all religions is also the most tolerant – in Nepal, at least, if not in India. In theory, Hinduism accepts all other beliefs as true and allows for forms of worship which range from simple animism to deepest philosophy. Its many paths even include *tantra* which maintains that enlightenment can come through absolutely anything in life; and that includes drink, drugs and sex.

Central to Hindu beliefs is reincarnation, the belief that all living things go through a series of rebirths which lead eventually to *moksha*, salvation in the form of escape from the cycle and unity with the Creator. What determines whether you're reborn in the next life as a flea or a wealthy landowner is *karma*. Good and bad karma are the direct result of good or bad actions during your lifetime.

The Hindu caste system still has a profound influence on the lives of most people in Nepal. It was actually extended by the Malla king, Jayasthiti, to bring Buddhists into this rigid form of social control. The main Hindu castes are the **Brahmins**, the priestly caste (some Brahmins are still priests but many are now employed in the civil service), **Chhetris** (warriors and rulers), **Vaisyas** (traders and farmers) and **Shudras** (artisans). Below them are the **untouchables** (butchers, tailors, sweepers and those who carry out other menial tasks).

The Hindu pantheon has three main gods, Brahma the creator, Vishnu the preserver and Shiva the destroyer and god of reproduction. Most Hindus are Vaishnavites (followers of Vishnu) or Shaivites (followers of Shiva). On the Jomsom-Muktinath trek you may meet *sadhus*, Shaivite pilgrims (carrying a trident as the symbol of Shiva) on their way to the temples of Muktinath.

Other popular deities include Saraswati (Brahma's consort and the goddess of science and wisdom), Kali or Durga (Shiva's blood-drinking consort, the goddess of death), Rama and Krishna (the seventh and eighth incarnations of Vishnu) and Hanuman (the monkey god).

> **Holy cows**
> The cow is sacred to Hinduism and Kathmandu's free-ranging herds take full advantage of their divine status, sunning themselves on the warm tarmac of the capital's main thoroughfares.
>
> If your taxi is held up, pray to Ganesh. He's Shiva's elephant-headed son, the god of wisdom and remover of all obstacles!

Buddhism

In its purest form Buddhism isn't actually a religion since it's concerned not with gods or the saving of the soul but with personal enlightenment dependent solely upon the works of the individual. Buddhism grew out of Hinduism in the 5th century BC and shares with Hinduism the belief in reincarnation. For Buddhists, however, escape from the cycle of rebirth brings *nirvana*, the extinguishing of self and desire.

The Buddha was born Prince Siddhartha Gautam in 560BC in Lumbini, southern Nepal. Overcome by all the suffering and pain in the world, he tried to find the reasons first in philosophy, then as an ascetic submitting himself to a round of tough penances. These included sitting on thorns, sleeping by rotting corpses and eating a diet so low in calories that he is reputed to have been able to feel his backbone when he grasped his stomach. He became so weak that one day, walking along a river near Bodhgaya in India, he fainted and fell into the water. Coming to he decided that enlightenment was not to be found in extreme deprivation. He restored himself with a good meal and sat down under a tree (the famous bodhi tree) to meditate.

• **The Middle Way** In his meditation, it was revealed to the Buddha that human desires cause people to be locked into the eternal circle of rebirth. Only when people cease to desire can they escape this cycle of suffering and achieve final peace. He realised that he couldn't have achieved enlightenment before because it was what he desired. He realised that extremes of self-mortification and self-indulgence were not the answer; the 'Middle Way' is the path to enlightenment. This involves mastering the four noble truths (that all life is suffering, that desire is the cause of all suffering, that it is possible to escape from this state and achieve nirvana, and that this can be done by following the Eight-Fold Path of right views, right thought, right speech, right action, right livelihood, right endeavour, right mindfulness and right concentration).

• **Buddhist sects** Soon after the Buddha's death in 480 BC, a schism occurred amongst his disciples that eventually divided Buddhism into two main camps, Theravada and Mahayana; but there are now many sects within these.

Theravada Buddhism ('the tradition of the elders') is closer to the Buddha's original teachings that enlightenment comes through your own endeavours, not through divine interference. Also known as Hinayana (the 'Lesser vehicle'), it's followed in Sri Lanka and the countries of South East Asia.

Mahayana Buddhism is entirely different. It's much more like a religion with a colourful pantheon of enlightened beings known as *bodhisattvas*. The Buddha himself is seen as a divine being, just one of a number of Buddhas who've come down to earth (and some who have yet to come) to help everyone achieve nirvana. Buddhism was given a much wider appeal because converts did not have to give up their old gods; they could continue to worship them as bodhisattvas.

Tibetan Buddhism or Lamaism is the main form of Buddhism practised in Nepal. When Mahayana Buddhism reached Tibet in the 7th century, it absorbed the deities of the native religion, Bon. Lamaism emphasises the importance of magic and the reciting of magical phrases from *tantras* (manuals) to achieve certain ends; it's often referred to as Tantric Buddhism. Tantrism was formerly popular also in Hinduism, and it taught that there are two parts to each deity, male and female. It was thought that a mystical union with one or other part of the deity was possible by mortals through sexual excess. In the 11th century, Tibetan Buddhism was purged of these extreme tantric elements by the monk, Marpa.

In Tibetan Buddhism, spiritual teachers are known as **lamas** and live in the **gompa** (monastery) that is usually attached to the temple. In the course of Tibetan history these lamas achieved greater power than the kings. There are four main orders of monks. The **Nying-ma-pa** (the Ancient Order or Red Hat school) was founded in the 8th century by the monk Padmasambhava (also known as Guru Rinpoche), who spent some time in Nepal. Most of the Buddhists in the mountain regions here are followers of this order. The **Sakya-pa** and **Kagyu-pa** (founded by the reforming monk Marpa) have few adherents in Nepal, although there are monasteries of the Sakya-pa sect in the north Annapurna region. The **Geluk-pa** (Yellow Hat school) is led by the Dalai Lama, the exiled Tibetan leader who now lives in India. Many of his followers came to Nepal as refugees after the invasion of Tibet by China in 1959.

Newari Buddhism, as practised in the Kathmandu Valley, is not derived from Tibetan Buddhism but from earlier influences from the south. The religion of the Newars is an interesting mixture of Hinduism and Mahayana Buddhism. Their Buddhist priests do not live in monasteries but marry and belong to a hereditary caste.

Om mani padme hum

The most famous *mantra* (prayer chant) of the Tibetan Buddhists is Om Mani Padme Hum', which means 'Hail to the Jewel in the Lotus', the jewel being the Buddha. It's believed that the more times this magical phrase is prayed, the greater protection against evil it affords. Enterprising worshippers have come up with some novel ways to do this. **Prayer flags** printed with the mantra release its magical powers into the winds. **Prayer wheels** contain the mantra on lengths of paper and come in a range of sizes from small portable models to huge painted drums. These must always be turned clockwise. The mantra is also carved onto rock faces and **mani stones**, which can be seen piled up into walls along the trails in the northern part of the Annapurna region.

Animism

Even older than the established religions of Hinduism and Buddhism in Nepal is a belief in the forces of nature which are able to affect human beings. The sun, the moon and the stars, mountains, rocks and rivers are all thought to have an *anima* (spirit) which needs to be placated or a delicate balance will be upset that will lead to some human misfortune. Particularly amongst the mountain people, there are still **shaman**, or faith-healers (*jhankri*) who intervene between the deities and mortals, especially when the latter are ill.

Practical information for the visitor

VISAS AND TREKKING PERMITS

Visas are required by all foreigners except Indian passport holders and as well as a visa every trekker is required to have a trekking permit. Visas are most easily obtained on arrival at the airport or border (US$25 for a 30-day visa, US$15 for 15 days – both single entry). A double entry 30-day visa costs US$40, and there's also another option: a 60-day multiple entry visa for US$60. Visas are also obtainable from Nepalese embassies abroad (see p236) but prices vary from country to country. In the UK, a visa currently costs £20 and takes 24 hours to process. One passport-sized photo is the official requirement; they don't seem to insist on this if you're getting your visa on arrival.

Visa validity and extensions

Visa extensions are available in Kathmandu and Pokhara and cost the equivalent in rupees of US$1/£0.67 per day for a total of 120 days. It's sometimes possible to get an additional 30 days in special circumstances. In any one calendar year no tourist may stay longer than 150 days.

Nepalese visa regulations and prices are subject to frequent changes. At one time you used to have to show bank receipts to prove you had cashed a certain amount of money through legal means (ie not the black market) in order to gain a visa extension. Although this is no longer the case you might be wise to keep all currency exchange receipts.

If you overstay the period on your visa you will be charged the regular extension fee plus 100%.

Trekking permit and ACAP entry permit

A trekking permit may be obtained only in Nepal, at the offices of the Department of Immigration in Kathmandu (see p108) or Pokhara (see p127). You must first be in possession of a visa valid for at least as many days as the trekking permit. Charges start at the equivalent in rupees of US$5 per week for the first month, US$10 per week thereafter. Permits are processed the same day but the offices are closed on Saturday. If you are stuck in Jomsom and need an extension to your trekking permit it's sometimes possible to get one from the District Officer. As well as the

---

(**Opposite**) Keeping watch with the gods and goddesses in Durbar Square, Kathmandu. (Photo: Henry Stedman). (**Overleaf**) The village of Jharkot (seen from below Muktinath) sits on a spur overlooking the barren valley.

trekking permit, trekkers in the Annapurna region are also required to pay an **ACAP entry fee** (currently Rs650) which goes directly to the Annapurna Conservation Area Project. In Kathmandu it's available in the National Parks Office, across the road from the Department of Immigration.

LOCAL TRANSPORT

• **Air** Since 1991, when the new government permitted the formation of private airlines, visitors have been offered alternatives to the national carrier, Royal Nepal Airlines (RNAC); they still have the largest number of routes and planes but the new airlines have provided much needed back-up on the popular routes. For the mountain routes STOL (Short Take-Off and Landing) planes, such as the Twin Otter or the Pilatus Porter are used. Taking off and landing in these tiny planes can be an exhilarating experience but it's quite safe. Helicopters are now also used on the flights to Jomsom.

For tourists, ticket prices are quoted in US$ and must be paid for with hard currency. Locals pay considerably less than foreigners but on popular flights tourists get precedence. Tickets can be bought for the same price from a travel agent as from the airlines companies. Check that the travel agent is not adding on a service charge; they get a commission from the airlines, anyway.

• **Bus** Long distance local buses are cheap and uncomfortable; night-buses pure torture. Unless you're really strapped for time it's far better to take a day bus; the views are spectacular.

There are three kinds of bus: cheap **private buses** which operate from the bus stations; government-run **Sajha** buses which leave from their own bus stops; and the more expensive **tourist buses**.

The two former are similarly priced but Sajha buses, usually newer Mitsubishis (part of a Japanese aid package) tend to be faster, more reliable and better maintained than the Indian Tatas run by private companies.

Some tourist buses are quite comfortable though not much faster than the Sajha buses. They do, however, have the advantage of leaving from the tourist areas in Kathmandu and Pokhara. Packed with like-minded foreign trekkers, they're not much of a cultural experience. Note that in Pokhara, the taxi mafia has ensured that buses go only as far as the bus station and don't take you to the hotel area. They do, however, allow the buses to leave from the hotel area in the morning.

(**Opposite**) The private chapel in the Red House Lodge, Kagbeni, contains a large gilt image of the Red Buddha Amitabha.

• **Taxi** The battered troupe of elderly Toyotas that for many years constituted Nepal's taxi fleet has recently been joined by some newer vehicles. As well as the black and yellow cabs there are also three new taxi companies. All taxis have meters although the drivers are reluctant to use them for tourists, despite a big rate rise in 1995. Most foreigners establish a price with the driver before getting in. Instead you could try offering Rs10-20 on top of the meter price or just get in and wait until you've got a short way down the road before threatening to get out if the driver doesn't turn the meter on.

• **Auto-rickshaw** These Indian-built Bajaj three-wheelers of Italian descent are about 25-50% cheaper than taxis. They have meters but the advice above also applies since drivers are not keen to use them. Unlike taxi meters, these meters need recalibrating so you should pay what's on the meter plus 40%. Drivers will ask for much more than this, though.

• **Tempo** Larger versions of auto-rickshaws, tempos have cramped bench seating in the back for up to eight people. They follow fixed routes and can be flagged down anywhere along them. Fares are only a few rupees.

• **Cycle-rickshaw** Environmentally friendly but bargaining is required before you climb in. Tourists have pushed prices up so that they're not much cheaper than auto-rickshaws.

• **Motorbike** A number of places in the tourist areas of Kathmandu and Pokhara have started motorbike rental. This costs around £5-7/US$3.50-4.50 per day for a 125cc Indian-built Kawasaki. Helmets are also available and are vital, given the appalling state of both the roads and the hospitals.

• **Bicycle** Renting a bike is a good way to get around Kathmandu or Pokhara and there are numerous rental shops. Heavy Indian Heros cost £0.60/US$0.88 per day for new models, £0.30/US$0.44 for older ones. Taiwanese mountain bikes are also available, for £1.40/US$2.20 per day. Try for a discount if you're renting for more than a day or two.

Check your bike's tyres, brakes, bell and lock before cycling off. You will be held responsible if your bike is stolen so take particular care with mountain bikes.

LANGUAGE

Nepali is the national language of Nepal but it is the mother-tongue of less than 60% of the population. It's a Sanskrit-based language similar to India's Hindi. There are two other important languages on the Terai, Maithili (spoken by 11% of Nepalis) and Bhojpuri (7.6%). Newari, a rich

Tibeto-Burman language, is spoken by only 3% of the population. Languages spoken in the Annapurna region tend to be of the Tibeto-Burman group and include Gurung (which has several dialects but no script), Magar, Thakali and Manangba as well as Nepali. Many other languages are spoken in Nepal.

Along the main trekking routes you'll always find someone who knows at least a few words of English but you should try to learn some Nepali phrases (see p249).

ELECTRICITY

Less than 10% of the population has access to electricity but some villages in the mountains are supplied by low voltage micro-hydro schemes. Bulbs glow rather than burn brightly and recharging batteries is difficult which fortunately discourages people from dragging their camcorders too far into the mountains.

In Kathmandu and other towns on the national grid the voltage is 220V, 50Hz. Sockets are of the old, round pin variety (2, 5 and 15 amp) as formerly used in Britain.

The little gadget (decorated in Heath Robinson style with dials, switches and lights) that you may see beside fridges in Nepal is a voltage regulator. It's necessary to protect against frequent power surges that would otherwise overload the circuitry.

Power cuts are frequent so a torch/flashlight is vital.

TIME & DATE

Nepal time

Nepal is 5 hours 45 minutes ahead of Greenwich Mean Time (GMT) which (to show the country's independence, no doubt) is 15 minutes ahead of India. Time calculations for the following cities are:
• London: -5 hours 45 minutes (Oct to Mar); -6 hours 45 minutes during British Summer Time (Apr to Sep)
• New York: -10 hours 45 minutes
• Los Angeles: -13 hours 45 minutes
• Sydney: +4 hours 15 minutes
• Auckland: +6 hours 15 minutes
• Lhasa: +2 hours 15 minutes (Oct to Mar); +3 hours 15 minutes (Apr to Sep)

Date

The Nepalis may be just a few minutes ahead of the Indians as far as the time goes but they're halfway through the 21st century according to their calendar. The official calendar is based on the Bikram era (**Bikram Sambat** or BS) and is 56 or 57 years ahead of the Gregorian calendar used in the West. The new year begins on 13 April and thus 1996 AD is 2052 BS until then, 2053 BS thereafter until 12 April 1997 AD.

The months run from the middle of months in the Gregorian calendar. They are Baisakh (Apr-May), Jestha (May-June), Asadh (June-July), Shraaun (July-Aug), Bhadra (Aug-Sep), Aswin (Sep-Oct), Kartik (Oct-Nov), Mangsir (Nov-Dec), Pous (Dec-Jan), Magh (Jan-Feb), Phalgun (Feb-Mar) and Chaitra (Mar-Apr). They vary in length from 29 to 32 days.

Religious festivals and many other ceremonies, including weddings and death anniversaries follow a **lunar calendar**. Months are 28 days long and are made up of a 'light' fortnight (Sukla Pachhi – when the moon is waxing) followed by a 'dark' one (Krishna Pachhi – as it wanes).

Date-keeping is further complicated by many of Nepal's communities operating their own systems. The Newar year starts around the end of October and is 880 years behind the Gregorian calendar. New Year's Day comes in February for the Tibetans.

HOLIDAYS & FESTIVALS

Office hours
Saturday is the day off during the week when all offices are closed, including the Department of Immigration where trekking permits are obtained. Business hours are from 10am to 5pm (to 4pm from mid-Nov to mid-Feb), Sunday to Friday, although many offices close at 1 pm on Friday. Embassies are closed on Saturday and Sunday.

Festivals
With the rich patchwork of cultures and religions in Nepal, there's a festival going on somewhere at least every other day. The main season for festivals, however, comes in August and September as the monsoon withdraws.

The principal festivals which are celebrated in Kathmandu or the Annapurna region are listed below. Since almost all are determined by the lunar calendar they occur on a different day each year. The Ministry of Home Affairs issues a list of the 25 official holidays at the beginning of each year.

• **Dasain** (Durga Puja) is the biggest of Nepal's festivals, lasting at least 10 days and beginning at the end of September or early October. The whole country grinds to a halt as people return to their villages for family reunions and feasts. It's a Hindu festival, which celebrates the triumph of good over evil, symbolised by the victory of the Hindu Rama over Ravana and the goddess Durga over Mahisasur, the devil who took the shape of a buffalo. Consequently numerous buffalo (and goats, sheep and cockerels) lose their heads during the eighth and ninth days of the festival and the roads literally flow with blood. Every form of transport, from the cycle-rickshaws of Thamel to Royal Nepal Airlines' Boeing 727s, has its wheels doused with sacrificial blood to bring good luck for the year ahead.

• **Tihar** (Deepavali) lasts five days and usually falls in November, two weeks after Dasain. It's known as the 'Festival of Lights' after the thousands of oil lamps that are lit in windows to welcome Lakshmi, the goddess of prosperity. Children go singing door-to-door for coins, houses are cleaned, sisters perform pujas for their brothers and everyone pujas the local cow.

Puja

A *puja* (act of worship) can be anything from a quick prayer to a festival of several days but offerings of some sort are usually involved. Hindus offer flowers, food and coloured powders and light incense and butter lamps. They receive a *tika* (a red mark on their forehead) as a blessing from the deity. Hindu pujas to mark the year's most important festivals require animal sacrifices (formerly human sacrifices) and at Dasain thousands of buffalo and goats are beheaded.

Buddhist pujas are rather more humane. Juniper is burnt as incense, mantras (see below) are chanted and prayer wheels are spun. Lamas are sponsored to say prayers and invoke the blessing of the gods on certain people. In Manang, on the Annapurna Circuit trail, there's a lama who will perform a puja to get the gods to help you over the Thorung La (see opposite p224).

• **Losar**, the Tibetan New Year, falls in February. If you're in Kathmandu at this time, Baudha is the place to be. On the fourth day thousands of Tibetans converge on the stupa for prayers.

• **Shivaratri** is celebrated in February at Pashupatinath in Kathmandu. It's a day of ritual bathing and puja that attracts Hindus to this Shiva temple from as far away as India.

• **Holi** If you're in any Hindu area in March you can't escape this boisterous spring festival. It involves tossing buckets of water over everyone and 'playing colours' (throwing handfuls of coloured powder). Westerners, particularly women, are favourite targets so put on your old clothes, stock up with bags of powder and water squirters and keep your camera covered.

• **Bisket Jatra** is Nepalese New Year's Day, which falls in April. Main celebrations are in Bhaktapur and then in Thimi the following day.

• **Raato Machhendranath** The god Raato ('Red') Machhendranath is the protector of the Kathmandu Valley, worshipped by both Hindus and Buddhists. Held in April or May to ensure that the monsoon will reach the Valley, this festival lasts at least a month. An image of the god is pulled on a huge chariot through the streets of Patan in a smaller version of the Jagannath procession that takes place in Puri in India.

• **Buddha Jayanti** is the birthday of the Buddha, celebrated in May. Conveniently, it's also the anniversary of his enlightenment and death. In Kathmandu the main celebrations take place at Swayambhunath but there will be pujas at most Buddhist temples.

• **The Dalai Lama's birthday** is on 6 July, celebrated particularly by Tibetans.

• **Janai Purnima** falls in August on the full moon of Shraaun and is centred on the Kumbeshwar temple in Patan. High caste Brahmins and Chhetri change the sacred red thread (*janai*) that they wear over their left shoulder and under their clothes. The festival also attracts shamans. The **Gai Jatra** ('Cow Festival') follows the next day, to honour those who have died within the last year.

• **Teej**, celebrated in August/September, is a women's festival that begins with a feast and is followed by a day of fasting. Husbands are honoured and women take ritual baths at Pashupatinath in Kathmandu to cleanse themselves from the 'sin' of touching a man during menstruation.

• **Indra Jatra** This important festival marks the end of the monsoon in September. It lasts eight days and in Kathmandu there are mediaeval pageants and masked dances. Prithvi Narayan Shah conquered Kathmandu to unify Nepal during Indra Jatra in 1768 and this historic event is remembered during the festival.

An important part of the festival is the appearance of the Kumari, the living goddess' (see p109), in Durbar Square. She rides in a chariot to greet the image of the god Bhairab in Hanuman Dhoka, whereupon beer flows from a pipe between his teeth. To get a sip of this brings good luck. On the last night of the festival the Kumari places a tika on the forehead of the King to give him the right to rule for the next year.

MONEY

Currency

The Nepali rupee (Rs) is issued in banknote denominations of Rs 1, 2, 5, 10, 20, 50, 100, 500 and 1000 and coins of 5, 10, 25 and 50 paise. There are 100 paise in a rupee. As in India, people won't accept notes with torn edges so check your change to make sure you're not being slipped some. If there's a hole in the note it does not matter.

Foreign exchange at a bank

When changing money at a bank keep the exchange certificate you are given. It's worth ensuring you're given some small change although on the main trekking routes during the season lodge owners are usually able to break larger bills for you. Rates do not vary greatly between banks, but they're a little better at the lesser-known Nepali banks (Nabil Bank) than at branches of Western banks (Grinlays). At the foreign exchange offices in Thamel rates are less good.

Travellers' cheques attract a better rate than cash, about 2% more. Current tourist rates are £1 = Rs85, US$1 = Rs54.5, A$1 = Rs41, DM1 = Rs38.5, and Indian Rs1 = Rs1.60.

Black market
Many travellers use Nepal's black market which is usually centred on the carpet shops in the tourist areas. Surprisingly, dealers accept travellers' cheques as well as cash in major currencies. Rates are about 5-10% higher than in the banks and best rates are for US$50 and US$100 bills. Note that using the black market helps the Indian carpet-sellers get their profits out of the country but does nothing to help the national debt.

International banks in Nepal
Nepal-Grinlays, Standard Chartered and American Express all have branches in Kathmandu. Nepal-Grinlays will give instant cash advances on Visa or Mastercard for as much as your credit agreement with these companies will stand, as will numerous other banks.

Tipping
Not a tradition in Nepal, tipping has come to be expected in the top hotels and restaurants. A service charge of 10% is, however, sometimes included in the bill. At smaller places tip 5-10% if the service was particularly good, although this is not necessary.

Porters expect tips of about an extra day's wages per week trekked. If you're trekking with a group, the agency will usually offer guidelines on how much to tip.

Bargaining
This is expected when you're buying souvenirs, fruit or, to some extent, for hotel rooms out of season. Westerners are notoriously bad at it forgetting that it's as much a form of social interchange as a way to get the price down. They tend either not to bother and pay the asking price (in which case for things like fruit they drive up the price for the local people) or else they bargain too aggressively.

It's best to treat it as a game and not to try to force the seller down to the lowest possible price. When shopping for souvenirs, decide what your maximum price will be before you start bargaining. Don't offer more than 50% of the seller's initial price as your first bid. Only start bargaining if you're actually interested and never back out of a deal once you've both agreed on a price.

POST & TELECOMMUNICATIONS

Postal services
Most travellers use the Poste Restante service at the GPO in Kathmandu and Pokhara to receive mail. Letters should be addressed with your surname underlined (or they may be mis-sorted), Poste Restante, The GPO, Kathmandu (or Pokhara). Since everyone is allowed to sift through the mail it's inadvisable to get anything valuable sent to you this way. American Express accepts mail for its clients.

Postage rates are currently Rs12 to the UK and Rs15 to the USA or Australia for a postcard; they take two to three weeks. For an aerogram it's Rs14 and Rs17 respectively and for a 20g letter by air, Rs18 and Rs20. When sending letters you should try to ensure they are franked or the stamps may be steamed off and reused. The numerous **communication centres** that have sprung up in the tourist areas sell stamps and take letters to the post office to have them franked. They can also receive mail for you.

Phone
The system now seems to work well, both within the country and for international calls. Local calls from a phone in your hotel room are usually free.

Fax
Sending and receiving faxes in Nepal is absolutely no problem. In fact it's so easy to do here you can run up a big bill faxing family and friends around the globe. The communication centres are the most convenient places to use. Prices vary between them but it generally costs about £2/US$3 per minute (enough for a short fax).

If you're trying to fax or phone into Nepal this is easiest to do when it's night-time in Nepal. The international dialling code for Nepal is 977; Kathmandu is 1 (01 within Nepal); Pokhara is 61.

E-mail
Several communications agencies in Kathmandu now offer to send and receive e-mail for customers. See p105.

THE MEDIA

Newspapers and magazines
According to the latest figures, Nepalis have 587 registered newspapers to choose from, although most of these are weeklies. The English-language daily, the *Kathmandu Post,* is what to peruse over your porridge in the mornings but you'll be eating long after you've finished reading. You could then move on to the *Rising Nepal*, once the mouthpiece of the monarchy and still adopting a squirmingly deferential attitude to the royal

family; the ins and outs of palace life continue to reduce world news to no more than a few columns.

Kathmandu's excellent bookshops also stock copies of the *International Herald Tribune, Asian Wall Street Journal* and *USA Today* plus international news magazines like *Time* and *Newsweek*. Pick up a free copy of *Nepal Traveller* at the tourist office at the airport. The bi-monthly environmental journal, *Himal*, has interesting articles.

The British Council Reading Room subscribes to many UK newspapers and magazines and is a good place to go if you want to know what the weather was like in Britain two weeks ago.

Radio & TV

Radio Nepal broadcasts the news in English at 08.00 and 13.05 hours.

Short wave radio frequencies for the BBC World Service are 15310, 11955, 11750, 17790, 9740 and 5975. Voice of America broadcasts on 1575, 6110, 7205, 9700, 11710, 15205 and 17735. Lower frequencies generally give better results at night, higher ones during the day.

On Nepal TV, the news in English is at 10.15 each evening. Satellite TV has caught on in Nepal and Star TV, BBC World Service TV and CNN are available in many hotels.

FOOD

Since Nepal is a cultural junction between the people of the north and the south, you might expect a wealth of culinary contrasts, as in Singapore which has a well-deserved reputation for the diversity of its food. In Nepal, however, the poverty of both the people and the ingredients means that for most of the population food is fuel not culinary art.

That having been said, the kitchens of Kathmandu and Pokhara have earned a reputation among travellers for being able to reproduce Western goodies like steak and chips, apple pie and chocolate cake. If you've been travelling round India for a while, you'll be very impressed by the food here. If you've just flown in from the West expecting Oriental delicacies you're likely to be disappointed.

Vegetarians, however, are well catered for in Nepal. Meat is an expensive delicacy for most Nepalis and is replaced by pulses, lentils in particular, and eggs. Cheese is sometimes available.

Daal bhat

The vast majority of Nepalis subsist on a couple of meals of *daal bhat* (lentils and rice) with *tarkari* (vegetables) each day, taken in the middle of the morning and in the early evening.

A good daal bhat can be delicious. You're given a *thaali* (stainless steel tray) with a heap of boiled rice, a bowl of soupy lentils and a small serving of lightly curried vegetables. You should wash your hands first

(Nepalis do), pour some of the lentils over the rice, add some vegetables and eat with your right hand only. Use your thumb to push the food off your fingers and into your mouth. Most trekkers find eating without utensils difficult so spoons are provided. Daal bhat is an all-you-can-eat meal and your plate will be topped up until you've eaten your fill. It's also cheap, nutritious and filling – ideal trekking fuel – but some trekkers find it tedious and go for the Western alternatives below.

Some restaurants in Kathmandu and Pokhara serve upmarket versions of daal bhat with many side dishes, some of them consisting of meat.

Other Nepali and Tibetan food

Rice is available along all the trekking routes in the Annapurna region but it is the staple diet for most Nepalis near the lower-altitude areas where it can be grown or cheaply portered. In the higher regions other grains take

---

Culinary expectations on the trek

• **Breakfast** Nepalis make do with a glass of sweet milky tea before hitting the trail early in the day. They'll stop for daal bhat between 10.00 and 11.00. If you've got a long day's walking ahead it's probably a good idea to start early after just a cup of tea, stopping for breakfast an hour or two later. Oat porridge, corn porridge, muesli (available with milk and diced apple), eggs (boiled, fried, poached, scrambled and as an omelette) all make a filling breakfast. Bread is rarely available, the alternatives being Tibetan bread (sweet, doughy and fried but good) and chapattis with jam, honey or peanut butter. A bowl of steaming porridge followed by an omelette placed between two chapattis makes an excellent breakfast.

• **Lunch** Although lodge owners will prepare the supper items listed below at any time in the day many trekkers prefer a light lunch. Noodle soup is one of the most popular items despite the fact that it comes out of a packet. It is, however, tasty and it's very quick to prepare so it uses little firewood. Vegetables are usually added to make it more interesting. Fried rice and chowmein are other popular lunchtime dishes; pancakes make a good pudding if you want one.

• **Supper** Most lodges have a good range of soups. Favourites include pumpkin, and garlic (although many cloves of garlic are used they're not strongly flavoured). There's also vegetable, and (usually from packets) tomato and chicken.

Meat is a delicacy that rarely appears on menus in trekking lodges although tinned tuna is sometimes available. Alternatives to daal bhat include pizzas, spring rolls, chopsuey, chowmein, Swiss rosti (potato, veg. and cheese), potatoes in a range of guises – mashed, boiled, lyonnaise, fried, au gratin – and Tibetan momos. Some of the more adventurous lodges in the Kali Gandaki even feature buritos, lasagne or miso soup on their menus.

Puddings included pancakes, apple pie, rice pudding, apple fritters, hot chocolate pudding or chocolate cake. Tibetan bread (fried) is good with honey or peanut butter.

The catering requirements of trekkers are placing a heavy strain on firewood resources in the Annapurna region. See p80 for information on how to limit your impact. Note that the three-course dinner is not part of the culture of Himalayan cuisine so don't expect your courses to come in any particular order and don't complain if you start with apple pie and finish with soup!

its place. Roasted flour made from millet, maize or, in the far north, barley, is made into *tsampa*. A versatile staple, it can be eaten on its own without cooking, mixed with Tibetan tea or made into porridge.

In the hills meat is rarely available but in Kathmandu and Pokhara chicken, goat and buffalo may be curried or may appear on tourist menus in a variety of guises including 'buff' steak. If you like biltong (jerky) you'll like *sukuti*, the Nepali/Tibetan equivalent. You may see it hanging in strings above the fire, being smoked. It's usually deep fried just before it's served and goes very well with beer or tumba (see below).

Tibetan food is popular and includes *momos* (meat- or veg.-filled pasta that are steamed and served with a chilli sauce). These are sometimes also fried; they're then called *kothay*. A favourite Tibetan soup is *thugpa*.

Cheese is good but not always available in the hills. It's made from the milk of buffaloes or naks (female yaks – the yak is the male). Many travellers eat yoghurt/curd although the containers this is stored in are far from spotless. Lassi is a delicious drink made from yoghurt but it's sometimes diluted with water and so not 100% safe. Order hot milk to ensure it's pasteurised.

Western food
Nepal's fame for apple pie and chocolate cake dates back to the 1960s when foreign volunteer workers encouraged the Freak Street lodge owners in Kathmandu to provide them with a taste of home. Aunt Jane's Place, started by the wife of a Peace Corps volunteer, has now passed into history but was among the first of the budget restaurants serving Western food.

What proves popular in one restaurant is quickly copied by most of the others and now it's possible to eat food that is at least recognisably Western along the main trekking routes in the Annapurna region. You can get passable Nepali versions of pizzas on the trail and in Kathmandu and Pokhara the have-a-go-at-everything menus feature pepper steaks, spaghetti bolognese, roast chicken and chips, lasagne, moussaka, quiche, tandoori dishes and even Mexican food (tacos, enchiladas and buritos).

Some dishes are simple to prepare and use ingredients that are easily available (pancakes, for example). Others require making do with whatever the restaurateur can get hold of in Nepal. Your taco shell may turn out to be nothing more than a dry folded chapatti!

Fruit and vegetables
Potatoes can be grown at high altitudes and are popular in the northern parts of the Annapurna region. They're small and tasty, served just with salt but sometimes also cheese. Vegetables include onions (onion omelettes are recommended), cauliflower, pumpkin and spring greens. In Kathmandu there's a far greater variety.

Fruit depends very much on what is locally available according to the seasons since distribution is costly. In the Annapurna region, apples, peaches and apricots are grown around Marpha and Chame and available in the summer and autumn. Mandarin oranges (*suntala*) are widely available in the winter and papaya and bananas can be found in Kathmandu and Pokhara throughout the year. Mangos and guavas are available during the monsoon.

DRINK

Don't drink the water' is the number one health rule for Nepal (and most of Asia). Drinks that have been boiled or bottled are generally safe and as trekkers will lose a lot of liquid at altitude and through sweating they must ensure they drink large quantities. Tea (*chiya*) is the national beverage but it bears little resemblance to what some people might drink with their cucumber sandwiches. It's produced by boiling tea-leaves, milk and sugar together into a strong unappealing orange liquid. Luckily there are other options: black tea, lemon tea (delicious) and tea with milk but without sugar. It's available by the glass or in small, medium and large pots. Other hot drinks include coffee (Nescafe), milk, chocolate and even cappuccino. Tibetan tea should be tried, though few Westerners develop a taste for it. It's produced by churning hot tea, salt and butter together.

Bottled fizzy drinks include Coke, Pepsi, Sprite, Fanta (orange and lemon) and 7-Up, all cheaply produced under licence in Nepal in reasonably hygienic conditions. Plastic bottles of mineral water are available but you should ensure that the seal is intact or they may have been refilled with tap water. Because of the difficulty of disposing of the bottles, mineral water is not an environmentally-friendly alternative to purifying water yourself (see p239).

Alcoholic drinks include locally-produced beers. Star and Iceburg have now been joined by the better and more expensive Tuborg and San Miguel, brewed under licence. There's a large range of local spirits including Snowland gin, Khukri rum, Three Lions whiskey. *Chang* is home-brewed beer and *rakshi* a potent liquor made from rice or millet. When you visit Baudha in Kathmandu, you should try *tumba*, fermented millet mixed with boiling water and drunk through a straw. In Tukuche and Marpha local distillers produce powerful apple, apricot and peach brandies that taste great when you're trekking but seem a bit rough if you try them when you get home.

THINGS TO BUY

The souvenir shops in Kathmandu and Pokhara are stuffed full of carpets, crafts and knitware, some of it very well made but there's also some real tourist junk. It's best to do your shopping near the end of your trip, once you've had a chance to see what's available. Compare goods and prices in a number of shops and always bargain. The tourist shops in expensive hotels are not a good place for a bargain but they may have some high quality goods.

Read Jeff Greenwald's *Shopping for Buddhas* for an amusing portrait of Western consumers in Nepal. If it's real antiques you're after note that you need an export permit for anything that looks as if it could be more than 100 years old. For other antiques a receipt from the shop will suffice as long as it contains a detailed description of the item. You should be aware that your own country will probably have some restrictions on the value of goods you import duty-free.

● **Clothes and sweaters** Clothes shops sell the latest trekking fashions, including loose-fitting cotton trousers which are recommended, and they also do a good line in embroidery. T-shirts are emblazoned with everything from 'Tintin in Tibet' to 'I love Kathmandu'. Woollen sweaters are a best buy. They're hand knitted in attractive colours but need careful washing as they lose their shape easily. Undyed Pasmina shawls, made from the highest quality wool, are expensive but luxuriously warm.

● **Carpets** The Tibetan carpet industry, started as a refugee relief programme in the early 1960s, has now expanded to become Nepal's largest exporter. Prices vary according to the number of knots per square inch – from about 50 up to 100 for the best quality. They're usually made from wool and colours are mainly pastel hues but there also are some bright striped tiger rugs. Kashmiri traders have also opened shops in Nepal selling rugs in Kashmiri, Indian and Central Asian styles in silk or wool.

● **Thangkas** There are many shops specialising in these Tibetan religious paintings. They're bright, highly detailed and done on cloth but may not be quite as old as you're led to believe. Some thangka painters are also producing humorous modern paintings in this style. There are some good shops off Patan's Durbar Square as well as in Thamel and Pokhara.

● **Jewellery** There's a wide range of jewellery available but you have to know your gems or you could be fobbed off with glass. Silver filigree bangles, earrings and coral and turquoise necklaces are all popular. Strings of colourful beads are sold at the bead market in Kathmandu.

If you can afford it, you could have some earrings made up by a goldsmith in Kathmandu, Pokhara or even the Annapurna village of Tatopani (see p143).

● **Trinkets and other souvenirs** There's a wide range of interesting little souvenirs including attractive papier mache boxes and vases in

Kashmiri shops. Puppets, masks, Nepalese caps, incense sticks, and Nepalese tea all make good presents.

Handmade paper is a traditional craft and you can buy block-print calendars, writing-paper and cards. There are also cloth-covered notebooks and photograph albums with traditional-style black paper leaves.

The streets of Thamel are thronged with boys hawking Tiger Balm, flutes and khukris. Some sell 'Nepali padlocks'. Made from brass in the shape of animals, these make interesting little presents.

Thimi, near Kathmandu, is famous for its pottery and makes an interesting bicycle excursion but most pieces are too large and heavy to be convenient souvenirs.

SECURITY

The towns in Nepal are considerably safer than many cities in the West, even at night, although it might be wiser for women to go out in a group after dark.

Security in hotels is generally good but you shouldn't tempt staff by leaving valuables around. Bigger hotels have security boxes at reception; they'll also store anything you don't want to take trekking.

Beware of pickpockets in crowded places, especially on buses, and keep your passport, travellers' cheques and airline tickets in a pouch around your neck or in a moneybelt. A photocopy of the personal information pages in your passport will speed up the reissue process should you be parted from your documents. Remember to keep the receipt for your travellers' cheques separate from the cheques themselves or getting a refund could prove extremely difficult. Keep other valuables (cameras etc) with you at all times.

On the trail there's a greater risk from nature than from man and violent attacks on trekkers are rare. You should, however, be careful in the forests around Gorepani: don't walk by yourself here. Generally, in case there's an accident, it's not a good idea for men or women to trek alone and it's imperative to get together a group of at least five people and to stick together when crossing dangerous passes such as the Thorung La. If one person falls ill or breaks a leg, one could stay with him or her and the others could go together to get help.

PART 3: MINIMUM IMPACT TREKKING

Minimum impact trekking

Nepal's trekking industry – the pros and cons

Tourism is a vital source of foreign exchange for Nepal. Directly or indirectly many Nepalis benefit from the increasing numbers of trekkers and tourists visiting the country even though most of the money they spend goes to just a few people: the trekking companies, the lodge owners and, of course, His Majesty's Government. How much of the money actually contributes to local village economies is debatable and one study places the figure as low as £0.14/US$0.20 out of the average £2/US$3 spent by a trekker each day. In a country where the annual average wage is just over £100 or US$160 and in a region that sees over 40,000 trekkers per year, however, this is not as inconsiderable as the statistic might suggest. Villages that are situated along the main trekking routes are generally more affluent than those that few trekkers pass through.

Much has been written about the negative effects of trekking. It is very true that trekkers place a far greater strain on local resources, firewood particularly, than do locals. According to ACAP, in one village on a main trail in the Annapurna region, up to one hectare (about 21 acres) of forest is cleared each year for use as firewood for the needs of trekkers. Forest clearance leads to soil erosion, already a major problem in the unstable Himalayan region.

Trekkers make a significant contribution to the pollution problem with streamers of pink lavatory paper and plastic mineral water bottles. Far less obvious are the negative aspects of the cultural impact made by trekkers on local communities.

In the tourist boom of the 1970s and 80s it was realised that the pressures of visitors in popular areas like the Annapurna region could eventually destroy the very environment that attracted the visitors in the first place. Several organisations, the Annapurna Conservation Area Project in particular, have done sterling work in conservation education. Their advice is well publicised but, sadly, not always followed; some trekkers behave as if having paid their trekking fees and lodge bills this gives them the right to behave exactly as they choose. The oft-repeated 'Nepal is here to change you, not for you to change it' may sound trite but it is all too true: responsible trekkers should follow this maxim.

The main areas of concern are environmental, economic and cultural. The simple steps that can easily be taken by trekkers to lessen their impact on the delicate ecological balance in the Annapurna region are detailed below.

ENVIRONMENTAL IMPACT

Forest clearance

About 95% of Nepal's energy comes from firewood and the country's forests are being cleared at a rate of 3% per year. Reforestation projects cannot keep pace with this deforestation and the subsequent erosion that often occurs may make the land unusable. A rapidly expanding population and a reliance on firewood for fuel are the main causes of the problem but in a few localised areas, the Annapurna region in particular, trekkers may be more to blame than local people. It's been estimated that a trekker requires up to ten times the amount of firewood that a Nepali would need. Complicated meals are requested at odd times, hot showers are required immediately and boiled water may be demanded for drinking. In winter, trekkers may want a warm fire to sit around at night.

In a country that has tremendous hydroelectric potential, electricity would seem to be the answer to the problem. At present, most of the power generated in this way is either consumed in the Kathmandu Valley or sold to India. There are a number of micro-hydro schemes in the hills but other than powering a few low-wattage cookers they're used mainly for lighting. It's been said that these lighting schemes may actually lead to a greater consumption of firewood since people are now able to stay up after dark and so keep fires burning for warmth.

In order to lessen your impact on the environment you should:

● **Have hot showers only at lodges with solar panels or back-boilers** Some lodges now have back-boilers installed in the cooking stove so that extra wood is not used to heat water. Other lodges have solar-panels for water heating that can be remarkably efficient (as long as you're not at the end of the queue for a shower). Patronise places like this if you want a hot shower and have a wash in a bucket of cold water in smaller places.

● **Order meals together and keep orders simple** Some of the complicated Western dishes that are requested by trekkers are far from fuel efficient, especially when they are ordered singly. Place your order for supper as soon as you arrive at a lodge so that the lodge owner can bulk dishes together. If you want something for pudding order this at the same time, even though you may prefer to wait until you've had your main course. Order simple things for lunch. Noodle soup is a good choice not only because it's fuel efficient but because it's very quick to prepare.

ANNAPURNA CONSERVATION AREA PROJECT (ACAP)

Origins

Set up in 1986 to help preserve this region in the face of the severe deforestation that was taking place to meet the needs of local people and trekkers, ACAP is a comprehensive programme of reforestation and forest management, alternative energy schemes, community development projects, wildlife studies and conservation education.

The ACAP region

This independent non-profit organisation opened its project headquarters in Ghandruk village in December 1986 to administer and protect an area of 2,600 square kms bordered on the west by the Kali Gandaki River, on the east by the Marsyandi and to the south by the Pokhara Valley. The area was extended in 1992 up to the border with Tibet to include the whole of Mustang and Manang districts. The project is directly funded by trekkers' contributions (the entry fee paid when applying for a trekking permit) and through its association with a number of international conservation organisations.

The ACAP approach – co-operation and integration

ACAP is currently regarded as one of the most successful conservation programmes in the country and its success is largely the result of a novel approach. Rather than establish the area as a traditional national park, relocating the inhabitants, it was decided that more could be achieved by co-operating with local people. The project's instigators were adamant that the concept of integrating the human and conservation needs of an area was a far better approach in a less developed country like Nepal where there is very little land that is not already occupied by people.

It was realised that trying to promote environmental conservation amongst very poor people would have little effect unless these people could see something in it for themselves. ACAP's initial drive was to help improve local living conditions to gain the respect and trust of the people. Sir Edmund Hillary, who founded the Himalayan Trust in the Khumbu region, was quick to realise that the projects that were most successful were those initiated by and for the villagers themselves. Like the Himalayan Trust, ACAP has provided the funding for schools, bridges, drinking water projects, health centres, micro-hydro schemes, reforestation projects, trail improvement and sanitation schemes. Local people must provide the labour if they want the projects to go ahead.

ACAP's conservation education projects have helped show local people, lodge owners and trekkers the importance of conserving firewood. Forests have been denationalised and self-regulation of forest resources is being revived with some success. Alternative energy sources have been developed and many lodges now have back-boilers or solar panels. Micro hydroelectric schemes have been established in some areas. Lodge management committees have been set up for each district within the ACAP area and these meet regularly to set prices for food and lodging in order to ensure a reasonable return for the lodge owners and reasonable standards for trekkers. Training schemes in food preparation, the running of lodges and in basic English are held and the certificates awarded on completion of these courses adorn the walls of most lodges.

ACAP now has visitor centres in many of the villages in the Annapurna region, among them Bhulebhule, Tal, Manang, Kagbeni, Jomsom and Ghorepani, as well as in Pokhara and at their headquarters in Ghandruk.

The Nepali staple of daal bhat is cooked in large quantities morning and evening, even in lodges largely patronised by Westerners. It's delicious, filling, cheap and arguably the most environmentally right-on dish you could choose.

• **Don't request boiled water for drinking** There are several perfectly good ways of purifying water (see p239) which render boiling unnecessary. If you treat water yourself you can also be absolutely sure that it has been purified, not simply warmed in a kettle. Iodine is available from the ACAP information offices in Ghandruk, Bhulebhule, Tal, Manang, Kagbeni, and Jomsom.

• **Put on extra clothes, not another log on the fire** Sitting round a fire toasting marshmallows on sticks may be all right in the West but in Nepal it's ecologically more sound to turn in early or put on extra clothes if you're cold.

• **Use kerosene if you're camping** Whilst most trekking companies now use kerosene for cooking for trekkers they do not provide such environmental luxuries for their porters who are forced to cook on fires. It's up to trekkers to lobby trek leaders and the trekking companies if this situation is to change. It has been calculated that to provide kerosene for everyone on the trek would increase the daily cost of a trekking holiday by only £1.50/US$2.25.

Kerosene is available in larger villages. There is a total ban on fires in the Annapurna Sanctuary and there's a kerosene depot in Chomrong on the route in. ACAP is setting up kerosene depots around the Annapurna Circuit.

Erosion
It's not only forest clearance that's to blame for the high incidence of erosion in the Himalaya. The world's youngest chain of mountains is still being formed, rising several millimetres per year as the Asian continental plate pushes up against the Tibetan Plateau. Monsoonal rain on the southern slopes causes further erosion as swollen rivers rush down to the lowlands.

This natural erosion makes the erosion caused by forest clearance all the more serious. Approximately 400,000 hectares of forest are cleared in Nepal each year, resulting in the loss of an additional twenty million tons of soil each year.

• **Stay on the main trail** Avoid steep shortcuts since their continued use may erode the hillside. Don't damage crops or the edges of rice fields: these surrounding ledges are designed to keep in the water when the fields are flooded.

• **Don't damage plants** The age of the Victorian plant-hunter is past and you're unlikely to get your rare rhododendron specimen through customs in Heathrow or Newark, so don't try.

Pollution

Litter is a modern problem. Before the 1960s there was virtually nothing available in the mountain villages that was non-biodegradable, apart from glass bottles. The few items that might be sold in the village shop were wrapped in paper or cloth not plastic. In the lowlands, take-away snacks and meals were and still are served on sal leaves, sewn together and pressed into the shape of a bowl.

In many villages, particularly those on the trekking routes, litter is now a significant problem. Trekkers are certainly to blame for the lavatory paper that may occasionally be seen along the trail and for the piles of plastic mineral water bottles since local people would not use either. A growing cash-based economy has led to greater local use of shops and some Nepalis are still unaware of the cumulative effect of discarding biscuit wrappers, cans or plastic fertiliser bags.

Faecal contamination of water supplies by humans and animals is, however, not a new problem although in many areas drinking water is now piped into the village from a relatively clean source. You should, nevertheless, purify all water for drinking.

• **Don't leave litter** Never drop litter on the trail but take it on with you and dispose of it at the next lodge. Picking up other people's litter would be helpful and set a good example to Nepalis and other trekkers.

If you're on an organised trek burnables should be thrown on the fire and, ideally, non-burnables should be carried out and disposed of outside the trekking area. More usually, non-burnables are buried in a pit dug at the campsite. Stress that this must be efficiently done; although this may be difficult since you will probably leave the site before the kitchen staff.

• **Avoid bottled mineral water** Soft drink bottles and some beer bottles are returnable and therefore environmentally-friendly. Mineral water is, however, sold in plastic bottles that are not only non-returnable but also non-biodegradable. Since, furthermore, you cannot be sure that the bottle hasn't been refilled from a tap (the seals are not 100% tamper-proof) it's far better to get water from lodges and purify it yourself.

• **Dispose of used batteries outside Nepal** In her useful booklet, *Trekking Gently in the Himalaya*, Wendy Brewer Lama has calculated that if every one of the 70,000 trekkers who come to Nepal each year disposes of four flashlight batteries during their stay more than a quarter of a million batteries would be left behind annually. Since the country does not have the facilities for their proper disposal many of these batteries land up polluting the environment or even as children's playthings. Small batteries for cameras could be even more dangerous as toys. Take all used batteries out of Nepal and dispose of them in the West.

• **Don't pollute water sources** If there's a latrine available, use it, otherwise ensure you're at least 20m from a water source and bury your faeces. If you're on an organised trek, a hole is dug and a latrine tent erected over it. Sprinkle some earth into the hole after each use and ensure that it is properly filled when you break camp.

Don't pollute hot springs with soap and shampoo, whatever local people are doing. Borrow a bowl or bucket from a lodge (or you could even use your mug) and wash away from the spring. Collapsible plastic buckets are available from camping shops in the West. These are particularly useful for clothes' washing by streams. Dispose of dirty water away from the stream.

• **Burn used lavatory paper** Few Westerners can adapt to the Nepali water-and-left-hand method. They should, however, ensure that the yards of pink Chinese loo paper that they require as an alternative are entirely incinerated or put in the bins provided for the purpose. Keep your roll of paper in a plastic bag with a cigarette lighter. Don't drop paper down a latrine as this may clog it.

ECONOMIC IMPACT

The economic importance of tourism for Nepal is undeniable. Until recently the people of Lo Manthang and Upper Mustang (closed to foreigners until 1992) must have looked with envy at their rich neighbours to the south in busy tourist villages like Marpha and Jomsom. Given the choice most Nepali village committees would opt to climb aboard the trekking bandwagon. The distribution of these tourist dollars is far from equal, though. Book an organised trek through a foreign operator and a proportion of what you pay stays in the West to pay the company's administrative costs. Book an organised trek in Kathmandu and a large proportion remains in the city. The trek personnel may not be from the Annapurna region and since virtually everything on an organised trek is brought into the area few local services are used and there may be little financial benefit to the region.

If you trek independently you will contribute more to the local economy but perhaps not as much as you might think, since the few services you use (lodges and shops) are operated by only the more wealthy villagers. They do, however, provide a certain amount of work for local people as porters for provisions and as helpers in lodge kitchens.

• **Use local services** The price of a Coke may be close to what you would pay in the West once you're several days' walk into your trek but it's largely composed of the porter's wages required to get it up here. Buying drinks and other things from shops not only helps local business but also helps provide employment for porters.

Using lodges rather than camping is an obvious way to patronise the local economy. When arranging a trek with an organised group you could request to spend some nights in lodges rather than under canvas.

If you're trekking independently employ a **local porter** to carry your pack, if only over part of the trek. Unfortunately, most independent trekkers feel that being weighed down by a heavy pack is all part of the trekking experience. Perhaps colonial guilt (a British trait) also has something to do with it. Arranged once you're on your trek, the services of a porter can cost little more than £3/US$5 per day. It's safest to ask your lodge to suggest someone, rather than to go off with a total stranger. Ensure your porter is clear about your route and the number of days involved, make certain all porters have adequate clothing and shoes if you're trekking at altitude and be sure everyone is clear about what the pay includes. If you are going to be paying for food as well as a daily wage stipulate exactly what this includes. It's probably better to pay a slightly higher wage and not also pay for food and lodging except in remote places (Thorung Phedi and the Annapurna Sanctuary, for example) where everything is expensive.

Take care of your porter on the trail. As yet, it's not easy for independent trekkers to take out insurance against the death of a porter in their employ.

• **Observe standard charges** To ensure a fair return for certain services lodge management committees have set prices for food and lodging that are listed on menus throughout each area. You should not attempt to bargain these down. Don't, however, believe the curio sellers who tell you that all their goods are 'fixed price'!

CULTURAL IMPACT

The people of the Annapurna region probably have a longer history of contact with the world outside Nepal than does any other group in the country. Pilgrims from as far away as South India have been visiting the shrines at Muktinath for hundreds of years. Thakali lodge owners have been providing food and shelter for Indian, Nepali and Tibetan traders on the great salt route along the Kali Gandaki for almost as long. The Manangba from the Marsyandi valley have been visiting distant Asian trading centres since the early 19th century when the king granted them special travel dispensations. Many of the men in the Gurkha regiments of the British and Indian armies come from villages in the south of the Annapurna region.

In the light of this history of contact with other cultures, the cultural impact of Western trekkers here is difficult to assess. Travelling in 1956, David Snellgrove visited many of the monasteries in the region and found most with almost as few monks as today's trekker will see. None had the large flourishing Tibetan-style communities that one might have imagined in the days before the trekkers arrived here.

Whilst for the older members of the villages on the main trekking routes, foreigners are probably nothing more than passing curiosities it is undeniable that we make a far deeper impression on younger Nepalis. Many now view West as best: Westerners are all rich, they can travel whenever and wherever they like and have girlfriends or boyfriends for casual relationships. It is unfortunate that Nepalis see us only when we are on holiday, intent on enjoying ourselves.

• **Encourage local pride** Try to give Nepalis a balanced picture of life in the West. If they ask you what you earn, try to put this into perspective by telling them how much it costs to rent a flat or buy a car, an air ticket or a week's supply of groceries. Let them know what you think is good about their way of life – the incomparable scenery, the low incidence of robbery and murder, the clean air. If you've enjoyed your stay in a lodge or had a particularly good meal, let the lodge owner know.

• **Discourage begging** Requests for 'one rupee', 'bon-bon' or 'school pen' from children or adults should all be ignored. Giving to beggars fosters an attitude of dependency. As ACAP's Minimum Impact Code (see p88) states, 'Begging is a negative interaction that was started by well-meaning tourists'. Giving sweets to children in a country with few dentists is not an act of charity. You may be approached by older children and asked to make a donation to their school. Whilst these requests may well be genuine, it's probably better to send a cheque, once you get home, to one of the aid agencies that operates in Nepal.

• **Respect holy places** Always pass to the left of Buddhist monuments (chortens, prayer-wheels and mani-walls) and turn prayer-wheels clockwise. Don't prop your pack (or yourself) up against a chorten or mani-wall. Take your boots off before entering a temple and always make a donation. There's usually a donation box. It's also customary to give a small sum of money, or food, to *sadhus*, Hindu holy men whom you may meet on their way to Muktinath.

• **Dress and behave modestly** Too many trekkers disregard local dress standards believing that Nepalis obviously don't mind what foreigners wear because there are never any complaints. Nepalis are far too polite to complain.

Women should wear loose trousers or calf-length skirts, not shorts or sleeveless blouses. Men should always wear a shirt and preferably long trousers; if you want to wear shorts these should be long shorts not jogging shorts. Avoid body-hugging lycra clothing and bright colours. Never bathe in the nude.

• **Don't flaunt your wealth** Your wealth, however poor you may be by Western standards, is way above the wildest dreams of most Nepalis so don't flaunt it. Don't leave valuable items like cameras lying around.

• **Respect people's privacy when taking photos** Before taking someone's photograph you should try to imagine how you would feel in their position. Always ask permission before taking a photo. Don't pay people for posing, rather you should suggest sending them a copy of the photo and get someone to write down their address. If you do do this, however, it is most important to follow through your promise. A British anthropologist working in a small Nepali village was visited by a friend who took photos of a number of the villagers promising to send copies. Each day one villager would trek down to the post office to see if the eagerly-awaited package had arrived but it never did. To allay the tremendous disappointment the anthropologist had to take a set of photos herself.

• **Respect local etiquette** Many of the do's and don't's concern parts of the body. The feet are considered the least clean or holy part of the body, the head the most. You should never touch someone on the head, not even children. Avoid sitting with your feet pointing towards another person but tuck them under you or point them towards a wall. Don't step over someone or put yourself in a position so that they are forced to step over you.

Eating is done only with the right hand. The left hand is used for washing after defaecating so is considered unclean. When being given something, however, you should receive it with both hands. When greeting people don't shake hands but bring both palms together as if praying and say 'Namaste' ('I greet the god within you'). Don't point at things or people but extend your right hand instead.

Don't share eating utensils or take food from someone else's plate. When drinking from a container that is shared you must not let your lips touch it. High caste Hindus (Brahmins) have a particularly strict concept of food cleanliness (*jutho*) and as an untouchable (if you're from the West and not also a Brahmin) you will be served outside the house if you're eating there. You're unlikely to be invited to sleep inside the house.

• **Don't play doctor** Some local people along the trail may ask you for medicines or to treat wounds. Except in the case of cleaning up a small

---

THE MINIMUM IMPACT CODE

Developed by the Annapurna Conservation Area Project, this code of conduct summarises the steps trekkers should take to minimise their impact on the environment and cultures of this area:

Conserve firewood

Be self-sufficient in your fuel supply and make sure your trekking staff uses kerosene and has enough warm clothing. Make no open fires. Limit hot showers. If possible, stay at lodges that use kerosene or fuel-efficient wood stoves and space heaters. Kerosene is available in Chomrong village near the Annapurna Sanctuary.

Stop pollution

Dispose of all trash properly: paper products, cigarette butts, toilet paper, food scraps etc should be burned or buried. Bottles, plastics and other non-biodegradable items should be packed out or deposited in rubbish pits if available. Use toilet facilities provided – if none exist, make sure you are 20 metres from any water source and carry a small shovel to bury wastes. Don't use soap or shampoo in any stream or hot spring. Supervise trekking staff to make sure they cover toilet pits and dispose of garbage properly.

Be a guest

Do not damage, disturb or remove any plants, animals, animal products or religious artifacts. Respect Nepali customs in your dress and behaviour – women should not wear shorts or revealing blouses and men should always wear a shirt. Avoid outward displays of physical affection. Ask permission to take photos and respect people's right to privacy. Begging is a negative interaction that was started by well-meaning tourists – please do not give **anything** to beggars. Don't barter for food and lodging. Many areas have lodge management committees that have set standard rates to ensure a more equal return for their efforts. Encourage young Nepalis to be proud of their culture.

Above all, remember that your vacation has a great impact on the natural environment and people who live off its resources. By assisting in these small ways, you will help the land and people of Nepal enormously.

Nepal is here to change you, not for you to change Nepal.'

cut and applying a plaster you should direct them to the nearest health post. In the Annapurna region there's one in most of the larger villages. If you try to administer to anything more complicated than a small cut and your efforts are not ultimately successful you won't help to build up faith in Western medicine. Locals may continue to patronise the local shaman rather than the health post.

• **Always keep your sense of humour** Nepalis very rarely lose their tempers and you should try hard to control yours when things aren't working out as you would wish. A smile costs nothing.

FURTHER INFORMATION

For more information on how to minimise your impact while trekking contact the **Kathmandu Environmental Education Project** (KEEP) at their offices near the Department of Immigration (see p107). Also in Kathmandu, **Himalayan Guides for Responsible Tourism** runs an eco-trekking workshop to teach conservation practices to trekking staff. They publish a bi-annual newsletter, *Ecotrek*, obtainable from Wendy Brewer Lama, GPO Box 1913, Kathmandu (☎ 414195; fax 1-418890) or Frances Klatzel, Box 1041, Canmore, Alberta T0L 0M0, Canada.

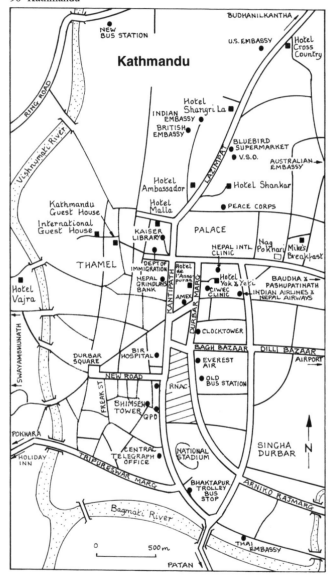

PART 4: KATHMANDU

Kathmandu

Nepal's capital city is a fascinating mélange of mediaeval and modern that combines astounding beauty with appalling squalor and poverty.

Time has stood still in parts of Kathmandu. In the narrow alleys, around the numerous temples and shrines and along the banks of the Bagmati River people go about their daily lives in much the same way as their ancestors did hundreds of years ago. Yet the contrasts between old and new become ever more bizarre. A porter struggles under the weight of two colour-television sets, carrying them in the traditional fashion – supported only by a *namlo*, the strap around his forehead. A couple of sacred cows doze on the warm asphalt in the middle of busy Durbar Marg. They block part of the road and slow the traffic but will not be moved on. A young Tibetan monk in ochre robes passes on his way to the great stupa at Baudha, his shaven head in the grip of the head-phones of his walkman.

For first-time Asian visitors, Kathmandu is a visual feast but for long-term travellers who've journeyed up from India it's also a feast of a more basic nature. The city has some of the best budget restaurants on the sub-continent dishing up everything from pepper steaks to enchiladas, chocolate cake to apfelstrudel. Accommodation, too, is excellent and can be better value than in India. Communications are good and you can make international phone calls and send faxes with the minimum of delay.

It's well worth setting aside at least a few days to see something of the city. On the bus route from India to Pokhara and back it is, however, possible to bypass Kathmandu entirely since trekking permits for the Annapurna region are easily available in Pokhara.

HISTORY

Origins

The name Kathmandu is believed to be a corruption of Kasthamandap ('square house of wood'), the 1000-year-old *dharamsala* (rest-house) that still stands in Durbar Square.

The first identifiable civilisation in the Kathmandu Valley was that of the Kirats, who occupied a number of sites in the region in the second half of the first millennium BC. They were succeeded by the Lichhavi in the second century AD and the Malla in the eighth century. The settlements were centred around religious sites known as *piths* or power places, usually on the tops of hills.

Early urban planning

Kathmandu was a town of almost 2000 houses by the beginning of the Malla period (13th century), centred on Pashupatinath. Like the other two large towns in the Valley, Patan and Bhaktapur, it was an independent kingdom. Religion controlled not only the lives of the people but also the layout of these towns. Wandering through the chaotic maze of streets and temples in modern Kathmandu, it's difficult to believe that there has ever been any town-planning here; but, in fact, centuries ago Hindu philosophy determined the design of whole towns based on the Vastupurusa Mandala, a complex layout in the shape of a square. This was composed of many smaller squares assigned to different deities and their temples. The main temple and palace, the centres of spiritual and temporal power, were symbolically placed at the very centre. Agricultural land surrounded each town.

Newar architectural heritage

The dominant culture in the Kathmandu Valley, until the unification of Nepal by the king of Gorkha in 1768, was that of the Newars. They are best known for their spectacular architectural legacy – the temples and palaces that surround the Durbar Squares in Kathmandu, Patan and Bhaktapur. They built with brick, wood and tiles and are said to have invented the pagoda. Until the introduction of reinforced concrete in Nepal just 40 years ago, Kathmandu was truly the Florence of the East. Visiting in 1959, Michel Peissel described the city as 'simply one vast work of art, from the humblest of the peasant's rectangular brick homes to the most impressive of the two-thousand-odd pagodas whose gilt roofs rise above the neat rows of houses. Each house, each temple, each shrine is decorated with delicately carved beams representing gods and goddesses, or animals drawn from reality and from fantasy, carved in dark wood that stands out against the background of pale pink bricks.' (*Tiger for Breakfast*, see p43).

Rigid town planning did not allow for the enormous growth that has taken place in the area. Satellite towns were developed to house the growing population and these often became associated with a particular industry. (Thimi, for example, is still a pottery centre). Most of the towns in the Kathmandu Valley did, however, manage to conform to their original plans at least until the time of the Ranas. Jung Bahadur, the first of this line of prime ministers, visited Europe in 1850 and introduced the bizarre neo-classical style of architecture exemplified in the vast whitewashed edifices that can be seen in various stages of dilapidation in the city. Large areas of agricultural land were taken over for their construction.

Modern Kathmandu

The real attack on the strongly inter-related cultural, social and religious framework of the Valley's urban centres did not, however, really begin until the 1950s after the restoration of the monarchy and the opening up of the country. The effects have been dramatic, though, and many parts of Kathmandu have degenerated into an urban sprawl of unsightly concrete-block buildings. The district of Thamel, that today looks no different from tourist ghettos in the other Asian capitals on the backpackers' route, was largely fields twenty years ago. The Kathmandu Guest House, opened in 1968 to house Peace Corps volunteers, was the first hotel here.

Kathmandu today is plagued with the problems that beset all rapidly expanding Third World cities: overcrowding, severe pollution and traffic congestion to name but a few. The population of the Kathmandu Valley now stands at 1.3 million, with a very high growth rate of almost five per cent. None of these problems seems to tarnish the allure of the city as far as the tourist is concerned. Kathmandu draws more than a quarter of a million tourists each year, most of whom, you'll no doubt be glad to know, venture no further than the capital.

ARRIVAL AND DEPARTURE

By air

• **Arrival** A twenty-minute taxi ride east of the city centre, the modern airport buildings of Tribuvan International Airport were opened in 1990. In the arrival hall there's a **duty-free shop** (sample prices: 200 Marlboro cigarettes US$9; French wine US$5-9, Haig whisky US$9 for 750ml) and a **foreign exchange counter**. If you'll be getting your visa in Immigration here, you can get the US$ bills required from this counter. There's also a bank in the departure hall. Across the hall at **Immigration** 30-day visas (US$25 cash) are issued to those who don't have them. Downstairs are the luggage carousels, staffed by predatory porters who expect at least Rs20 if you use their services.

You pass through **customs** into the main hall. Pick up a free city map at the **tourist office** here and a copy of *Traveller' Nepal* magazine. There's also a **post office**, **communications agency** (for telephone calls and faxes), **bank** and **hotel reservations counter**. If the airport bus is running (unlikely), tickets are sold at the booth here. Some hotels (and even some of the budget places) offer free transport from the airport.

To get out of the airport you need to push your way through an enthu-siastic mob of hotel touts and taxi drivers crowding round the entrance. Taxis to the city centre and Thamel cost Rs150 if you get your own out-side, or Rs200 if you arrange one with the pre-paid taxi desk in the main hall. If you're really counting the pennies you can reach the bus stop for the crowded local bus (Rs 2) by walking to the end of the airport drive and turning left.

• **Departure** A hefty airport departure tax of Rs700 (Rs600 for SAARC countries) for international flights is payable, in local currency only, before you check in. At the bank here you can convert into hard currency (usually US$) only up to 15% of the rupees for which you have encashment certificates. Alternatively you can dispose of surplus rupees at the shop in the corner of the departure hall, that sells gift packs of tea and Coronation Khukri rum in exotic khukri knife shaped bottles. There's not much worth buying in the duty-free shop (see 'Arrival' above): fans of the Nepali royal family may be interested in the china plate commemorating the coronation in 1977. Originally retailing at US$120 this is now a snip at US$50.

By land
Some of the tourist buses will take you all the way to Thamel. Most go no further than the new bus station about 3km north of the city on the ring road. Buses from the Everest region still use the old bus station by the clock tower in the centre of town. Frequent shuttle buses (Rs2) link the two, passing by the northern end of Thamel.

The blue-and-white Sajha buses usually stop at the GPO, which is closer to Thamel.

ORIENTATION
Greater Kathmandu, which includes Patan as well as Kathmandu itself, lies at about 1400m/4593ft above sea level. The Bagmati River runs between these two cities. The airport is 6km to the east, near the Hindu temple complex of Pashupatinath, with the Buddhist stupa at Baudha 2km north of Pashupatinath. The other major Buddhist shrine, Swayambhunath, is visible on a hill in west Kathmandu. The third city in the Valley, Bhaktapur, is 14km to the east.

Within Kathmandu, most hotels and guest houses and the Department of Immigration (for trekking permits) are to be found in Thamel, north of the historic centre of the city, Durbar Square. Freak Street, the hippy centre in the '60s and '70s which still offers some cheap accommodation, is just off Durbar Square. Some of the top hotels and the international airline offices are along Durbar Marg which runs south from the modern royal palace.

WHERE TO STAY
Hotel areas
• **Thamel** Most travellers find Thamel the most convenient area to stay in, although it's now largely a tourist ghetto. Everything you could want is available here, with a vast range of accommodation (from £1/$1.50 to £50/$75 per night), good restaurants, souvenir shops, book shops and

travel agencies. It's also very close to the Department of Immigration, for trekking permits.

• **Freak St** In the halcyon days of the 60s and 70s when Kathmandu was a major stopover on the hippy trail, Freak St, just off Durbar Square, was the place to hang out. With the government crackdown on the drug scene Freak St lost out to Thamel and many of the hotels closed down. There are still about 10 places to stay here, mostly in the bottom end of the budget bracket. Freak St is far less touristy than Thamel but some of the hotels are not what you'd call spotless.

• **Other areas** Although the above alternatives are probably the most convenient areas in which to stay there are other options. In Patan, there's a youth hostel near the zoo and also a few expensive hotels. At Baudha, there are several cheap hotels; Westerners studying Buddhism rent rooms from Tibetans here.

Prices

Prices given below are for the high season (Oct-Nov/Mar-Apr) for single/double/triple rooms, with common (com) or attached (att) bathrooms as indicated. You may be able to get a discount of anything up to 50% on the prices below outside the high season, depending on the length of your stay. Many hotel owners quote their prices in US dollars; you pay in rupees, though. Given the high rate of inflation in the country, this is a sensible idea so US dollars are used here. The dollar/pound exchange rate hovers around US$1.50:£1. Hotels are keyed to the map on p99.

Budget guest houses (US$5/£3 or less)

• **Thamel** There are around 40 places to choose from in this price bracket, and in some you'll also get an attached bathroom for this price. Try to get a room that faces away from the roads – Kathmandu is plagued by noisy dogs.

Well-run by a friendly Tibetan family is the **Hotel Potala** [12] (☎ 416680), more of a guest house than a hotel. All rooms are doubles with shared bath and cost from US$2-5. Nearby, the **Memorable Guest House** [31] (☎ 243683) is another cheerful cheapie with rooms for US$2/4 (com). There's a good range of rooms from US$4-12 at **Earth House** [28] (☎ 418197), and a roof-top terrace. Also efficiently run is the **Marco Polo Guest House** [50] (☎ 227914) with rooms for US$3/4 (com) and US$5/7 (att). The rooms at the back are quietest.

Other recommendations in this price range in Thamel include the **Buddhist Guest House** [15] (☎224189), the spotless **Kathmandu Guest Home** [16], the friendly **Rainbow Guest House** [41] (☎ 410182), the **Pooja Guest House** [22] (☎ 416657) - popular with overlanders, the **Mont Blanc Guest House** [24] (☎ 222447) which is good value, as is the **Guest Palace Guest House** [28] (☎ 225593).

The **Kathmandu Peace Guest House** [53] (☎ 415239) is, as the name suggests, located in a peaceful area – a short walk north-west of Thamel in Paknajol. Rooms are US$3/4 (com) and US$5/8-15 (att), and there are even mountain views from here.

• **Freak St** The best of the cheap places here is the **Travellers' Paradise Guest House**, above the Paradise Vegetarian Restaurant. At US$4 for a double with common bath it's more expensive than other hotels in Freak St but very clean; the restaurant is excellent. The **Buddha Guest House** (☎ 240071) is also clean and has rooms for US$1.50/3 (com) or US$4 (att). It's down a side street past the Jasmine Restaurant.

Annapurna Lodge (☎ 213684) is a popular friendly place with rooms for US$3.50/4.50 for doubles/triples with common bath. With attached bath doubles are US$5. There's still a whiff of patchouli in the air at **Century Lodge** (☎ 214341), good value at US$1.25/3/4 (com). There's a notice board where you can arrange to meet trekking partners and you can rent bikes here.

Cheap hotels in Thamel

With rooms from US$5/10 (att), the **Hotel Jagat** [68] (☎ 227701) is good value, although it's on the southern outskirts of Thamel. An excellent choice is the friendly Tibetan-run **Mustang Holiday Inn** [88] (☎ 226 538), not to be confused with the Mustang Guest House. Rooms are US$8-20/US$10-30 (att). **Hotel Utse** [114] (☎ 226946) is nearby and similar, priced from US$13/20 (att); next door the **Hotel Norling** [109] (☎ 240734) offers stiff competition at US$10/18 (att). In the heart of Thamel is the **Hotel Garuda** [113] (☎ 416340), with clean rooms from US$13/17 (att).

The best known of the cheap hotels in Kathmandu must be the long-running **Kathmandu Guest House** [82] (☎ 413632), a landmark in the city. Popular with expeditions it's often fully-booked in the high season. They have a few rooms from US$6-8/8-10 (com) but most accommodation here is US$17/20 (att) in the new wing.

Moderately-priced hotels

There are numerous reasonable hotels in the US$15-30/£10-15 price range. Most have attached restaurants. All rooms have attached bathrooms with hot water. The **Hotel Karma** [116] (☎ 417897) is a friendly place that's recommended; rooms cost from $15/20 (att). Also good, and at the same price, there's **Hotel Buddha** [120] (☎ 413366) nearby, and **Hotel Moonlight** [119] (☎ 419452), situated in Paknajol. There's free snooker and billiards here. There is, however, one hotel in this category that stands out above the others, chiefly for its unique atmosphere. The

---

(**Opposite**) From the hill above the city, Swayambhunath looks out over the Kathmandu Valley. (Photo Henry Stedman).

Hotel Vajra (☎ 272719, fax 271695) is located on the western side of the river, equidistant between Thamel and Swayambhunath. Unlike virtually all the other hotels in the city, the Vajra is not a concrete block but built in brick and wood in the classic Newar style. It was conceived and paid for by a Texas billionaire, and built by Newar craftsmen, with wall-paintings by Tibetan and Tamang artists. It has its own Avant-Garde theatre group, Studio 7, which performs occasionally. There's also a restaurant, a well-stocked library, and a roof-top bar with views over the city. Room prices are US$14/16 for singles/doubles with wash-basins, US$33/38 with attached bathroom and US$53/61 for rooms in the new wing.

Expensive hotels

Until its unfortunate demise in 1970, the top place to stay was the Royal Hotel. Its success was largely due to its proprietor, the legendary White Russian émigré, Boris Lissanevitch. It was the country's first Western hotel, opened in 1954 in a wing of the palace that is now the Bahadur Bhavan. Virtually everything for it had to be imported from Europe, shipped to India and then carried in by porters. Staying here you'd be guaranteed to meet interesting people and many of the mountaineering expeditions made it their Kathmandu base.

Most of the city's top hotels are now much like expensive hotels anywhere in the world. The **Hotel Yak & Yeti** (☎ 413999, fax 227782) is probably the best place to stay, with rooms from US$150/160 to US$450 for a suite. Centrally located, it has everything you'd expect from a five-star hotel, although the modern wings don't exactly blend with the old Rana palace which forms part of it. The Yak & Yeti Bar with its Chimney Restaurant was moved here from the Royal Hotel when it closed. Rich Nepalis, however, consider the **Soaltee Holiday Inn Crowne Plaza** (☎ 272550, fax 272205) as the best hotel in Nepal (rooms from US$150/160-675) but it's not so well located, in the west of the city, in Kalimati.

Near the Hotel Yak & Yeti, on Durbar Marg is the **Hotel de l'Annapurna** (☎ 221711, fax 225236) with rooms from US$125/135-300, a large pool and casino. Similarly priced but inconveniently located is the **Everest Hotel** (☎ 220567) on the road to the airport.

The **Hotel Malla** [140] (☎ 410320) is very pleasant, just north of Thamel with rooms from US$100/110. The overpriced **Hotel Shanker** (☎ 410151) in a converted palace in Lazimpat, costs US$90/105.In the same price range are the **Hotel Kathmandu** (☎ 418494) along Maharajganj, in the far north of the city, and the **Hotel Sherpa** (☎ 227000) on Durbar Marg. The best value in this group is the **Hotel Shangri La** (☎ 412999, fax 414184), in Lazimpat, with rooms from US$100/115.

(Opposite) Top: Winnowing the modern way in the streets of Thimi. **Below:** Tourist trophies in Durbar Square, Kathmandu. (Photo Henry Stedman).

Thamel Accommodation In ascending order by price for singles/doubles with common (c) or attached (a) bathroom. Prices in US$ but payable in rupees.

01 Chitwan Tulsi $1.50/2 (c)
02 MK GH (212866) dbl: $2 (c), $3 (a)
03 Norling GH (221534) $1.50/3 (a)
04 H. Aroma (222229) $1.50/3 (c), $2/4 (a)
05 Green Land GH (244553) $1.50/3 (c)
06 Htl Mercy Palace $2/2, $3 dbl (a)
07 Pheasant Lodge (417415) $2/2.50 (c)
08 Cosy Corner (417799) $2/2.50(c) $5 (a)
09 Fishtail Home $2.50 dbl (c), $3 dbl (a)
10 Machhapuchhare Guest House
    (410875) $2/2.50 (a)
11 Continental GH (221446) $2/3 (a)
12 Hotel Potala (416680) $2/3 (c)
13 Friendly GH (414033) $2/3 (c)
14 Kunal's (411050) $2/3 (c), $4 dbl (a)
15 Buddhist GH (224189) $2/3 (c), $4 (a)
16 Kathmandu Guest Home $2/3 c, $3/5 a
17 Hotel Silk Rd (212224) $2/3 (c), $4/6 a
18 Hotel Star (411004) $2/3 (c) $6/8(a)
19 Dolpo GH (224367) $2/3 (c), $6/8 (a)
20 Everest GH $2/3 (c), $4 (a)
21 Namaste GH $2 (c), $3/4 (a)
22 Pooja GH (416657) $2/3 (c), 3/4 (a)
23 Yak Lodge (224318) dbl: $3.50c $4.50 a
24 Mt Blanc GH (222447) $2/3 c, $3/5a
25 White Lotus GH (224563) $2/3c $4/5 a
26 Htl Florid (416155) $3 (c), $5 (a)
27 My Mom's House $2/3 (c), $4/5 (a)
28 Guest Palace GH (225593) $2/3c, $5 a
29 Souvenir GH (416416) $2/3 (c), $4/7 (a)
30 Hokkaido GH $2.50/3 (c)
31 Memorable GH (243683) $2/4 (c)
32 Skala (223155) $2/4 (c), $3/5 (a)
33 Ajanta GH (411023) $2/3 (c) $4/6 (a)
34 Gurkha Soldier GH (230666) $3/4 (c)
35 King's Land GH (417129) $3/4 (c)
36 Blue Sky GH $3/4 (c)
37 Mini Om GH (229288) $3/4 (c)
38 Polo GH (212256) $3/4c, $4/5a
39 Centre GH (223109) $3/4 (c), $5 dbl (a)
40 Namaskar GH (410182) $4/5 (a)
41 Rainbow GH (410182) $3/4 c, $4/5 (a)
42 Fuji GH (229234) $4 s (c) $5/6 (a)
43 Gorkha (214243) $3/5 (c), $6 (a)
44 Hotel Oshin (417157) $3/5 (c), $3/6 (a)
45 Tibet Home (224986) $4/6 (a)
46 LP GH (412715) $3/4 (c), $5/6 (a)
47 Tourist GH (418305) $4 (c), $6 dbl (a)
48 A-One GH (229302) $4 (c), $6 (a)
49 Tibet Peace GH (415026) $3/4c, $4/7a

50 Marco Polo (227914) $3/4 (c) $5/7 (a)
51 Tara GH (220634) $3/4 (c), $5/8 (a)
52 Htl Puska (225027) $3/5(c),$6/8(a)
53 Ktm Peace GH (415239) $3/4c, $5/8a
54 Holy Lodge (416265) $3.50/5c, $8/12a
55 Hotel Angel (227916) $3/4 (c), $6/10 (a)
56 Shangri-La Guest House (227388)
    dbl: $5 (c), $10 (a)
57 Earth House (418197) $4/6c, $6/12a
58 Valentine $4/6 (c), $8 dbl (a)
59 Deutsch Home (415010) $4/5c, $7/10a
60 Shiddartha Guest House (227119)
    $5(c), $7/10/12 (a)
61 Hotel Shakti (410121) $4/6c, $6/12a
62 Htl Iceland (416686) $4/6, $11/14a
63 Lhasa GH (226147) $5/6 (c), $7/10
64 Hotel Horizon (220904) $6-20 dbl (a)
65 Down Town GH (224189) $5/7 (c)
66 Thahity GH $5/8 (a)
67 Mustang GH (419789) $5/8c, $9/12a
68 Htl Jagat (227701) $5/10 (a)
69 Htl Mt Fuji (413794) $6/8 (a)
70 Htl Eyeball (226048) $6/10 (a)
71 Acme GH (414811) $6/8 (c), 14/18 (a)
72 Holyland GH (411588) $6/10 (a)
73 Hotel Namche Nepal (417067)
    $5/6 (c), $6/7 (a)
74 Universal GH c$5/10 (a) opening soon
75 Hotel Mughal Durbar (222176)
    c$6/10 (a) opening soon
76 Damaru GH (244063) $4/6c, $6/12a
77 Green Peace Ktm GH $4/6 (c), $10/12a
78 My Home(231788) $5/8 (c), $7/10 (a)
79 Capital GH (414150) $5/8 (c), $9/15 (a)
80 New Tibet Rest House (225319)
    $6/9 (c), $8/12 (a)
81 Hotel White Lotus (226342)
    $6/10 (c), $10/14 (a)
82 Kathmandu Guest House (413632)
    $6/8 (c), $17/20 (a)
83 Sagarmatha GH (410214) $6/10c,
    $14/20a
84 Potala Tourist Home (410303)
    $6/10 (c) $10/15 (a)
85 Wayfarer's Inn (413471)
    $7/10 (c), $10/15 (a)
86 Shakya GH (410266) $7/10c, $10/12a
87 Htl Nana (418633) $8/10 (a)
88 Mustang Holiday Inn (226538)
    $8-20/10-30 (a)

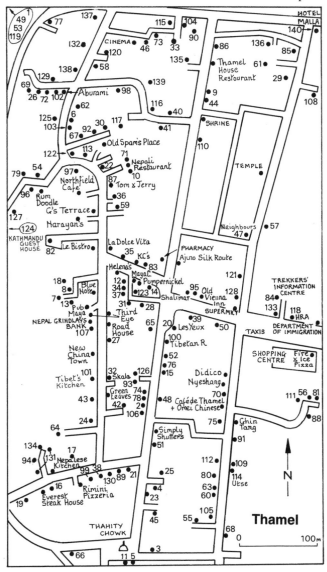

HOTEL
MALLA

1
49
53
119

77
137
115
104
140
132
CINEMA
73
90
120
46
33
86
136
85
138
58
135
Thamel
House
Restaurant
61
29
129
139
69
26 72 102
Aburami
98
9
44
62
116
108
125
6
40
103
30
117
SHRINE
67 92
41
122
113
Old Spam's Place
71
110
79
54
97
22
Nepali
Restaurant
TEMPLE
96
Northfield
Café
87
10
Rum
Doodle
36
Tom x Jerry
127
G's Terrace
59
124
Narayan's
Neighbours
47
57
KATHMANDU
GUEST
HOUSE
82
Le Bistro
La Dolce Vita
35
KC's
83
PHARMACY
Ajno Silk Route
18
Helena's
MayaC.
Pumpernickel
121
8
Blue
Note
12
95
Old
128
TREKKERS'
INFORMATION
CENTRE
7
34
123 14
Shalimar
Vienna
Inn
84
13
Pub
Maya
37
31
28
SUPERMKT
133
118
HRA
NEPAL GRINDLAYS
BANK
107
Third
Eye
Road
House
65
39
20
Les Yeux
50
DEPARTMENT
OF IMMIGRATION
27
100
Tibetan R
TAXIS
New
China
Town
52
76
SHOPPING
CENTRE
Fire
x Ice
Pizza
Tibet's
Kitchen
101
32
Skala
126
15
Didico
Nyeshang
43
93
74
70
111 56 81
Green
Leaves
78
48
Café de Thamel
+ Omei Chinese
42
2
24
106
75
Chin
Tang
88
64
Simply
Shutters
91
134
94 131
17
Nepalese
Kitchen
51
99 38
25
112
109
16
130 89
21
80
114
Utse
19
Rimini
Pizzeria
4
63
Everest
Steak House
23
60
45
55
105
THAHITY
CHOWK
68
66
11 5
3
N

Thamel

0   100m

89 **Potala GH** (220467) $8-10/15-20 (a)
90 **Pilgrims Htl** (416910) $8/10 (c), $15a
91 **New Tibet Cottage** (226577) $8c, $15a
92 **Yeti Guest Home** (419789)
  $8/12 (c), $12/16 (a)
93 **Thorong Peak Guest House** (224656)
  $8/12 (c), $14/18 (a)
94 **Tibet GH** (214383) $9/10c, $13/15a
95 **Newa GH** (415781) $8/15 (a)
96 **Prince GH** (414456) $10/15 (a)
97 **Htl Himal Home** c$10/15 (a) open soon
98 **Hotel Shree Tibet** (419902) $10/15 (a)
99 **Khangsar GH** (216788) $10/15a
100 **Lovers' Nest** (220541) $10/15 (a)
101 **Sherpa GH** (221546) $8 (c) $10/15 (a)
102 **Hotel Lily** (413184) $10/15 (a)
103 **Hotel Bikram** (417111) $10/15 (a)
104 **Htl Greeting Palace** (417212) $10/15a
105 **Hotel New Gajur** (226623) $10/16 (a)
106 **Hotel Pisang** (220097) $12/15 (a)
107 **Hotel The Earth** (228890) $12/15 (a)
108 **Htl Yeti** (414858) $8/10 (c), $12/16 (a)
109 **Hotel Norling** (240734) $10/18 (a)
110 **Hotel Sonna** (418399) $11/18 (a)
111 **Imperial GH** (229339) $12/15 (a)
112 **Htl Blue Diamond** (226320) $12/15 (a)
113 **Hotel Garuda** (416340) $13/17 (a)

114 **Hotel Utse** (226946) $13/20 (a)
115 **Htl Gauri Shankar** (417181) $14/19 a
116 **Hotel Karma** (417897) $15/20 (a)
117 **Htl Tashi Dhargey** (415378) $15/20 a
118 **Hotel Tilicho** (410132) $15/20 (a)
119 **Htl Moonlight** (419452) $15/20 (a)
120 **Hotel Buddha** (413366) $15/20 (a)
121 **Htl MM Internatl** (411847) $15/20 (a)
122 **Hotel Mona** (412380) $15/20 (a)
123 **Hotel Excelsior** (410853) $15/22 (a)
124 **International GH** (410533) $16/19
125 **Hotel Mandap** (413321) $18/24 (a)
126 **Htl Tashi Dhele** (217446) $18/25 (a)
127 **Hotel Shikhar** (415588) $18/26 (a)
128 **Hotel Tridevi** (416742) $20/25 (a)
129 **Hotel Rimal** (410317) $20/25 (a)
130 **Hotel Tayoma** (211149) $15/30a
131 **Trans Himalayan G**(214683)$20/25a
132 **Hotel Tenki** (414483) $25/35 (a)
133 **Tibet Holiday Inn** (411453) $20/35 (a)
134 **Nirvana Garden H** (222668) $30/40 a
135 **Hotel Thamel** (417643) $30/40 (a)
136 **Htl Norbu Linka** (414799) $30/45 (a)
137 **Hotel Manang** (410993) $35/50 (a)
138 **Htl Marshyangdi** (414105) $50/60 (a)
139 **Htl Vaishali** 4* opening 1996
140 **Hotel Malla** (410320) $100/110

WHERE TO EAT

Kathmandu's restaurants are renowned amongst travellers throughout South Asia for their ability to serve passable approximations of Western dishes. You will, however, probably be more appreciative of Kathmandu's apple-pie cuisine after a long, hard trek rather than on arrival direct from the West. It's surprising how quickly you forget how things are really supposed to taste! The cost of meals in restaurants doesn't vary as greatly as hotel prices. Most main courses cost less than US$3/£2, often much less.

Be especially careful about what you eat before you set out on your trek; you're probably more likely to pick up a stomach bug in a Kathmandu restaurant than in the hills. A recent test on the quality of the tap water in Thamel showed it to contain more than ten times the WHO recommended safe maximum level of faecal matter. Don't believe restaurants that tell you their salads are washed in iodine. If they're busy they may not have time for Western 'idiosyncrasies' such as this. It's best also to avoid ice cream (although you're unlikely to be attracted to the Nepali choc-bar that's marketed as 'Shital'!) and everything else that has not just been cooked and is still hot. Stick to bottled or hot drinks. Unless otherwise indicated the restaurants described are in Thamel (see map p99).

Breakfast

Even the smallest guest houses now offer breakfast and snacks either as room service or in their own snack bars. Most of the Thamel restaurants have set breakfasts that can be good value but there are a few places worthy of special mention.

The **Pumpernickel Bakery** does a roaring trade in cinnamon rolls, bagels and other pastries and cakes. There's a pleasant garden behind it and the noticeboard here is a good place to track down trekking partners. **Helena's** (see below) is equally good for breakfasts.

For many years the place to go for a long, relaxing start to the day has been **Mike's Breakfast**, although it's now quite expensive. You breakfast on authentic American fare (hash browns, pancakes and syrup, fresh coffee with free refills etc) in a garden, serenaded by the sounds of the ex-Peace-Corps owner's classical record collection. The breakfast special is Rs130. The main branch is in Naxal (north east of Thamel) but there's a second branch, the **Northfield Cafe**, near the Kathmandu Guest House. In the main season, both places are open for supper as well as breakfast and lunch.

Lunch and dinner

• **Western** The cheapest restaurants in Kathmandu serving 'Western' fare are in and around Freak St, although a slice of hippy history died in 1995 with the closure of the infamous Lunch Box. The **Jasmine Restaurant**, just off Freak St, still has a nice mellow atmosphere and does veg fried rice for Rs25. The **New Mandarin** is popular, breakfast costs Rs28. In the Annapurna Lodge, the **Diyalo Restaurant** offers main courses from Rs35-60 and shows free videos at 5.30 and 7.30pm. The **Oasis Garden** is more expensive but does, as the name suggests, have a pleasant garden. Steak and chips are Rs80. Opposite, the **Paradise Vegetarian Restaurant** is probably the best place to eat in Freak St. Their crêpes with garlic cheese are recommended but will set you back Rs75.

Back in Thamel, restaurant prices can be much higher, but there are still places where you'll get a cheap meal that's reasonably filling. **Lips Cafe** at My Mom's Home offers chicken fried rice for Rs25. **Neighbours' Restaurant** in the Tourist Guest House does a filling egg curry rice for Rs27. Nepal's answer to McDonald's is **Nirula's** on Durbar Marg. Beef-burgers are out of the question, mutton Maha-burgers being the alternative.

Helena's is a popular place, main dishes are Rs80-140, there's good cappuccino and a wide range of cakes and pies. Nearby, the **Clay Oven** has outdoor seating in a small garden. Main dishes here range from Rs55 to Rs125. **Narayan's**, in Chetrapati, is also popular. The **Road House Cafe** is a rather self-consciously cool terrace-diner with a have-a-go-at-anything menu. The food's quite good and there's sometimes a live band.

Many places have steaks on the menu, usually (but not always) buffalo steak. It's often served as a 'sizzler' and arrives in front of you on a heated cast-iron plate doing just that. **The Third Eye** is an excellent place for a steak (around Rs200) and in the back room you can recline on the cushions while you eat. It's a very popular place, however, so you need to come early. The **Everest Steak House** is also good, with a wide range of steaks, from Rs130 right up to Rs600 for chateaubriand.

Now in its 19th year, **KC's Restaurant & Bambooze Bar** is as much a Thamel institution as the Kathmandu Guest House. The food's good but prices are distinctly up-market. A sizzling steak from the people who introduced the 'sizzler' to Kathmandu now costs Rs195; and if that doesn't fill you up you can round off your meal with their cheese board (yak mozzarella and cottage cheese with whole wheat bread and pickles – Rs100). Another Kathmandu institution recommended for its food is the **Rum Doodle** (see Nightlife, below).

There are numerous pizza places around Thamel; several also show videos in the afternoons and evenings to pull the customers in. One pizza place stands way above the rest, however. **Fire & Ice Pizzeria & Ice Cream Parlour**, just opposite the Department of Immigration, has to be experienced to be believed. Run by an Italian woman who's imported her own computer-controlled Moretti Forni pizza oven, some of the best pizzas on the subcontinent are now turned out here – to the sound of Pavarotti. Prices range from Rs150-250 and there's wine by the glass for Rs130. It's very popular but closed on Sunday.

G's Terrace is another Western-Nepali joint venture and authentic Bavarian cuisine is served in this pleasant roof-top restaurant. There's Bavarian homemade potato soup with sausage and specialities like French pepper steak in cognac and cream. Most main dishes are over Rs200. **Old Vienna Inn** serves Austrian cuisine for similar prices. You can buy delicious salami rolls (Rs42) to take away both here and in their **Delicatessen Center** on Kantipath. The Delicatessen Center stocks a surprisingly wide range of imported cheeses and other delicacies, at unsurprisingly high prices.

Simply Shutters Bistrot (☎ 226015) is a recommended place for a special occasion. The menu is sensibly limited to a few choices on a set menu (Rs340) and the quality of the food is high. A sample menu might include chicken liver paté, boeuf bourguignon and vodka orange sorbet. There are also tasty sandwiches served with salad (Rs90) at lunchtime. The restaurant is closed on Tuesday; reservations are essential in the evening as there are only a few tables.

In the five-star hotels there are some excellent Western-style restaurants, some run by Western chefs. The buffet lunch or dinner at the **Hotel Yak & Yeti** costs Rs537 including tax.

● **Nepali & Newar** Although most Thamel restaurants will serve daal bhat, it's usually at grossly inflated prices. There's a cheap Nepali place (no name), serving daal bhat for Rs30, by the entrance to the Acme Guest House, and another, **Nepali Foods Restaurant**, near the Tourist Guest House.

The **Nepalese Kitchen** has a range of daal bhat specials (Rs80-165) that are far superior to the daal bhat that most Nepalis consume twice a day. There's live music several times a week.

Thamel House Restaurant (☎ 410388) is set in a renovated 100-year-old Newar house. Opened recently with an eye to attracting the tour groups it's an interesting place for a celebratory dinner. Main dishes range from Rs80-130 and the nine-course set meal costs Rs450.

● **Tibetan** restaurants are amongst the cheapest places to eat in Thamel. The **Tibetan Restaurant** in the same building as the Lovers' Nest Guest House is excellent value and is run by very friendly Tibetans. You can get a plate of ten momos here for Rs15; buff chowmein costs Rs20. In the Kingsland Guest House, **Tashi Deleg** is popular and also does Western food that's good value.

The best-known Tibetan place here is **Utse**, now relocated to the hotel of the same name. The pingtsey soup (meat soup with wontons) is excellent, as are their momos (vegetable, mutton, buffalo or pork) which cost Rs37 for ten. They also do Chinese food, buffalo steak and chips for Rs77 and, given a couple of hours' notice, will prepare complete Tibetan meals (Rs860 for four people).

● **Chinese** Most restaurants have spring rolls and chowmein on their menus although what appears on your plate is usually unmemorable. The **New China Town Restaurant** is recommended – there's a Chinese chef; main dishes here range from chicken fried rice (Rs55) to prawn in black bean sauce (Rs150). Probably the best Chinese restaurant is the **Mountain City** at the four-star Malla Hotel, just north of Thamel.

● **Thai** Now in larger premises in Lazimpat, **HimThai** still has a pleasant garden setting and a good reputation. Prices have risen, though; chicken satay is Rs140 and most main dishes are around Rs160.

● **Israeli** Catering to the large number of Israeli visitors that the country is now attracting, **Aburami** opened in 1992. The food is quite authentic and good value. Hummus with chapattis costs Rs48, Israeli salad with chapattis is Rs94, and they do some of the best chips (Rs36) in town. It's a popular place and they put on special meals for Jewish festivals.

● **Japanese** Catering to the ex-pats, there are a number of Japanese restaurants here and some of the dishes are surprisingly authentic. The best place is said to be the newly-opened **Tamura**, in the south of the city off the Arniko Highway near the UMN. The other places are nearer Thamel. **Fuji**, pleasantly located just off Kantipath, is also very good. Assorted tempura costs Rs180 and set meals range from Rs230-550. **Koto**, on Durbar Marg, is slightly better value.

• **Indian** Mughal/tandoori dishes appear on many menus but can be disappointingly unlike what you would reasonably expect south of the border. In Thamel the **Shalimar Restaurant** does chicken masala that's good value at Rs35; chicken tikka costs Rs75 and the chef is from India. There's Kashmiri food, including rogan josh, at the newly-opened **Hotel Mughal Darbar**. On Durbar Marg, there's the **Amber Restaurant** which is popular with local people.

The top Indian restaurant is the Hotel de l'Annapurna's **ghar-e-kebab** (☎ 221711). It specialises in the rich cuisine of North India, main dishes are around Rs200 and there's live music in the evenings. You may need to book in advance.

• **Vegetarian** Most restaurants have some dishes for vegetarians who are sick of daal bhat but there are also some places that specialise in Western-style vegetarian food. **New Nirmala** has brown bread, garlic toast (Rs8) and excellent cream of spinach soup for Rs35. Tofu lasagne al forno is Rs89. **Skala Vegetarian Restaurant** is set in a pleasant garden and has an imaginative menu (herb roulade with mushrooms and brown bread for Rs80).

If it's Indian vegetarian food you're after, try the excellent **Foodsmen Maharaja Restaurant** near Hotel My Home. The owner, a Sikh, supervises the production of delicious Punjabi cuisine. A cheese paratha is Rs18, egg curry Rs35. On Freak St, **Paradise Vegetarian Restaurant** is an excellent place to eat.

NIGHTLIFE

Pubs & bars

Kathmandu turns in early although there are a few bars in Thamel that stay open late for the tourists.

Rum Doodle Restaurant & 40,000'/₂ft Bar is a Kathmandu institution, with yeti prints on its walls inscribed by the members of many mountaineering expeditions. It's named after the book, *The Ascent of Rum Doodle*, a send-up of the mountaineering account genre. As well as a wide range of drinks (hot buttered rum at Rs70, for example) the food here is good; main dishes are Rs100-150.

The **Tom & Jerry Pub** is noisy and popular, an old favourite. There are pool tables and satellite TV. **Pub Maya**, **Maya Cocktail Bar** and **Ground Round** are all similar. Particular tastes of music are catered for at the **Reggae Pub** (above Aburami Israeli Restaurant) and the **Blue Note**

Jazz Bar. **Old Spam's Place** is the closest you'll get to a British pub in Kathmandu. You can drink your brew out of a beermug and bar snacks include chip butties (Rs50) and almost Cornish pasties (Rs95).

SERVICES

Banks
There are several bureaux de change in Thamel. Nepal Grindlays has a counter (open 09.45-16.15, Sun to Fri) near the Kathmandu Guest House. There's also a bureau de change in the Department of Immigration. It's open during normal banking hours (10.00-14.30, Sun to Thurs, 10.00-12.00 on Fri).

The American Express office (☎ 226172, open Sunday to Friday 10.00-13.00 and 14.00-17.00) is by the Mayalu Hotel. You can get credit card cash advances on Mastercard or Visa at many banks.

If you want to do your financial transactions on the black market (see p71) it'll find you soon enough if you wander past the carpet shops in Thamel.

Bookshops & libraries
Kathmandu has some excellent bookshops, including many small secondhand shops where you can trade in your novel for another.

You can catch up on what happened in Britain two weeks ago in the papers and magazines at the British Council Reading Room on Kanti Path. The Kaiser Library, Kaiser Shamsher Rana's private collection, is worth visiting as much for the building as for the 30,000+ musty volumes. This Rana palace is now the Ministry of Education & Culture, just west of the modern royal palace.

Communications
• **Telephone & fax** The phone system in Nepal works quite well both for internal and international calls. Since the Central Telegraph office is inconveniently far from Thamel, it's best to use one of the many communications agencies. You can make international calls and send and receive faxes at these places, which charge only a small commission. L'Autre Monde Public Services (LAMPS), near Pub Maya in Thamel, is a small reliable operation. Their fax no is (+977)-1-226763.

• **E-mail** Several of the communications agencies are now offering this service. Currently, the cheapest place is Global Communications (glocom@glopc.mos.com.np) in the shopping centre opposite the Department of Immigration. They charge Rs60 per kb to send (Rs30 if on disk) and Rs20 to receive.

• **Post** The GPO is in the south of the city, a twenty-minute walk from Thamel. Poste Restante letters are held here and you need to show your passport to claim mail. When sending letters you should try to get them franked or the stamps may be removed and resold. Alternatively, for a small commission, the Thamel communications agencies will handle this for you.

Embassies
- **Australia** (☎ 411578), Bansbari
- **India** (☎ 410900), Lainchaur
- **Israel** (☎ 411811), Bishramalaya House, Lazimpat
- **New Zealand** (Honorary Consul ☎ 412436), Dilli Bazaar
- **Sweden** (☎ 220939), Khichapokhari
- **Thailand** (☎ 213910), Thapthali
- **UK** (☎ 410583), Lainchaur
- **USA** (☎ 411179), Pani Pokhari

Left luggage
All hotels and guest houses are happy to store excess luggage for free while you go off on your trek, although they expect you to stay with them on your return.

Massage
To relax those après-trek aching limbs a number of places offer massages. Stated charges are from around Rs500 for an hour but if business is slack you could try to bargain this down a bit. The number of massage parlours has mushroomed in recent years and the women that purport to be masseuses have become younger and more attractive; the whole business appears to be taking its lead from Bangkok.

Medical clinics
CIWEC (☎ 228531, open Monday to Friday 09.00-12.00, 13.00-16.00) is the best place to go for medical treatment in Kathmandu. It has now moved to a more convenient location just off Durbar Marg, near the Hotel Yak & Yeti. Consultations cost US\$35 or equivalent in any currency. **Nepal International Clinic** (☎ 412842, open Sunday to Friday 09.00-17.00) is also excellent and consultations cost US\$30 or equivalent. It's opposite the Royal Palace, slightly east of Durbar Marg.

Cheaper clinics in Thamel include **Synergy** (☎ 413503), opposite Blue Note Bar; **Everest International** (☎ 411504) on the square north of Les Yeux; and **Himalaya International** (☎ 225455) near Hotel Utse.

Supermarkets
Best Shopping Centre near Marco Polo Guest House has lots of imported goodies. Bluebird Supermarket in Lazimpat has a wider stock.

Swimming-pools
The top hotels all have swimming-pools and will allow non-residents to use them for a price. The largest is at the Hotel de L'Annapurna but it'll

cost you Rs350 to swim here. The small pool at the Hotel Shangrila costs Rs250 and is set in very pleasant gardens.

Trekking agencies

All the treks described in this guide can be done independently but for the side trip into the newly-opened north Mustang region (see p32) you are required to use a trekking agency. There are more than 100 trekking agencies in Nepal, most based in Kathmandu. The top outfits have their offices on Durbar Marg but there are many other reputable companies based in Thamel. They can organise anything from a porter-guide to accompany one person on a tea-house trek to complete expeditions with sirdar (trek leader), sherpas (assistants), cooks and porters. For an organised trek, expect to pay anything from £13.50/US$20 to £60/US$100 per person per day depending on the number of members. Be sure you know exactly what will be included and that your porters will be adequately clothed for high passes like the Thorung La.

Trekking equipment rental

There are numerous trekking equipment rental shops in Thamel where you can hire sleeping-bags (check that these are clean and give them a good airing in the sun before use), boots, rucksacks, and down jackets as well as camping gear and mountaineering equipment (of variable quality). Deposits are required.

Himalayan Rescue Association & Trekkers' Information Centre

If only for their own safety, all trekkers should visit these two organisations (conveniently near the Department of Immigration) before hitting the trail.

The **Himalayan Rescue Association** (HRA) was founded not just to rescue injured mountaineers and trekkers but to conduct research into the causes and prevention of altitude sickness (AMS). The reduction in the numbers of deaths from AMS, when the numbers of visitors have vastly increased, bears witness to their impressive success. Two health posts are operated during the trekking season, one in Pheriche (Everest region) and the other in Manang (Annapurna region). Every afternoon, there are lectures on how to minimise the risks of AMS. It's a better idea to attend one of these here rather than at the HRA health post in Manang because you can then spend the time in Manang exploring the area. You can also register with your embassy using forms provided here. This will facilitate procedures should a helicopter rescue be needed.

KEEP (Kathmandu Environmental Education Project) run a **Trekkers' Information Centre** around the corner from the HRA, by the Potala Tourist Home. The centre was opened in 1992 with the aim of encouraging trekkers to adopt a more responsible attitude to the cultural and natural environment. The centre can give you advice on routes and information about conditions on the high passes. There's a coffee shop here and a noticeboard where you can advertise for trekking partners. They also sell environmentally friendly soap, recycled paper products and iodine for water purification.

Since both the HRA and the Trekkers' Information Centre are operated as charities, donations are always welcome.

Trekking permits

These are obtained from the **Department of Immigration** (☎ 412337), located just east of Thamel. It's open for applications for trekking permits and visa extensions between 10.00 and 14.00 from Sunday to Thursday, 10.00 to 12.00 on Friday. The forms for the three main trekking areas are colour-coded: you need a yellow one for the Annapurna region. Two photos are also required (available instantly in several photographers' nearby). You also need to pay the Annapurna Conservation Area Project entry fee in the National Park Office located in the basement of the shopping centre across the road. See p64 for visa extension and trekking permit fees.

Permits and visas are usually ready the same day in the afternoon between 14.00 and 16.00 Sunday to Thursday, 12.00 to 15.00 on Friday. At the height of the season you may have to wait until the following day so make your application as soon after the office opens as possible.

TRANSPORT

By **bicycle** is definitely the best way to get around although traffic and pollution problems get worse each year. There are lots of rental stands around Thamel. No deposit is required; you sign the book and pay the first day's rental. Be sure you check the tyres, brakes, lock and bell before you cycle off. Lock the bike whenever you leave it as you'll be held responsible for its replacement if it gets stolen. You can rent an old Indian Hero with patched tyres for Rs30 per day or a smart new Chinese Flying Pigeon for Rs40. Some places also have Taiwanese mountain bikes for Rs80-100. If you're renting for more than one day (a good idea as you can keep the bike overnight at your guest house) you can usually negotiate a lower rate.

A number of places in Thamel now rent out **motorbikes**, mostly 100-250cc Japanese bikes made under licence in India. They cost Rs350-450 per day, plus Rs25 for a helmet; a cash deposit is sometimes required, usually they simply want to know where you're staying. You're supposed to have either an international driving licence or a Nepali one.

There are lots of **taxis** around Kathmandu but it's difficult to get drivers to use their meters, especially if you pick one up in a tourist district like Thamel or Durbar Marg. You won't get away paying less than Rs150 for the ride in from the airport to the city centre although the metered fare would be about half this. There are also **auto-rickshaws**, metered and costing about a third less than taxis. Auto-rickshaw meters need recalibrating so you currently have to pay what the meter reads plus 40%. Taxi meters were all recalibrated in 1995.

Kathmandu's **cycle-rickshaw** wallahs understand just how your delicate Western conscience ticks, so hard bargaining is required if you're going to pay anything like local prices. There are extensive **bus** routes around the city and out to the airport but this is a very slow and crowded transportation option.

WHAT TO SEE

You could easily spend a week in the Kathmandu Valley, such is the rich concentration of sights here. Several companies operate bus tours (ask in the larger hotels and travel agencies) but renting a bicycle and wandering round independently is rather more rewarding. Getting lost is all part of the fun.

Durbar Square

First stop on the Kathmandu sightseeing trail is Durbar Square, also known as Hanuman Dhoka. This complex of ornately carved temples and monuments includes the old royal palace (closed Tue), the Kumari Bahal (the home of the Kumari, the 'living goddess', a young girl chosen as the incarnation of the Hindu goddess Durga), the Kasthamandap (the wooden pavilion from which the city's name is said to have been derived) and the tall Taleju temple, built in the 16th century. The best time to be here is early in the morning when people are going about their daily pujas.

Baudha (Bodhnath)

This Buddhist stupa is one of the largest in the world. Seven kms from the city centre, it's a major place of pilgrimage, especially for Tibetans. There's a large Tibetan community here and several monasteries.

From dawn to dusk the faithful make their circumambulations (always in a clockwise direction) under the fluttering prayer-flags and the all-seeing eyes of the giant white stupa. It's a fascinating place to visit, especially at the time of a new or a full moon when there are special festivities. Nourishment of a more basic nature is available at the Oasis Restaurant and a number of other places near the stupa. There are also a couple of bars serving momos and tumba (see p76) just around the corner from the Oasis. Look for a curtain across a door; there are no signboards. Order a plate of *sukuti* (dried meat) to accompany your tumba and momos. It's all ridiculously cheap but not terribly hygienic – probably best enjoyed when you come back from your trek.

Swayambhunath

Visible from many parts of the city, this ancient stupa is the second most important Buddhist shrine in Kathmandu. It's a 40-minute walk west of Thamel. The steep climb up through the woods is certainly good practice for a trek and there's a good view from the top but Swayambhunath has little of the atmosphere of Baudha. It's also known as the 'Monkey Temple' on account of the troupes of macaques here. Don't feed them as they can get vicious when your supplies of biscuits run out.

Pashupatinath

Hindu pilgrims come from all over the sub-continent to this Nepalese Varanasi (Benares). It's a very extensive complex of temples beside the Bagmati River, six km from the city centre.

Pashupatinath derives its fame from the metre-long linga, carved with four faces of Shiva which is kept in the main temple (closed to non-Hindus). The whole complex is dedicated to Shiva and is a focus for sadhus, wandering ascetics, some of whom may have walked here from as far away as south India.

As at Varanasi, people perform their early morning ablutions from the ghats here. It's also the most auspicious spot to be cremated in the country. The funeral pyres by the river have become something of a tourist sight, attracting coachloads of scantily-clad foreigners who behave with astounding insensitivity, firing off rolls of Kodachrome at the burning bodies.

Patan

Also known as Lalitpur, the second of the three main city-states in the Kathmandu Valley is now just a suburb of the capital. Patan's Durbar Square is probably the best collection of late Malla architecture in the country and rather less touristy than Durbar Square in Kathmandu. A taxi from Thamel should cost around Rs60 using the meter.

It's also worth visiting Kumbeshwar Square, which boasts the only five-storey temple in Patan. Water in the pond here is said to flow directly from the holy lake of Gosainkund in Langtang. At the north-east corner of the square is Kumbeshwar Technical School. Visitors are welcome at this school and orphanage set up to help the lowest castes in the area. Tibetan rugs and sweaters of considerably higher quality than those on sale in Thamel can be purchased here.

Bhaktapur

The third city, Bhaktapur, is a mediaeval gem, visited only fleetingly (if at all) by tourists. Fourteen km east of Kathmandu, it's an almost entirely Newar city that is strongly independent of Kathmandu. Some of the people who live here can't even speak Nepali. Much more than in Kathmandu or Patan, an atmosphere of timelessness pervades this place. Bhaktapur's main attraction is its Durbar Square, with its Palace of Fifty-Five Windows, but here, as in the rest of the city, many buildings have been damaged by earthquakes. The major 'quake in 1934 affected more than half the buildings. Much of the reconstruction work has been done by the Bhaktapur Development Project, a sensitive urban renewal programme sponsored by the German government.

It's a dusty hour-long cycle-ride to Bhaktapur from Kathmandu or you can take the electric trolley-bus from Tripureshwar which will drop you across the river, a 15-minute walk from Bhaktapur's Durbar Square.

Thimi
This small Newar town is famous for its pottery and the streets and squares are lined with recently thrown pots drying in the sun. Ten km from Kathmandu, Thimi makes a pleasant cycle-excursion and can be combined with Pashupatinath and/or Baudha.

Nagarkot
The most popular mountain-viewing spot near Kathmandu is Nagarkot, 32km from the city on the road that passes Bhaktapur. Since the view, which includes Everest and four of the other ten highest peaks in the world, is best in the early morning, most people spend the night here. There are lodges to suit all pockets from less than US$1 to over US$25. There are, however, tours that leave Kathmandu before dawn to catch the sunrise from Nagarkot. You can also get here by bus from Bhaktapur (three per day, two hours), on foot or by mountain-bike.

Mountain flight
A more expensive alternative to mountain-viewing from Nagarkot is to take one of the early-morning mountain flights operated by RNAC, Everest Air and Necon Air. The flight costs US$99 (refundable if clouds cause it to be cancelled).

Other entertainment
Several of the top hotels put on evening **cultural shows**, some including dinner. There's a nightly floor-show in an impressive Rana palace theatre, now the Naachghar restaurant at the Yak & Yeti Hotel. It's expensive and you must book (☎ 413999).

Look out for posters in Thamel advertising Chris Beall's **slide shows** covering the main trekking regions of the country. He's a professional photographer and lecturer and the slide shows, held in the Kathmandu Guest House, are well worth the ticket price.

For many years the Soaltee Holiday Inn was Nepal's only **casino**, very popular with visiting Indians. Foreigners who have arrived in Nepal within the last seven days are given Rs100-worth of chips free. It's open 24 hours a day. All the top hotels now have casinos.

Everest Snooker has seven tables and charges Rs120 per hour for their use. Follow the winding road out past Holy Lodge and it's on the right almost opposite Hotel Shikhar. The Hotel Moonlight also has tables; there is no charge if you stay there.

GETTING AWAY

By air
Nepal's air transport system has expanded rapidly since the government allowed the formation of private carriers in 1991. There are now at least four companies to choose from but all charge the same rate for the routes

AFTER YOUR TREK

Chitwan National Park

In this nature reserve on the low-lying Terai you may see one-horned rhino, rhesus macaques, langur monkeys, chital (Indian spotted deer), gharial (rare fish-eating crocodile) and if you're extremely lucky, a Bengal tiger. Even if you don't see a thing the excursions into the park are enjoyable. Elephants are the standard form of transport in the park.

There's a wide range of accommodation at Sauruha, the village near the park, from US$2. The top safari lodge, Tiger Tops, is actually inside the park and a wonderful place to stay but it'll set you back at least US$250 per night. Elephant safaris cost US$7 per person per hour

There are buses from Kathmandu and Pokhara to Tadi Bazaar ($6^1/_2$-$7^1/_2$ hours from either town). Tadi Bazaar is 8km from Sauruha. For Tiger Tops you fly to Meghauli (US$72) and transfer to the lodge by jumbo!

Rafting

A few days' rafting has become a very popular adjunct to a trek and Nepal has some of the best white water in the world.

Trips last anything from a day or two to a week or 12 days and all equipment (including life-jackets and food) is supplied by the rafting agencies. The day is spent floating down the river, shooting rapids from time to time, stopping for lunch and paddling when the going gets slow. At night you camp on the river bank. Rafting is now possible year round, on different parts of the river but the best months are September to November and March to May.

There are now numerous local companies offering trips and a lot of cowboys amongst them who give scant regard to the important safety aspect of rafting. Daily charges range from £10-40/US$15-60. Make sure you discuss all the details with the operator to find out exactly what you'll be getting for your money. Ultimate Descents (☎/fax 411933) is a knowledgeable and reliable operator; for other recommended outfits, ask recently-returned rafters. Some of the operators give free slide shows in the evening in Thamel to try to drum up custom.

Tibet

A visit to this still exotic corner of the world is highly recommended. The main drawback is that, from Nepal, you may only be able to visit as part of an organised tour. The regulations for foreign visitors seem to vary from year to year. In 1987 and 1988 Tibet was open for independent travel and more than a few intrepid souls set off to mountain bike from Kathmandu to Lhasa. Since then the Chinese, despite officially opening Tibet several times, have unofficially done their utmost to discourage individual travellers. In 1994 several cyclists made the Lhasa-Kathmandu trip, but in mid-1995, during the 'celebrations' in Lhasa marking 30 years of Chinese rule, it was visas for groups only.

From Nepal, there are four-day and eight-day group tours, run every Saturday, from around US$800/£500. These are easily arranged in a week from many travel agents in Kathmandu, who can also obtain a Chinese visa for you. Trekking tours are expensive but it's possible and rewarding to trek to the north side of Everest. One of the best all-round operators is Arniko Travels (☎ 421861, fax (+977) 1-414594), opposite the Chinese embassy in Baluwatar.

they share. Routes and schedules are subject to change as the new companies settle in. **Royal Nepal (RNAC)** (☎ 220757) flies from Kathmandu to Pokhara (US$61, 35 minutes) several times daily, with extra flights in the tourist season. They have connections to Jomsom and Ongre/Manang from Pokhara (see p130) and flights to many other towns in Nepal.

Everest Air (☎ 222290) flies from Kathmandu to Pokhara (US$61, 35 minutes) daily at 09.45 and direct to Jomsom (US$110, 45 minutes) on Thursday, Friday and Sunday at 07.05. This company now also has helicopters which it may use on some flights to Jomsom. **Nepal Airways** (☎ 416575) has morning flights to Pokhara and daily helicopter flights direct to Jomsom in the trekking season. **Necon Air** (☎ 472542) have morning flights to Pokhara daily except Sunday.

By bus

• **Pokhara** The easiest way to get to Pokhara is on one of the tourist buses that run from Thamel, leaving in the early morning. Tickets can be bought at most travel agents for around Rs225-275. More interesting since they're also used by Nepalis are the Sajha buses (Rs 74, seven hours) which run from near the GPO at 07.00. Tickets can be bought up to 2 days before departure from the kiosk here. The Sajha night bus (departing at 19.00, Rs77) is not recommended since the buses currently used don't have reclining seats.

Buses from the new bus station north of Thamel are cheaper and considerably more crowded. There are ordinary buses to Pokhara (Rs85, 10 hours) from 06.30-09.00 and deluxe ('Swiss') buses (Rs132, 7 hours) at 07.00. The original 'Swiss Bus' was operated by an aid project funded by the Swiss but it no longer runs. The appellation is now indiscriminately applied by Nepalis to any 'luxury' bus service.

• **Besisahar** Direct services run from the new bus station to Besisahar (Rs105) taking anything up to 12 hours. They leave at 06.30 and 08.30. You should book one day before at the fourth window from the right at the bus station.

• **Other destinations in Nepal and India** From the new bus station there are buses to most towns in Nepal, many departing early in the morning. Avoid the night buses, not only because they don't exactly make for a restful night but also because you'll miss some spectacular views. For the Everest region, buses use the old bus station in the centre of town.

If you're going on to India watch out for 'through' tickets. Since everyone has to change into an Indian bus at the border, there's actually no such thing. Travel agents give you a bus ticket to the border and a voucher to exchange with an Indian bus company with whom they've got an arrangement. Since things don't always run as smoothly as they might it's safer, cheaper and just as easy to buy the tickets as you go along. It also gives you a choice of buses and the option to stop off where you want.

The best crossing point into India is via Sunauli for Gorakhpur, Varanasi or Delhi. From the main bus station for Sunauli ordinary buses (Rs98-118, nine hours) leave 06.00-09.00 and there are also night buses. Similarly-priced Sajha buses leave from near the GPO.

For Patna and Calcutta it's better to go via Birganj/Raxaul (Rs113, eleven hours). Buses leave from the main bus station. For Darjeeling you'll have to make the gruelling trip to Karkabhitta (Rs 255, 12-14 hours) on overnight buses leaving between 15.00 and 16.30.

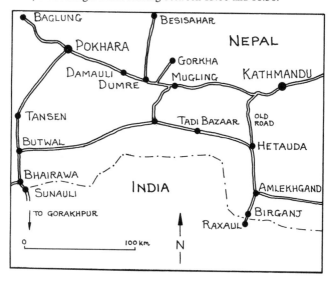

PART 5: POKHARA

Pokhara

In all my travels in the Himalaya I saw no scenery so enchanting as that which enraptured me at Pokhara. **Ekai Kawaguchi** *Three Years in Tibet*

Pokhara's superb mountain scenery has been enrapturing foreign visitors since Ekai Kawaguchi, the town's first foreign visitor, came this way in 1899. Modern travellers are no less impressed; there can be few other towns that are so close to such high mountains. Pokhara (pronounced 'POKE-rah') lies at 850m/2789ft yet peaks of over 8000m/26,267ft rise above it in a breathtaking panorama.

Two hundred kilometres (125 miles) west of Kathmandu, Pokhara is the starting and ending point for most of the treks in the Annapurna region, except the Annapurna Circuit (usually started from Dumre). It's also the perfect place to rest weary limbs after a trek and the town's relaxed atmosphere causes many travellers to stay rather longer than they'd originally planned. Along the eastern shore of Phewa Tal (Lake) a waterside version of Thamel offers accommodation to suit every budget.

The joy of Pokhara is that there really is very little to do here except laze around by the lake and over-indulge in those culinary delights you may have been pining for while away on your trek.

HISTORY

Origins

Probably at the same time that the Kathmandu Valley was a lake (about 200,000 years ago) the Pokhara Valley was also under water. Now just a few lakes remain: Phewa Tal in Pokhara, and Begnas Tal and Rupa Tal 10km to the east are the largest.

Very little is known about the early history of this area but Pokhara's location between the mountain passes and the plains has made it a focal point for peoples from both sides of the Himalaya for centuries. The area was controlled by numerous small kingdoms, usually situated on hilltops around the valley, populated by people who had migrated from Tibet. They were the ancestors of the Gurung who now live in Pokhara and the surrounding hills.

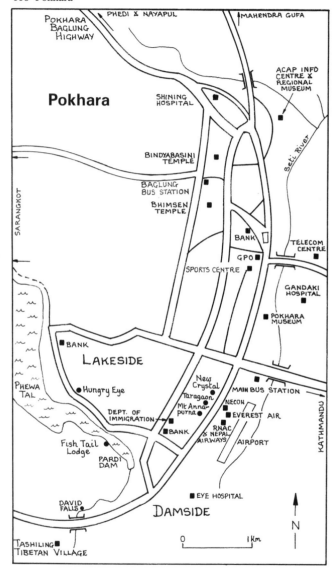

In the 14th century, Moghul persecution of Hindus in India forced refugee communities north into Nepal and some settled in the Pokhara area. Rajput princes from Rajasthan brought their entire courts and armies with them to carve out their own principalities. These Indo-Aryans developed the agriculture of the Pokhara Valley and whilst the high caste Brahmins and Chhetries remained in their mountain strongholds, the lower castes were sent to work the land below.

Shah Rulers of Kaskikot

In the 17th century, Pokhara was being ruled as part of Kaskikot, one of the most powerful of the Chaubise kingdoms in Central Nepal. These Chaubise kings were cousins of the Shah kings of Gorkha, Nepal's current royal family. Kulmandan Shah is the best known of Kaskikot's kings and also the first of the Shahs to rule a Nepalese kingdom. He is credited with establishing a winter capital in Pokhara and he encouraged trade along the Kali Gandaki Valley through Mustang to Tibet. Mule trains brought salt and wool down from Tibet to exchange for grain from Pokhara.

By the late 18th century the Chaubise kingdoms were no longer closely united. Prithvi Narayan Shah, the king of Gorkha who had conquered the Kathmandu Valley, turned his attention west to these kingdoms, sweeping through with his powerful army to conquer Kaskikot in 1785. In the period of peace and stability that followed Pokhara quickly grew to become the major trading town in the region.

The Ranas

Although the Rana prime ministers who ruled Nepal from 1846 to 1950 could claim ancestral connections to the Kaskikot area, only Jung Bahadur, the first of the Ranas, showed any particular interest in the region, declaring himself Maharaja of Kaski and Lamjung. None of the Ranas ever visited the Pokhara area.

Under the Ranas, Pokhara became the capital of Kaski and Lamjung districts. That there are few old buildings to see in Pokhara today is the result of a devastating earthquake in 1934, and in 1948 of a fire offering being made by a priest in the Bindyabasini temple that got out of control and reduced much of the town to ash.

Pokhara since 1950

Until the middle of this century, the only way to reach Pokhara from Kathmandu was on foot, a six or seven day journey. In 1951, the airfield was built but it was not until 1973 that the road linking Pokhara with the capital was finished. Another major communications project, the Pokhara-Baglung highway, is now also complete. This new highway has already sliced a day off the trekking schedules for the Annapurna region; it is hoped that the plans that it might at some time be extended up the

Kali Gandaki all the way to Jomsom will never leave the drawing board.

Improved communications brought people from the surrounding villages to swell Pokhara's population from just 5400 in 1961 to over 120,000 in 1995. The Chinese invasion of Tibet in 1951 brought 15,000 exiles to Nepal, many to Pokhara. Dervla Murphy spent some time working with Tibetan refugees in the 1960s and *The Waiting Land: A Spell in Nepal* provides an interesting description both of her experiences and of a Pokhara before apple pie and chocolate cake were being served on the shores of Phewa Tal. Numerous international aid agencies now have their regional headquarters in Pokhara.

Pokhara is the main recruiting area in Nepal for troops for the Gurkha regiments in the British and Indian armies. Together with tourism, army wages and pensions form the mainstay of the local economy.

ORIENTATION

The lake is the main focus for travellers. It's on the western edge of town and there are two main accommodation areas here, Lakeside (Baidam) and Damside (Pardi). Lakeside is one strip of hotels, guest houses, restaurants and shops with more places to stay up the paths among the trees. Damside is the smaller district beside Pardi Dam, to the south of the lake.

The airport and bus station are also in the southern half of the town, a long walk or a short taxi ride from the lake.

In the centre of Pokhara is the modern town; the old bazaar is to the north. Pokhara is a surprisingly spread-out town, sprawling for several kilometres down an incline that is unnoticeable until you try to ride your gearless Indian Hero from the lake to the bazaar.

WHERE TO STAY

Hotel areas

There are now more than 170 hotels in Pokhara so you shouldn't have any difficulty finding a place to stay except in the high season. Most are simple guest houses with just a few rooms, many run by ex-Gurkhas.

Although there is also some accommodation near the bus station and in the centre of Pokhara, everyone heads for the lake. Lakeside has the greatest choice of places to stay and almost all the restaurants and shops. Damside is quieter and it has better views of the mountains; many of the guest houses here also have dining rooms so you don't have to go to Lakeside to eat.

Prices

The prices given below are for single/double/triple rooms, with common (com) or attached (att) bathrooms, at the height of the season. At other times you should bargain. For the cheaper places you may get 20-40% off but for mid-range hotels you should be able to get a discount of up to 60%, depending on how many people are chasing rooms at the time. There is a 10% tax on accommodation for non star hotels, 11% for 1-3 star, and 13% for 4-5 star places: make sure you ascertain whether this is included in the price agreed upon.

Budget guest houses and cheap hotels
• **Lakeside** There are many places to stay in this price range and most are very similar: basic, cheap and cheerful. The two cheapest, the **Garden Guest House** [2] and its neighbour, the **Garden Rest House** [1], stand on a quiet lane about five minutes' from the lake, and both offer adequate standards of accommodation from US$1.50/3 (com). In a similar price range, **Heaven's Gate Guest House** [3] is a little nearer the action, and nearby the trendy **Holy Lodge** [16] has a friendly atmosphere and a pleasant garden. Moving north, another place that's been highly recommended is the **New Traveller Guest House** [4] with rooms from US$2 for a single with shared bathroom, to US$8 for attached doubles.

Particularly for women travelling alone, the friendly **Chetri Sisters' Guest House** is recommended. There are rooms from about US$1.50/3 and if you're interested in arranging for a woman porter to accompany you on your trek they should be able to help. The guest house is in the north of Lakeside, along the road that runs parallel to the lake, just off the map (see p121).

The New Zealand connection at the **Kiwi Guest House** [7] is that the manager spent two years there as a student. It's cheap, clean and very popular. Next door the immaculate **Stay Well Guest House** [13] is well maintained and the manager very helpful. Just opposite, the Indian and Dutch couple who own the **Nightingale Lodge** [31] offer not only spacious well-kept rooms but may even give a post-trek massage if required.

Hidden away in a beautiful garden, the **Gurkha Lodge** [37] is an excellent choice. There are five doubles at US$11 each in the bungalows here. On the main street, the **Rainbow Hotel** [21] offers basic cheap accommodation. To the north, the **Hotel Buddha** [28] is a large friendly place, and the nearby **Hong Kong Hotel** [23] has some budget accommodation amongst its pricier rooms, starting at US$4 for a single.

One place that looks certain to be very popular in the future is **Keiko's Cottages** [25], situated a little further on from Fewa Annex, boasting a library, the use of fishing equipment, games and a cottage on the opposite side of the lake. The double rooms cost from US$5 and are all individually decorated, most even having their own aquarium!

• **Damside** The most competently-run places here seem to be those owned and operated by ex-Gurkhas. The wonderful Captain DB Gurung

KEY In ascending order by price for singles/doubles with common bathroom (c) or attached bathroom (a). In some cases, space below permits only a price range from the cheapest single (c) to a double (a). Phone numbers are given in brackets. Prices in US$ but payable in rupees.

Lakeside

01 Garden Rest House (21862) $1-10 c/a
02 Garden GH $1.50/4 (c), $2/5 (a)
03 Heaven's Gate GH (21435) $2-5 c/a
04 New Traveller GH (21930) $2/4 c, $6-8 a
05 New Annapurna GH (21963) $2c,$6/10a
06 New Tourist GH (21479) $2-12 c/a
07 Kiwi GH $2/3 (c), $5-15/9-19 (a)
08 Dharma GH $2/3 (c), $15/20-35 (a)
09 Trekkers Retreat Lodge (21458) $3-4 c/a
10 Shining Lotus (21966) $3/4 (c), $4/6 (a)
11 Hotel Eyeball (21431) $ 3-5 c/a
12 Fewa Annex (21394) $3-7 c/a
13 Stay Well GH (21707) $3 (c), $6-8 (a)
14 Pancha Koshi GH $3 dbl (c), $6/12 (a)
15 New Friendly Home $3/5 (c), $6/10 (a)
16 Holy Lodge (21435) $3/5 (c), $10/15 (a)
17 MidnightWell dbl from $4
18 Pushpa GH (20332) $4-7 c/a
19 Santosh GH $2 dbl (c), $10 dbl (a)
20 Himalayan Country $4-6/6-8 (a)
21 The Rainbow Hotel $4/5 (c), $10/12 (a)
22 Hotel Asia (21159) $4/8 (c), $8/18 (a)
23 Hong Kong Hotel (21202) $4-30 c/a
24 Vienna Lodge dbl from $5 (a)
25 Keiko's Cottages dbl from $5 (a)
26 Pokhara Peace Home (21599) $5-15 c/a
27 Gaurishanker (21750) $5-30 c/a
28 Buddha GH (21428) $5-25 (c/a)
29 Tranquility Lodge (21030) $5-30 c/a
30 New Lake View GH $6/10 c/a
31 Nightingale Lodge (20338) $6-12 (a)
32 New Hotel Woodland (21970) dbl $7
33 Chalet de Pokhara (21707) $8-10 (a)
34 Hotel Lake Side (20073) $8c $15-24 (a)
35 Hotel Johnny Gurkha (21713) $8-25 c/a
36 Hotel Cordial $8-30 (c/a)
37 Gurkha Lodge $10-12 (a)
38 Hotel Motherland $10-15/15-20 (a)
39 Hotel Dreamland (21755) $10/15-20 (a)
40 Hotel Avocado (21183) $10-24 (a)
41 Blue Heaven GH $10-25 (a)
42 Hotel Meera (21031) $10/15 (c),$25/30a
43 Fairmount Hotel (21252) $10-30 c/a
44 Hotel Shikhar (21966) $10-37 c/a
45 Hotel Sitara (21579) $12-30 (a)
46 Mountain Top (20779) $12-30 (a)
47 Mandala Rest House (21478) $13/18 (a)
48 Hotel Full Moon (21511) $15-30 (a)
49 New Pokhara Lodge (20875) $15/35 (a)

50 Hotel Barahi (21879) $15-50 (a)
51 Mountain Villa (21954) $16/20 (a)
52 Nepal GH (21963) $16-22 (a)
53 Moonlight GH $18/23-30 (a)
54 Hotel Shamrock (21027) $18-35 (a)
55 Baba Lodge (20981) $20/25 (a)
56 Hotel Fewa (20151) $20-25 (a)
57 Hotel Glacier (21722) $20-30 (a)
58 Hotel Sahana (21229) $20-25/25-30 (a)
59 Hotel Bedrock (21876) $20-48 (a)
60 Hotel Monal (21459) sgl/dbl from $25
61 Thorung La (21157) $35/55 (a)
62 Hotel Pumori (21462) $40/50 (a)
63 Base Camp Resort (21226) $61/66 (a)
64 Fishtail Lodge $99 (a)

Damside

65 Hotel Green View (21844) $2c, $10/15a
66 Hotel Jamu (20930) $2-4 c/a
67 New Hotel Nascent (21719) $2.5-5 (a)
68 Sherpa GH $2/3 (c), $8/10 (a)
69 New Hotel Sunlight (21800) $2c, $5/10a
70 Indra Niwas (21719) $3/5 (a)
71 Super Lodge (21861) $3/5 (c), $7/12 (a)
72 Hotel Peaceful (20861) $3/4 (c), $8-15 (a)
73 Hotel Sakura (20924) $3-5 (c), $8-15 (a)
74 Purna GH $3/5 (c), $10/12 (a)
75 New Friendly GH $3-15 c/a
76 New Hotel Pagoda (21802)$3/4c,$10/13a
77 Hotel Siddhartha (20052) $3-20 c/a
78 Hotel Himalayan (21643) $3-20 c/a
79 Hotel Mary Ward $3-25 c/a
80 Hotel Garden (20870) $3/4 (c), $5-30 (a)
81 View Pt Hotel (21787) $4-10 c/a
82 Hotel Monalisa (20863) $6/10 (c), $20-35 (a)
83 New Hotel Anzuk (21845) $7/10 (a)
84 Hotel Blue Sky (21425) $10/15 (a)
85 Hotel Try Star (20930) $10/15 (a)
86 Ashok GH (20374) $15/20 (a)
87 Hotel Annapurna (21723) $15/20 (a)
88 Hotel Holiday (21763) $15/25 (a)
89 Tibet Resort (20853) $10/14 (c), $23/34 (a)
90 Hotel Jharna (21925) $19/24 (a)
91 Hotel Mt Manaslu (20953) $20/25-35 (a)
92 Pacific Hotel (21719) $30-50 (a)
93 Pokhara Resort (21043) $35-45 (a)
94 Dragon Hotel (20391) $40-50 (a)
95 Hotel Tragopan (21708) $40-80 (a)

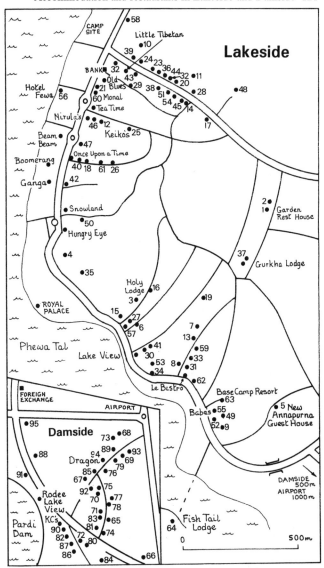

runs the spotless **New Hotel Sunlight** [69], charging a very reasonable US$2 for singles, US$10 for attached doubles. **The New Hotel Pagoda** [76] and **Mary Ward Hotel** [79] nearby are both of a similar standard to this, and are equally good value.

Considering that he supports Aldershot, the soccer-mad Captain KB Gurung remains remarkably cheerful, and his **Hotel Anzuk** [83] is a warm and friendly place to stay. For US$7/10, the captain will supply you with comfortable rooms, hot showers, and most of last weekend's English Premier League scores. Opposite, the excellent **Hotel Green View Lodge** [65] is amazing value. Set back in a very pleasant garden, this delightful family-run lodge offers some of the cheapest accommodation on Damside, with rooms at US$1.50/2 (com), US$10/15 (att).

On the waterfront, the **Monalisa Hotel** [82] has a few cheap single rooms for US$6, and doubles from US$10 with common bath.

Moderately-priced hotels

Several of the hotels which used to offer rooms for just a few dollars a night have spruced them up and dramatically increased their prices. Outside the high season, when many of these rooms are empty, you can get equally dramatic discounts if you bargain.

The recently renovated **Full Moon Hotel** [48] is full of character and offers delightful rooms with excellent views of the lake from its hilltop location. More centrally located, the **Hotel Barahi** [50] is now nearing completion and there are plans to establish tennis courts, whilst the immaculate **Thorung La Hotel** [61] continues to offer very high standards of comfort. The **Hotel Monal** [60] (☎ 24159) is well located on the main drag in Lakeside. It's run as a German-Nepali partnership and rooms here begin at US$25. **Baba Lodge** [55] (☎ 20981) is popular and has rooms from US$20/25. It's also worth checking out the **Hotel Hungry Eye**, a Lakeside landmark that was being rebuilt in 1995.

In Damside, rooms in the **Hotel Dragon** [94] (☎ 20391) cost US$40/50 with bathtubs in the attached bathrooms.

Expensive hotels

Opposite the airport, the recently-extended **New Hotel Crystal** (☎ 20035) has rooms for US$45-56/58-125, all with attached bathrooms. The restaurant here is good. In Lakeside, the **Base Camp Resort** [63] (☎ 21226) is the most up-market accommodation and even has satellite TV, should you want it. Rooms are US$61/66.

The top hotel in Pokhara is the **Fish Tail Lodge** [64], operated by Kathmandu's Hotel de l'Annapurna. It's worth visiting just for the superb view of the mountain panorama reflected in the water. All rooms have attached bathrooms and cost US$82/93. It's set in well-kept gardens and reached by raft across a narrow stretch of the lake. For reservations phone Kathmandu (01-221711).

WHERE TO EAT

Calorie after delicious calorie line the main street of Lakeside, from the cake shops laden with waist-expanding chocolate croissants, to the larger establishments offering ever more scrumptious ways of putting the wobble back in your walk after weeks on the trail.

It's difficult to give specific recommendations for restaurants: things change so fast. Some of the old favourites are listed below.

Breakfast

Many guest houses have a limited breakfast menu including porridge, muesli, toast and eggs. There's also great competition amongst the restaurants along Lakeside to provide all-inclusive breakfast specials. These range from Rs35 for a more than adequate set meal of eggs, toast, hash browns, tomatoes, and coffee, up to Rs100 for an 'American' or 'Trekkers Special', a huge feast that usually includes steak.

For those who find even that feast unfulfilling the **Fishtail Lodge** provides, for Rs375, an all-you-can-eat breakfast in Pokhara's most genteel surroundings, with incomparable mountain views thrown in.

Lunch and supper

• **Western/Have-a-go-at-anything** 'Tourist-friendly' restaurants now proliferate on Lakeside's main street. Characterised by thatched roofs and Western music, a new addition to one restaurant's menu is quickly emulated by the other places here, thus most menus now look decidedly similar. That said, the food is usually of a fairly high standard, the attempts at copying different national cuisines continue to achieve higher levels of authenticity – and the beer's always cold.

One restaurant that is consistently recommended by Westerners living in Pokhara is **Once Upon A Time**. The food, in particular the steaks (from Rs100) is always thoughtfully prepared. To the north is the **Pyramid**, a similarly large establishment with similar standards of food, but with the added distinction of offering spiritual enlightenment to accompany your enchilladas (Rs95): the manager teaches meditation and Buddhism.

A number of smaller places, such as the **Tequila**, **Phewa Beach** and **Moondance**, have similar fare at cheaper prices. The long-established **Tea-time Bamboostan** is still going strong, and if one of the ultra-hip waiters deigns to serve you, the food isn't bad at all.

Away from these trendier joints, many people's choice for a delicious meal is the smallish **Ganga Restaurant**. Their succulent fresh fish, caught from the lake and cooked in a rum butter sauce (Rs105), is truly mouth-watering. Opposite, the **Garlic Garden Restaurant** is of a similar standard but considerably more expensive, although it also offers a nightly cultural show.

Moving north, many restaurants now have gardens stretching down to the lake. Very pleasant in the early evening as the egrets swoop by, these places are also good for dinner, provided the mosquitoes don't devour you completely first. **Fewa Park** and **Beam Beam** are both recommended, with the latter serving some delicious curries.

In south Lakeside, **Baba's Restaurant** has been popular for many years. Main dishes (Rs75-150) include chicken cordon bleu and spinach mushroom lasagne. Nearby, **Le Bistro** has a good reputation and serves fish from the lake, steaks, and a range of cakes and pies. The **Hungry Eye** should now have reopened; it was always a good place for steaks and tandoori dishes.

In Damside, **KC's Restaurant**, whose delicious flame-grilled steaks are now legendary, continues to prosper. Nearby the **Rodee Lake View Restaurant** is the closest you can get to the water and serves excellent tandoori food. It's also the place for serious post-trek celebrations, as they reward anybody who drinks five bottles of beer with a free sixth one!

• **Nepali/Tibetan** There are several small Nepali/Tibetan places offering daal bhat or momos at give-away prices. More upmarket, the **Little Tibetan Tea Garden**, serves momos and many other Tibetan dishes. **The Lhasa Tibetan Restaurant** is also recommended, and you can try gyakok here (four hours' notice required).

• **Chinese** Although there are no specialist Chinese restaurants on Lakeside, a large selection of Chinese food can be found at many of the places here. Usually these are just variations on fried rice but are nevertheless tasty and filling. The **Ganga Restaurant** has a wide selection.

•**Austrian** At the part Austrian-owned **Little Vienna Restaurant** it's possible to dine on Weiner schnitzel, salad and French fries, and to follow that up with topfenpalatschinker (Austrian pancakes) all washed down with excellent filter coffee. It's part of Vienna Lodge.

• **Japanese** Next door to the Rodee Lake View Restaurant in Damside is the **Yamoto Restaurant** which serves Japanese food 'under Japanese direction'. Try the oyakodon (meat and egg over rice).

• **Indian** Most of the restaurants make decent attempts at Tandoori dishes. The **Gorkha Palace Restaurant** at the Lake View Resort has been recommended by many. For a taste of modern India, the sub-continent's fast-food chain **Nirulas**, purveyors of scrumptious sundaes and the famous footlongs, has opened a branch in central Lakeside.

• **Vegetarian** All restaurants have some vegetarian dishes. The restaurant at the **Shining Lotus Hotel** is exclusively vegetarian and has been recommended in particular for its South Indian dishes.

SERVICES

Banks

Nepal Grinlays Bank (open Sunday to Thursday 10.00-16.00, Friday 10.00-15.00, closed on Saturday) now has a branch on Lakeside. They will do cash advances on Visa or Mastercard. Nearby a couple of exchange counters have opened. Double check your money here as short-changing always seems to work in their favour. The main branch of **Nepal Rastra Bank** is in the centre of Pokhara.

Bookshops

As in Kathmandu, there's no difficulty in finding something to read with numerous bookshops and kiosks in the Lakeside area. They stock new and secondhand titles and most operate book exchanges.

Communications

• **Post** The GPO is a long bike ride into the centre of town. If you want your postcards to reach their destinations you should, however, bring them here and watch them being franked. Poste restante letters are held here. It's open from 10.00 to 17.00 Sunday to Friday.

• **Phone** In Lakeside and Damside it's easiest to use the phones in guest houses, shops and kiosks for international calls (most charge about Rs175 per minute). For a three minute international call, the Telecommunications Centre is cheaper, charging Rs576 for a person-to-person call, plus Rs144 for each extra minute and a Rs50 cancellation charge if you don't get through. It's open from 07.00 to 21.00 but is inconveniently located near the GPO.

• **Fax** There are now many fax offices in Pokhara. You can also use the Telecommunications Centr, but they have a three minute minimum charge.

Left luggage

As in Kathmandu, most hotels and guest houses will store excess baggage for free. Keep all valuables with you, though.

Massage, haircuts and spiritual well-being

For some unknown reason, the fresh juice bars on Lakeside also do massage as a sideline. The options are confusingly varied: half-body, full-body, American, Japanese, German or Indian and they charge around Rs250 per hour. Next to the Tequila Restaurant is an Ayurvedic Massage Centre, which charges similar rates.

To the north of Lakeside, on the road heading towards Prithwi Chowk, is Yogi's Yoga Centre, which offers a three day introductory course to yoga for Rs1000, as well as more advanced classes.

Barbers do haircuts for Rs25-50 and will then try to throw in a little manipulatory massage to push the price up. If this isn't what you want, say so or be prepared for a larger bill than you'd intended. If you want a shave, ensure that a new blade is used since Aids is on the increase in Asia. For 'facials, waxing and pedicure' try Venus Beauty Parlour, near Once Upon A Time.

Medical clinics

There are a number of clinic/pharmacies in Lakeside that do stool tests and also the Western Regional/Gandaki Hospital (☎ 20066), near the Telecommunications Centre. If you're hospitalised in Pokhara you may need a friend to bring you food and help look after you as nursing is minimal. For specialist eye treatment, the Himalaya Eye Hospital (☎ 20352) regularly treats foreigners for a nominal fee. Staffed by one Dutch and two Nepali opthalmologists, it's to the south of the airport.

Shopping

Pokhara is the perfect place to browse and there are rows of kiosks and small shops in which to do it. All the goods on sale here are also available in Kathmandu.

Few travellers escape the charms of the Tibetan curio-sellers who work the streets in pairs with considerable success. You can watch carpets being woven at Tashiling and Tashipalkhel Tibetan villages. Also worth visiting is the group of thangka shops just north of Lakeside, near the Hotel Sahana.

For supplies the grocery shops in Lakeside (Safeway, Saveways, Saleways, etc) stock everything a trekker could wish for: from Mars Bars (Rs50) to Mills and Boon romances (Rs125), for those cold, lonely nights in the mountains. Some of the bakeries sell delicious wholegrain trekking bread too. It's worth pointing out, however, that for most treks you don't really need to stock up on anything.

Tourist Office

The small tourist office is opposite the airport. It's open 10.00-16.00 daily except Saturday and closes at 15.00 on Friday.

Trekking agencies

There are a number of agencies here who will happily organise a complete trek, should you want their services. To hire a porter, it's usually cheaper to cut out the middleman and arrange things yourself. See p85 for more information. If you're a woman looking for a woman porter contact the Chhetri Sisters Guest House (see Where to stay).

Trekking equipment rental

As in Kathmandu, it's possible to rent most things from down jackets to sleeping-bags but don't expect any fancy climbing gear. If you've lost your camera you can rent one from the Photo Sunrise camera shop near the Hotel Tragopan for Rs75 per day.

Trekking permits

The Department of Immigration has a branch in Pokhara (☎ 21167), open from Sunday to Thursday from 10.00-13.30 for visa extensions and trekking permit applications and from 16.00-17.00 the same day for collections. On Friday you must get your application in before 12.00 for collection between 14.00 and 15.00. Visa extensions and trekking permits are issued for Annapurna and Jumla for a maximum of six weeks. It's not yet possible to get visas for the north Mustang area here.

Just outside the office here are a number of photo shops that will do instant passport photos.

Working in Pokhara

There are numerous aid agencies operating here but they're unlikely to recruit foreigners locally unless you have very special skills.

TRANSPORT

Taxi

Taxis are meterless and you pay as much as the driver thinks you will stand. Between the airport or bus station and Lakeside you probably won't get away with paying less than Rs50.

Bus

Local buses are slow and crowded. There's a loop service that runs between the bazaar, the airport and Lakeside. Lakeside to the airport costs Rs2.50. A shuttle bus links Prithwi Chowk Bus Station in the centre of town with Besi Bus Park (for buses to Nayapul for Birethanti etc).

Bicycle and motorbike

The best way to get around Pokhara is by bike. There are lots of places to rent them from and prices are around Rs20-30 per day for the cheapest, to around Rs80 for the latest edition mountain bike.

In Lakeside you can now rent motorbikes. An Indian Escort RX100 (licence-built Yamaha) costs around Rs500 per day.

WHAT TO SEE

There really are very few 'sights' in Pokhara so you needn't feel guilty if you spend your time lazing around by the lake.

Mountain viewing

The Pokhara panorama is undeniably impressive and dawn is the best time to view it; Fish Tail Lodge is the best place to view it from. Machhapuchhre is the most easily recognisable peak. From Pokhara it has a classic pointed shape; it looks like a fish tail only from the north. From left to right the major peaks you can see from Pokhara are

Dhaulagiri (8167m/26,795ft), Annapurna I (8091m/26,545ft), Machha-puchhre (6997m/22,942ft), Annapurna III (7555m/24,767ft) – shaped like an elephant, Annapurna IV (7525m/24,688ft) and Annapurna II (7937m/26,041ft).

Museums and exhibitions

Most interesting is the **ACAP Information Centre** which has displays about the work currently being done as part of the Annapurna Conservation Area Project. You can buy post-cards, T-shirts and books here. It's part of the **Annapurna Regional Museum**, which has a small display of local flora and fauna and an impressive collection of butterflies. They're both open daily (09.00-13.00 and 14.00-17.00) except Saturday and located on the university campus in the far north of the town. There are plans to move the ACAP Information Centre to Lakeside.

The Pokhara Museum (open 10.00-17.00 daily except Tuesday) has a small dusty archaeological and ethnographic display that's probably worth the Rs5 entry charge but not the Rs10 camera fee.

Temples

The most important Hindu temple here is the **Bindyabasini Temple**, just above the old bazaar. It's dedicated to Durga, the goddess of death and manifestation of Parvati, Shiva's consort. She is appeased by the sacrificing of goats, cocks and buffaloes and, especially during festivals such as Dasain, the streets flow red around this temple. South of Bindyabasini is the smaller **Bhimsen Temple**. You can visit the **Varaha Temple**, on an island in Phewa Tal, by boat.

There are modern **Buddhist temples** at the two Tibetan villages and a gompa one km east of the telecommunications centre.

For the energetic, there's a monastery to the south of Lakeside on top of the hill. It's visible from Lakeside, and the views of Pokhara and the mountains from there are stunning.

Bicycle excursions

Pokhara's other sights make pleasant bicycle excursions. In the south there's **David/Devi Falls**. The origins for its name get more confused with each guide-book that's published. A tourist named David, Davy, Devi or Miss Davis is said to have been swimming here when the sluice-gates on Pardi Dam, a couple of km upstream, were opened. He (or she) was drowned. The falls are quite impressive after the monsoon; much less so in the winter and spring. Nearby you can visit the **Tashiling Tibetan Village**, where there's a carpet factory. Tibetan trinket sellers will soon home in on you here and you'll also meet them in Lakeside.

(Opposite) Small hotels and restaurants line the main street in Pokhara's Lakeside.

TOURIST INFORMATION MAP BOARD

MENU
LUNCH, DINNER, BREA

HOT DRINKS
MILK TEA
BLACK TEA
LEMON TEA
HOT LEMON
MILK COFFEE
BLACK COFFEE
DRINKING CHOCOLATE
* HOT DRINKS ARE AVAILABLE IN CURDS/CHILL MT/CUSTARD

NEPAL
RICE PLA
RICE FRIE
RICE FRIED
RICE FRIED
RICE PUDDI
RICE DAL
PUMKIN P

PORRIDGE & MUESLI
PORRIDGE PLAIN
PORRIDGE W/ MILK
CORN PORRIDGE PLAIN
CORN PORRIDGE W/ MILK
MUESLI PLAIN
MUESLI W/ MILK
MUESLI W/

BREAD
TIBETAN
TIBETAN BR
CHAPATI P
CHAPATI W
PANCAKE P
PANCAKE W
CORN BREA
CORN BREAD
EGG/LEMON

EGGS
VEG. OMLET W/ EGG
EGG BOILED
EGG FRIED
ONION OMLET
POTATO OMLET

POTA
POTATOES
POTATOES
POTATOES
POTATOES
MASH POTA

SOUPS
NOODLES SOUP
VEG.   SOUP
POMKEEN SOUP
ONION   SOUP
EGG   SOUP
GARLIC   SOUP
CHICKEN SOUP
TOMATO   SOUP
POTATO   SOUP

HARD
XXX RUM
PINEAPLE W
RAWSI

COLD D
COCA-COLA
FANTA-LEM
BEERS
YAK CHEW

NOODLES
NOODLES FRIED PLAIN
NOODLES FRIED W/ EGG
NOODLES FRIED W/ VEG.
RARA/MAGI NOODLES W/VEG.
RARA/MAGI NOODLES W/EGGS
MACARONI
MACARONI VEG
MACARONI EGG
MACARONI TOMATO

PIZZA
MIX PIZ
VEG. PIZ
SPRING
VEG.
CHEESE
CHICKEN
PLATE

STOP LOCK

LEGEND
1 TRAIL
2 RIVER
3 BRIDGE
4 LODGE
5 ACAP HQ
6 HOT SPRING
7 POST OFFICE
8 ACAP HQ
9 KEROSEN DEPO
10 TOURIST INFORMATION
10 CHECK POST
11 HEALTH POST

DISTANCE IN HOUR
1 TOLKA - LANDRUK   1:30
2 LANDRUK - JHINU   2:30
3 JHINU - CHHOMRO
4 CHHOMRO - KHULDI
5 KHULDI - HIMALAYA
6 HIMALAYA - MBPC
7 MBPC - APBC
8 TOLKA - GHANDRUK
9 GHANDRUK - T-PAHI
10 DEURALI - DHOBILE
11 DEURALI - GHOREPANI   6 HRS
12 TOLKA - POTHANA
13 POTHANA - DHAMPUS
14 DHAMPUS - POKHARA   1:30
15 TOLKA - BIRETHANTI

YOU ARE HERE

KANDGO

To the north you could visit **Tashipakhel Tibetan Village** which has a restaurant, guest house, gompa and carpet factory. Follow the Pokhara-Baglung Highway for three km to reach it. Also in the north but past the British Gurkha camp is **Mahendra Gufa**, a large dark cave full of bats that's not really worth the long ride up.

The **Seti Gorge** is very impressive and deep but so narrow you may not be aware of its existence. You get a good view of it from the bridge between the GPO and the telecommunications centre.

ENTERTAINMENT

Boating and swimming
Hiring a boat to paddle yourself around the lake or out to the small temple on the island helps pass the time until the next meal. There are lots of boat hire places in Lakeside and owners will begin the bargaining at around Rs100 per hour or Rs200 'with driver'. The royal guards will wave you away if you stray too close to the King's palace, although he's hardly ever at this summer hideaway.

You can swim in the lake (best from a boat in the middle – but wear a swimsuit) and the water can be surprisingly warm.

If there's enough wind (there usually isn't) you can rent windsurfers and a small sailing dinghy from Hotel Fewa or Hotel Monal.

Sport
A new **Sport & Fitness Centre** has opened in Pokhara near the GPO in Mahendrapaul. There's a gym, sauna, tennis and aerobics. For a small fee you can hire racquets etc. It's open from 06.00 to 19.00 every day except Monday. Phone ☎ 21756 for information/bookings.

Cultural show
There are nightly cultural shows at many places on Damside; look for advertisements. The shows at the **Hotel Dragon** and **Garlic Garden Restaurant** have been recommended. Tickets are sold at the hotels or in some travel agents and bookshops.

GETTING TO THE START OF YOUR TREK

The new Pokhara-Baglung Highway has cut a day off most of the treks in the Annapurna region. For Birethanti it's best to get to Nayapul, past Lumle. The buses leave every 45 minutes from the Besi Park (Baglung) Bus Station and cost Rs23 for the $1^1/_2$-2-hour trip. Buses to Begnas Tal (Rs6, 1 hour) and Dumre (Rs25, 2 hours) leave from the main bus station.

(Opposite) Top: A typical tea-house menu, displayed beside a trekking map. **Bottom:** Despite icing piled higher than the snows on Annapurna, the famous cakes of Kathmandu and Pokhara do not always taste quite as good as they might look.

GETTING AWAY

By air

Get to the airport early as flight departure times are approximate. It's not unknown for a flight to leave early. With several new airlines now offering services on these routes timings are likely to change.

Royal Nepal (RNAC) (☎ 21021) has daily flights to Kathmandu, (US$61, 35 minutes) at 09.30, 11.25, 12.20 and 14.55 with extra flights in the tourist season. There are at least two early-morning flights to Jomsom (US$50, 25 minutes) daily and flights to Manang/Ongre (US$50, 25 minutes) on Monday, Wednesday and Friday at 07.00. Note that both these routes are subject to delays or cancellations if the weather is not perfect. The Manang route is not operated during the monsoon. The ticket office is at the airport. The Royal Nepal office just south of Prithwi Chowk can also re-confirm international flights for Rs35.

Everest Air (☎ 21883) flies to Kathmandu (US$61, 35 minutes) daily at 10.40 and to Jomsom (US$50, 25 minutes) on Thursday, Friday and Sunday at 09.00. **Nepal Airways** (☎ 21178) has a single daily flight to Kathmandu at 11.45 and **Necon Air** (☎ 20256) flies an Avro or Twin Otter to Kathmandu daily except Sunday at either 11.45 or 13.05.

By bus

• **Kathmandu** Simplest is to get a ticket from one of the agencies that operate tourist buses from Lakeside and Damside. They all charge from Rs175 for a large coach and up to Rs250 for the slightly faster minibuses and will pick you up at your hotel. The journey takes 7-9 hours.

Of the public buses, Sajha day buses are the best. They leave from outside the GPO, four km from the lake. From the ticket office here you can make reservations up to three days in advance for Kathmandu (Rs74 for day bus, Rs85 for the night service) or Sunauli. Buses to Kathmandu leave at 06.30, 07.30 and 19.00. Note that the night bus currently used doesn't have reclining seats. From the bus station there are lots of buses for Kathmandu (Rs75 daytime; Rs85 night service, ten hours) between 05.30 and 11.00 for the day buses, 19.30 and 20.45 for the night buses.

• **Other destinations** From the main bus station there are two buses direct to Gorkha (Rs44, four hours), at 07.00 and 09.30 but most other buses will get you to the turn-off to Gorkha from where you can get a connection. For Dumre (Rs25, two hours), you have a wide choice of buses: most pass through this town. For Tansen (Rs52, six hours), the direct bus leaves at 07.00. To Begnas Tal (Rs6, one hour), there are buses every couple of hours from 07.00. The direct bus to Tadi Bazaar (Rs52, six hours) for Chitwan, leaves at 07.30. To reach the border with India, the best route is through Sunauli (Rs85, nine hours). There are numerous buses from 05.00 to 10.00. There's also a Sajha bus from by the GPO.

PART 6: TRAIL GUIDE AND MAPS

Using this guide

The main trekking routes in the Annapurna region are described below and detailed on the accompanying maps. For route planning see the **Annapurna regional map** (pp26-27).

These route descriptions have not been laid out on a day-to-day basis since people walk at different speeds and will have different aims for their trek. Walking times for both directions along each path are given on the maps enabling you to plan your own itinerary. Some guidance is obviously necessary: suggested itineraries are given on p237. For an overview of each of the treks see pp25-33.

ROUTE DESCRIPTIONS

The route descriptions can be followed in either direction but are set out as follows:

ROUTE MAPS

Scale and walking times

These maps are drawn to an approximate scale of 18mm to one kilometre (about one inch to one mile) but with so many hills and valleys these measurements are actually of little use to the trekker. Time taken to cover the distance is of far greater interest, although this does vary considerably from person to person. Walking times are given along the side of each map and the arrow shows the direction to which the walking time refers. Black triangles point to the villages between which the times apply. Note that the **time given refers only to time spent actually walking**, so you will need to add 20-30% to allow for rest stops. When planning the day's trekking, count on between five and seven hours actual walking. Give yourself rest days and allow days for acclimatisation.

Up or down?

The trail is shown as a dotted line. An arrow across the trail indicates a slope; two arrows show that it is steep. Note that the arrow points towards the higher part of the trail. If, for example, you were walking from A (at 900m) to B (at 1100m) and the trail between the two were short and steep, it would be shown thus: A - - ->>- - - B.

Lodges and tea-houses

Lodges are marked as black squares on the maps and their names are also given. Some lodges are mentioned in the text but you should not take this to mean that if a lodge isn't mentioned it's not worth staying at. You must expect changes since new lodges are springing up every few months; older lodges change hands and are often given new names, too. The other trekkers you meet on the trail are the most up to date source of information as to which are the best places to stay or eat.

Tea-houses are marked with a 'T'. It's often also possible to stay at them, although accommodation is generally much more basic than at a lodge.

Village names and other symbols

Village names may be transliterated in a number of ways. The variants are given in the text, the most common option being used on the map. Altitudes are given in metres on the maps and also in feet in the text. Places where you can get water are shown by a 'W' within a circle. Post offices are marked 'PO', in the same style.

Chautara

Constructed at convenient points along the main trails in Nepal and in every town and village, you'll find these stone resting platforms. Although paid for and maintained by a philanthropic local, chautara are much more than the Nepalese equivalent of a park bench. They are designed with ledges just the right height off the ground for porters to rest their loads.

   Trees are planted in the middle of the chautara to provide shade. In the subtropical climatic zone, these are two sacred trees, the banyan (easily identifiable by the roots that trail down from its branches) and the pipal, symbolising the female and male, respectively. They stand side by side in 'wedlock'. In the village, the chautara is an open air community hall where people congregate to hear the latest gossip.

Pokhara to Ghorepani

POKHARA TO BIRETHANTI   [MAPS 1-2, p135, p137]

The main route

Before the Pokhara-Baglung road was built it was a long day's trek from Pokhara to Birethanti. From the Shining Hospital in the north of Pokhara you made the hot three-hour walk past the Tibetan village at Hyange and across the fields of the Yamdi Khola Valley to Phedi. A stiff climb of $1^1/2$ hours brought you up to Naudanda and from here it was a further three hours' walk through Khare and Lumle to Chandrakot, perched above Birethanti.

The new road has effectively ruined this first part of the trek and the best advice is to get past it as quickly as possible by taking a bus or taxi from Pokhara (see p129) 41km to Nayapul, twenty minutes' walk from Birethanti. Alternatively, you could get off at Lumle, from where it's a two-hour walk to Birethanti via Chandrakot.

Many of the lodges in the villages that lie along the road have now closed down. There's a tea shop in **Phedi (1130m/3707ft)** – the name means 'bottom of the hill'. The views from **Naudanda (1430m/4692ft)** above it are still good and if you want to stay here the best place is **View Top Lodge & Restaurant**, on the hill at the western edge of the village. There's a **police checkpoint** in Naudanda, where you're required to stop and register.

The road bypasses **Lumle (1610m/5282ft)** and at the southern end of the town not far from the road is the **Lumle Guest House**, which was always the best place to stay. Lumle is famous for the fact that it has the country's highest annual average rainfall and, no doubt as a result of this, it is the home of the nationally famous Lumle Agricultural Centre. The project was started as part of a British aid programme and currently employs more than 300 people.

Chandrakot (1580m/5183ft)   Most of the half-dozen lodges in Chandrakot are still operating and there are also a number of tea-shops here. Trinket-sellers display their wares by the tree at the northern edge of the village. One tea-shop has erected a small platform here from which its customers can admire the superb mountain views up the Modi Khola towards the Annapurna Sanctuary. A steep trail drops down to Birethanti.

Alternative route via Sarangkot   If you want to walk all the way from Pokhara, rather than going along the road from the Shining Hospital it's more interesting to go via Sarangkot. Follow the main road along Lakeside north until it becomes a path on the north shore of the lake (see map, p116). After 20-30 minutes it leaves the lake and climbs to a small plain before continuing steeply upwards.

There's a confusing number of paths here so you should ask directions frequently although it's difficult to get lost as Sarangkot is at the top of this hill, overlooking the Pokhara Valley. It may take you anything up to three hours to reach the village since this is probably your first day trekking. If you're coming down, Sarangkot to Lakeside takes at least an hour.

In **Sarangkot** the **View Top Lodge** is the most popular with good food and the best view of Pokhara below. From Sarangkot the path follows the ridge to Kaskikot, $1^1/_2$-2 hours beyond. It was the old capital of the region. There are another four lodges fifteen minutes further on at Kaskikot Deurali. Continue along the ridge for just over an hour to reach Naudanda.

Birethanti (1050m/3449ft)

Across a big suspension bridge, by the confluence of the Bhurungdi Khola and the Modi Khola, lies this large bazaar village. It's a pleasant enough place but, being so close to Pokhara, it receives more than its fair share of tourists.

Although there are several good places to stay here, you should be aware that the hardest section on the Pokhara to Jomsom trek is the 1200m/4000ft climb from Tirkhedunga to Ghorepani. Since it's really worthwhile spending a night at Ghorepani for the views at dawn from nearby Poon Hill, and since Birethanti to Ghorepani is either one very long or two rather short days' walking, you may prefer to press on to Hille or Tirkhedunga.

Accommodation The top place to stay in town is the impressive **Laxmi Lodge**, built by British poet, Dominic Sasse, who was tragically killed in the PIA air crash near Kathmandu in 1992. Efficiently presided over by Bugle Major, many of the employees here are ex-Gurkhas. As well as providing luxury accommodation for wealthy trekkers, the lodge operates a charity that helps improve local health care and develop reforestation programmes in the area.

In the tourist season Laxmi Lodge provides accommodation for Foreign Window clients but, if there is room, independent trekkers can stay here (see p30) in comfortable bedrooms with sheets and blankets on the beds. The bathrooms are spotless; the loos sparkle like the set for a

---

Walking times on trail maps
Note that on all the trail maps in this book the times shown alongside each map refer only to time spent actually walking. Add 20-30% to allow for rest stops.

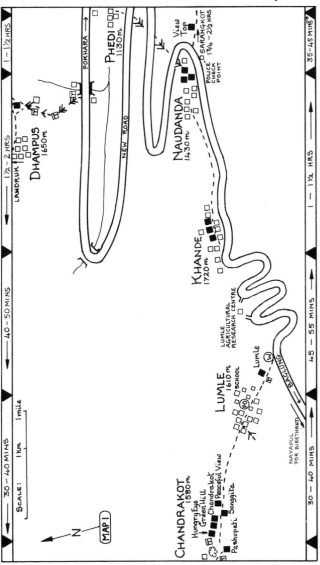

MAP 1

Harpic ad. There's a large sitting and dining room with a central fireplace, a well-stocked library and a photo of Bugle Major meeting Prince Charles.

For budget travellers the **New Gurkha Lodge** has high standards of hygiene, and boasts of a 'trained cook' amongst its staff, for a tenth of the price of the Laxmi. The food is indeed good, although for Western fare the **Hotel Sunrise** is a better choice and even lists whole grilled chicken under 'Super Fantastic Food' on its menu. The **Riverside Lodge** has a pleasant dining area by the river. Over the bridge, the **Fishtail Lodge** is quieter.

Other services   You can cash travellers' cheques at the **bank** (open Sunday to Thursday, 10.00-14.30 and on Friday until 12.30). There's a **post office** and several well-stocked shops. At the western end of the village you should stop at the **police checkpost** and sign the book. This apparent bureaucracy is essential practice since, if you go missing, the search party will have some idea of where to look.

A 10-15 minute walk along the Ghorepani trail brings you to a waterfall with a **pool**, a pleasant place to swim if it's hot enough; but you should be discreet and wear a swimsuit.

BIRETHANTI TO ULLERI   [MAP 2: p137]

The trail to Hille climbs gently and is easy to follow although landslides cause occasional detours. There are two suspension bridges across the Bhurungdi Khola which you should pass by and several tea-shops at the settlements of Ramgai and Sudame.

Hille (1500m/4921ft) and Tirkhedunga (1540m/5052ft)

In Hille, **See You Lodge & Restaurant** is well-run by a friendly guy, whilst nearby the **Laxmi Lodge** serves a good breakfast. About 15 minutes beyond, you reach the village of Tirkhedunga. The **Indra Guest House** here has hot showers and an extensive menu including Japanese food, whilst in between the two bridges the **Tirke Dunga River Lodge** even boasts its own swimming pool.

After the second suspension bridge, 3318 stone steps stand between you and the breathtaking views from Ulleri. It's best to pace yourself, climbing 500 steps or so at a time, then stopping to admire the view and remind yourself that trekking is not a race.

Ulleri (2070m/6791ft)

This pretty but not exactly spotless slate-roofed village is largely comprised of Magar people. They are Tibeto-Burman in origin and, as well as being skilled craftsmen in stone and wood, constitute the largest Nepali sub-group serving in Gurkha regiments abroad. In spite of having high

earning husbands, many Magar women are financially independent through their involvement with the rug-weaving trade.

The reward for scaling the 3318 steps to reach Ulleri is good views of Annapurna South and Hiunchuli, as well as the Bhurungdi Valley below. Many lodge owners have situated their dining areas to take advantage of the scenery. **Pratap's Guest House** is particularly pleasant, and the proprietor, Hitraj, is a good source of local information.

Ten minutes beyond the village, above a chautara, is a memorial to the young son of an anthropologist who died here in 1961: 'Benjamin Jeninis Hitchcock, Benbahadur. Once sweet bright joy, like their lost children an Ulleri child'.

ULLERI TO GHOREPANI   [MAP 3: p139]

Banthanti (2300m/7546ft)
The trail climbs less steeply now, and you soon encounter the first few lodges of the elongated settlement of **Banthanti**.

Passing the suitably named **Green Hill View Lodge**, the path climbs to the equally appropriately titled **Fishtail-Top View Lodge**, before rounding the corner to, what the lodge owners here call, the 'real Banthanti'. After the last lodge, Mr Pun's efficiently-run **Deepak Guest House**, the rhododendron forest begins. Spectacular in March and April when the whole hillside is cloaked in blossom, during the monsoon it's more renowned as a haven for millions of leeches. It's not a good idea to trek alone here as there have been recent reports of robbery in the forest surrounding Ghorepani.

Ghorepani (2750m/9022ft)
To watch the sun rise across a spectacular Himalayan panorama from the summit of Poon Hill, 450m/1475ft above this village is the main reason for coming up here. This famous dawn pilgrimage has brought tens of thousands of trekkers to Ghorepani, with disastrous consequences for the surrounding rhododendron forests. When I first came here, twelve years ago, Poon Hill was almost entirely covered in forest. It has now been stripped virtually bare. ACAP made the village an early focus for their conservation measures, moving the lodges down from the hill and persuading many of the lodge-owners to install back-boilers.

Accommodation The lodges of Ghorepani are in two groups. The first group is below the ridge in the older part of the town where the water troughs that gave the village its name ('place for watering horses') are still used by the mule trains. The **See You Lodge** is a well-run, pleasant place here.

Most trekkers, however, choose to climb the 100m further to Ghorepani Deurali (Pass) where the main part of the village, and most of the

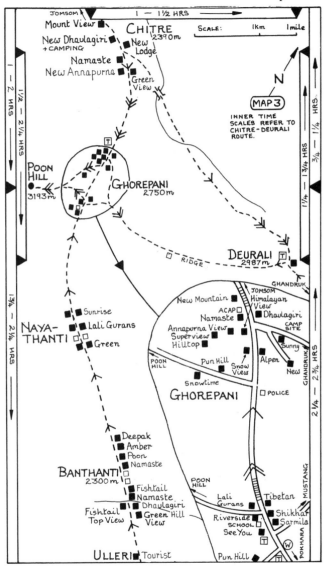

JOMSOM
1 — 1½ HRS
Mount View
CHITRE 2390m
SCALE: 1km 1mile
New Dhavlagiri + CAMPING
New Lodge
Namaste
New Annapurna
Green View
N
MAP 3
INNER TIME SCALES REFER TO CHITRE – DEURALI ROUTE.

1 — 2 HRS
1½ — 2¼ HRS

Poon Hill
3193m
GHOREPANI 2750m

1¾ — 1¼ HRS
¾ — 1¼ HRS

1¼ — 1¾ HRS

RIDGE
DEURALI 2987m

GHANDRUK

1¾ — 2¼ HRS

New Mountain
JOMSOM
Himalayan View
ACAP
Namaste
Dhavlagiri
CAMP SITE
Annapurna View
Superview
Hilltop
Sunny
Alpen
POON HILL
Pun Hill
Snow View
New
Sunrise
NAYA- THANTI
Lali Gurans
Green
Snowtime
GHOREPANI
POLICE

2¼ — 2¾ HRS

GHANDRUK

MUSTANG

Deepak
Amber
Poon
Namaste
BANTHANTI 2300m
POON HILL
Fishtail
Namaste
Dhavlagiri
Fishtail Top View
Green Hill View
Lali Gurans
Tibetan
Riverside SCHOOL
See You
Shikhar
Sarmila
ULLERI Tourist
Pun Hill
POKHARA
W

lodges, are situated. Many of the lodges here are fancy affairs with view towers and large dining areas, and the imminent arrival of electricity to the village will add to the comfort still further. The **Himalayan View** and **Snow View** lodges have both been recommended for their food, whilst the latter has also been praised for its hot showers.

Other services You must stop at the **police checkpost** to sign the book here. The **ACAP office** has information on current projects in the area.

Poon Hill (3193m/10,476ft) The wooden partitions in the lodges here are very thin and you'll be woken long before sunrise by the sounds of trekkers preparing for the pre-dawn assault on Poon Hill. If the sky is clear you should join them; if it's heavily overcast go back to sleep.

You may meet several people with the surname 'Poon' in the area; the Poons are a large Magar family and the hill was named after them. Take great care on the path up the hill as it can be slippery in places and you could lose your footing in the half light. It takes about 45 minutes to climb to the top.

The views are literally breathtaking, a wide Himalayan panorama stretching from Dhaulagiri (8167m/26,794ft and the world's seventh highest peak) to Manaslu (8156m/26758ft, the eighth highest) in the east, with the Annapurna range between them.

Route to Ghandruk and Chomrong see p171.

Ghorepani to Jomsom and Muktinath

GHOREPANI TO TATOPANI   [MAPS 3-4: pp139, 141]

The trail out of Ghorepani drops steeply down through the rhododendron forest into the Kali Gandaki Valley, which you follow all the way to Jomsom. There are good views of the solid lump that is Dhaulagiri as you descend and no need to hurry since you will probably want to spend the night in Tatopani (about five hours from Ghorepani) and soothe your aching limbs in the hot springs there.

There are tea shops strung out along the whole of this route but **Chitre (2350m/7710ft)** is the first village you come to. There are several lodges and in the middle of the village is a junction with the path to Ghandruk via Deurali (see p171).

Chitre merges into the village of **Phalate/Phalante (2270m/7448ft)** and after about 90 minutes of walking past small farm buildings and over the occasional landslide, you arrive at the more substantial settlement of

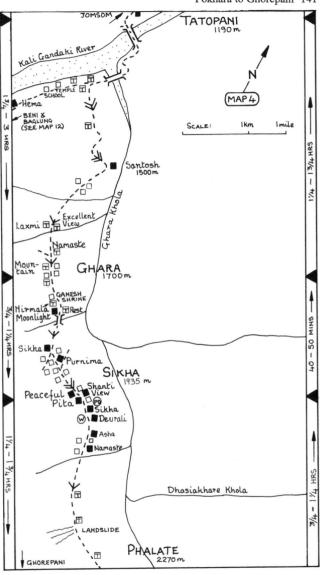

Sikha/Sauta (2000m/6562ft). The higher part of the village is known as Sikha Deurali, the lower simply Sikha. There's a post office here (open Sunday to Thursday, 10.00-17.00 and on Friday until 14.00). In the lower part of the village, **Purnima Lodge** is a pleasant place to stay.

Soon after **Ghara (1700m/5577ft)** you come to a lookout point where the **Santosh Hill Top Restaurant** can supply you with liquid refreshment while you admire the views up and down the valley.

A steep descent brings you down to the Kali Gandaki and the junction with the path to Jomsom to the right, and Baglung to the left. Turning right and crossing the bridge over the Ghara Khola and, shortly afterwards, a second bridge over the Kali Gandaki, you reach Tatopani in about 20-30 minutes.

▲ **Tatopani to Ghorepani** If you're following this section in the opposite direction you should be aware that much of this stiff climb is not through forests (unlike the Ghorepani-Ulleri path) and can be very hot. It's worth making an early start from Tatopani.

Tatopani (1190m/3904ft)   [Map 5: p145]
The name means 'hot springs' and these, with the sub-tropical gardens of this little riverside village, have been attracting trekkers since the 1960s. Even though it's getting a little touristy now, it's still a very mellow place to stay especially outside the main trekking season.

The village is a meeting-point for Magars and Gurungs from the south and Thakalis from the north. Some of the lodges here are run by Thakalis (see p152), accomplished hoteliers who have been catering to the needs of foreign travellers along this trading route to Tibet for several hundred years.

Bagh Chal

Also known as Tigers and Goats (the Nepali name translates as 'Moving the Tigers), Bagh Chal is rather like draughts. Tigers move along the lines on the board killing the goats by jumping over them. Attractive brass boards and pieces are sold in the tourist shops but the game can be played just as well with a 'board' drawn out in the dust and different sized stones to represent the four tigers and twenty goats.

The rules There are two players. The player who is the tiger places them on the four corners of the board. The other player puts one goat on the board and play commences with one tiger being moved and then one goat being placed on the board. No goat may move until all the pieces are on the board. When a tiger is beside a goat and there is a space on the other side of it the tiger may jump over it, removing it from the board. They may, however, only follow the straight lines. The art to defending the goats is obviously to try to ensure that they can never be jumped, by giving the tigers no open point on which to land.

The game is won by the tigers as soon as they have removed five of the goats; and by the goats if they can encircle all the tigers to stop them from moving.
Rosemary Higgs (Nepal)

A few of the lodges have their own methane gas plants that have proved remarkably efficient in providing fuel for cooking and lighting.

Accommodation When the owner of the **Dhaulagiri Lodge** married the French doctor from the health post this place soon became the best place to eat for miles around, although it already had an excellent reputation for its food.. There's a beautiful garden with tables and chairs set out amongst the tangerine trees and flowering plants, and views up the valley to Nilgiri South Peak. The rooms are better at the **Trekkers' Inn**, however, the food's also excellent and there's a peaceful garden here, too. Renovations at the **Kamala Lodge**, at the northern end of the village, should now be completed. They promised some double rooms with attached bathroom.

Other services There's a **bank**, several shops (one of which operates a book exchange) and a **police checkpost** as you enter the village from the south. Tatopani now has electricity from the micro-hydro scheme upriver.

Rather than an 'I Love Tatopani' T-shirt, you could have a pair of earrings handmade for you by the gold- and silver-smiths who have their workshops in Tatopani. In Nepal gold, like hashish, is measured in tolas (one tola being about 11.5g) and there is a standard rate which corresponds to the price on the world market.

A large pair of Nepalese-style earrings weighing about half a tola would cost £50-75/US$75-110 – a lot of money, maybe but a unique and lasting souvenir. Wearing Nepalese earrings helps bridge the cultural gap between Nepali and foreign women and a gold pair will be admired by every Nepali woman you meet.

Cassie Cleeve (Australia)

Hot springs The main spring is by the river, just below the Dhaulagiri Lodge. There are a couple of pools and they can be incredibly hot. The river, on the other hand can be painfully cold. Try to borrow a bowl from the lodge if you want to have a pleasant wash and don't pollute the spring or river with soap and shampoo, even if this is what the local people are doing. During the trekking season the pools are regularly cleaned and a small charge (Rs5) is made.

If the river is low you can get to the second spring just to the north of the village but it's very small, often not much more than a trickle.

About 30 minutes downstream, along the trail to Baglung, there's another hot spring, with a pool right by the river, below Hema Guest House (see Map 12, p166).

Walking times on trail maps
Note that on all the trail maps in this book the times shown alongside each map refer only to time spent actually walking. Add 20-30% to allow for rest stops.

TATOPANI TO RUPSE CHHAHARA [MAP 5: p145]

Following the Kali Gandaki north you pass **Jhatare** and just above it you go through a small tunnel, the only one on the trek. In many places along this trail you can see older paths cut high into the rock that are now disused following the landslides that frequently occur in this unstable region.

A bridge leads over the river to the Tatopani Small Hydel Project, a micro-hydro electric scheme that was financed by Saudi Arabia.

Dana (1400m/4593ft)

In the centre of the town several impressive houses with delicately carved windows indicate that Dana was once a place of some importance. It was, in fact, the capital of Mustang District until the early 1970s, when Jomsom succeeded it. In the days when Tibetan caravans brought salt through Dana from the deserts of Western Tibet it was an important trading town and a collection point for salt taxes. The customs post closed in 1931.

Amongst the old merchants' houses look out for a building known locally as the Bardali Ghar, which has a splendid carved window. It's probably the finest piece of wood-carving in the region and was moved to this house in the 1940s. It's said to have been made from over 100 pieces of teak and assembled in the traditional way without using nails. It dates from the early part of this century.

Dana is still quite a big place and there are a number of lodges here as well as a post office. **Kabin Guest House & Restaurant**, to the south of the town, is a pleasant place to stay. About an hour and a half to the north, **Rupse Lodge** is also recommended. The rooms are spotlessly clean and the food good.

As recently as the 1950s the trail to the north was said to have been frequented by robbers, according to Giuseppe Tucci who passed through Dana on his way to Lo Manthang in 1952.

Karam
You'll see this game, a kind of 'flick snooker', played in teahouses or street corners throughout Nepal. It's played on a board with coloured counters, by two or four players. One red counter is used as a cue and one black one as the final play.

The rules Place all pieces except the red in the centre. Player one puts the red counter on the home line and flicks it into the centre to spread the other counters. Player two takes the red and tries to put his or her own coloured counters in the corner pockets. Take turns at doing this.

If your opponent's counter goes into the pocket, it must be placed back in the centre of the board together with one of your counters that has already been pocketed. When you've got all your counters into the pockets you must finish with the black counter. **Tara Winterton** (Nepal)

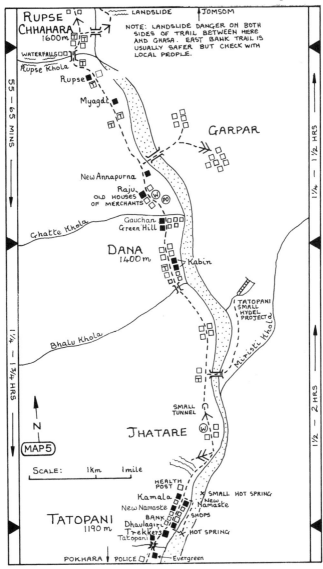

RUPSE CHHAHARA 1600m

↑ JOMSOM

~ LANDSLIDE

NOTE: LANDSLIDE DANGER ON BOTH SIDES OF TRAIL BETWEEN HERE AND GHASA. EAST BANK TRAIL IS USUALLY SAFER BUT CHECK WITH LOCAL PEOPLE.

WATERFALLS

Rupse Khola

Rupse

Myagdi

GARPAR

New Annapurna

Raju
OLD HOUSES OF MERCHANTS

Chatte Khola

Gauchan Green Hill

DANA 1400 m

Kabin

TATOPANI SMALL HYDEL PROJECT

Bhalu Khola

Miristi Khola

SMALL TUNNEL

JHATARE

N

MAP 5

SCALE: 1 Km 1 mile

55 – 65 MINS

1¼ – 1¾ HRS

¼ ↑ 1½ HRS

1½ ↑ 2 HRS

HEALTH POST

Kamala

× SMALL HOT SPRING

New Namaste

New Namaste

BANK

SHOPS

TATOPANI 1190 m

Dhavlagiri

Trekkers

Tatopani

× HOT SPRING

POKHARA ↓ POLICE

Evergreen

The waterfall at **Rupse Chhahara (1600m/5249ft)** is particularly impressive during or just after the monsoon. There are several water-powered mills grinding corn beside the river here and a couple of tea-houses.

RUPSE CHHAHARA TO LETE   [MAP 6: p147]

In Rupse Chhahara ask local people if you should continue on this side of the river or cross the small wooden bridge high over what is probably the narrowest point on the Kali Gandaki to reach the east bank. There are frequent landslides in the area and the path has to climb high to pass them. Take great care on the steep east bank trail: you pass a memorial to a young trekker who slipped off the path here in 1994.

Passing through fields of marijuana, you reach **Kopche Pani**, a grubby village set amongst grey boulders. Climbing high above the landslide (the path is set higher each year as more of the hillside falls away) a welcoming signpost alerts you to the fact that you're now in the district of Mustang. Soon after there's the **Bimala Lodge** run by a very friendly family; the father speaks excellent English. It's an entertaining place to stop for lunch or to spend the night.

Ghasa/Gansa (2010m/6594ft)
Crossing the big suspension bridge and climbing up to join the west-bank trail, you come into the long village of Ghasa.

This region is both a cultural and geographical watershed. You're now in the lower reaches of Thak Khola, the area inhabited by the Thakalis (see p152). The climate is cooler than in Tatopani and there are pine trees here. Rainfall is lower and this is reflected in the Tibetan-style flat-roofed houses you begin to see in Ghasa. The Thakalis are Buddhist and just past the Solo Restaurant there are two chortens in the middle of the trail. As with all Buddhist monuments you should pass to the left of these. At the northern end of Ghasa you go through a large entrance gate that is typical of the Thakali villages to the north.

The **Eagle's Nest** is the first lodge in the south of the village and the best place to stay. The rostis here are recommended. The **Kali Gandaki Lodge & Solo Restaurant** is also recommended for its food. Many of the lodges sell apricot brandy ('appriciate brandy' on the menu of the Solo Restaurant!) which comes from the distilleries in Tukuche and Marpha. The **Saugat**, at the northern end of the village, is a friendly place with a very pleasant roof-top terrace.

Climbing gently through forests of pine you reach **Belbahadur's Inn**, a newly-constructed lodge in a peaceful location. The trail crosses another landslide to reach the bridge over the Lete Khola. The **Namaste Lodge**

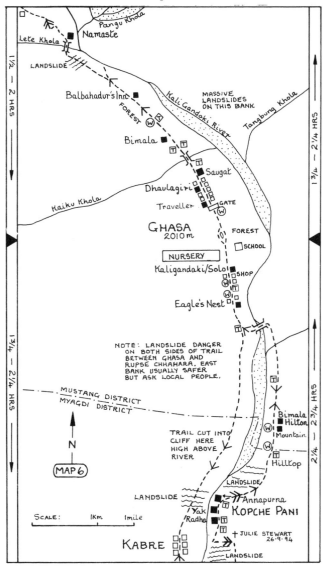

MAP 6

& Restaurant is craftily located to gather in those who cannot face the stiff but short climb up to Lete. It's not a bad place, though, and there are solar water heaters.

LETE TO LARJUNG   [MAP 7: p149]

Lete (2480m/8136ft) & Kalopani (2530m/8300ft)
This is really just one long village with Lete at the southern end, Kalopani to the north with the houses, many more of which are now flat-roofed, strung out between the two.

The views of Annapurna I (8091m/26,545ft) are good from here but even better if you climb for about 30-40 minutes behind the school.

Accommodation The lodges here are all good perhaps because, except during the high season, competition between them is intense. Their advertising placards line the trail. **Lete Guest House** has a table with a charcoal-filled foot-warmer beneath it, an innovation shared by the other lodges. It makes a very pleasant and fuel efficient way to keep warm on a cold evening. The **Kalopani Guest House** has solar heated showers and is so popular it's sometimes impossible to get in here. They even have two canoes for hire.

Other services There's a small **post office**, a government **health post**, a **police checkpost**, and the newly-constructed technical school.

From Kalopani to Larjung there are two trails: the marginally shorter but busier east bank trail which all the mule caravans take and the quieter west bank route.

On the west bank trail you pass a memorial to the five Americans and two Nepalis who died in an avalanche while climbing Dhaulagiri in 1969. Crossing the Ghatte Khola (the start of the route to the Dhaulagiri Ice-fall described below) you reach Larjung 20 minutes beyond. Note where local people walk to ford the Ghatte Khola if you don't want to get your feet wet.

It's at around this point, the bend in the river between Kalopani and Larjung, that you're at the bottom of the world's deepest valley. The two highest peaks in the area, Dhaulagiri (8167m/26,794ft) and Annapurna I (8091m/26,545ft) are 35 kms (22 miles) apart on either side of the valley. You're standing at an altitude of about 2540m/ 8333ft, which is $5^1/_2$ km or $3^1/_2$ miles below the summit of Dhaulagiri.

Larjung (2550m/8366ft)
Larjung and Khobang are separated by only a stream and a few fields but are, in fact, two different communities.

Larjung is a place of religious and ancestral significance for Tamang Thakalis since the masks of the presiding deities of the Tulachan and

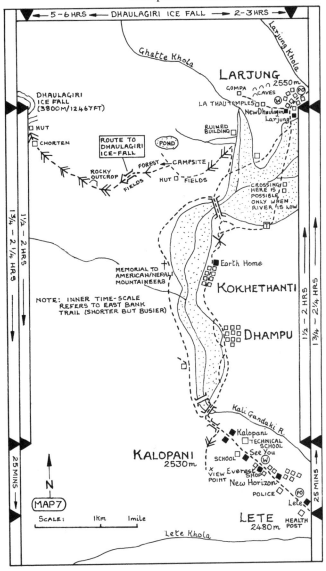

5-6 HRS ← DHAULAGIRI ICE FALL → 2-3 HRS

Ghatte Khola

Larjung Khola

LARJUNG 2550M

GOMPA
CAVES
LA THAU TEMPLES
New Dhaulagiri
Larjung

DHAULAGIRI
ICE FALL
(3800M/12467FT)

HUT
CHORTEN

ROUTE TO
DHAULAGIRI
ICE-FALL

RUINED
BUILDING

POND

FOREST   CAMPSITE
ROCKY
OUTCROP   HUT   FIELDS
FIELDS

CROSSING
HERE IS
POSSIBLE
ONLY WHEN
RIVER IS LOW

13/4 - 2 1/4 HRS

1/2 - 2 HRS

MEMORIAL TO
AMERICAN/NEPALI
MOUNTAINEERS

Earth Home

KOKHETHANTI

NOTE: INNER TIME-SCALE
REFERS TO EAST BANK
TRAIL (SHORTER BUT BUSIER)

DHAMPU

1/2 - 2 HRS

13/4 - 2 1/4 HRS

Kali Gandaki R.

Kalopani
TECHNICAL
SCHOOL
SCHOOL   See You
KALOPANI
2530m
X   Everest
VIEW   SHOP
POINT   New Horizon
POLICE
Lete

25 MINS

25 MINS

N
MAP 7
SCALE: 1km   1mile

LETE
2480m

HEALTH
POST

Lete Khola

Sherchan clans are kept in the Lha Thau temples just above the village. A major festival, the Lha Phewa ('the Appearance of the Gods'), takes place every 12 years in honour of the deities (next due at the end of 2005). The masks are taken out of the temple and paraded through surrounding villages in 17 days of music, dancing and hard drinking. Above Larjung are the abandoned caves once inhabited by Buddhist monks on retreat. Some are very difficult to get to and there's little to see in those you can reach. There's a post office here and two lodges.

The **Larjung Lodge** is popular and also sells provisions. Their Wall Drop Salad sounds interesting. If there have been any changes to the route up to the Dhaulagiri ice-fall you may find some thoughtful trekker has left updated directions pinned to the wall here.

Side trip to Dhaulagiri Ice-fall The climb up to the glacier below Dhaulagiri is very worthwhile for the tremendous views back across the Kali Gandaki towards the Annapurnas. Maurice Herzog must have followed part of this route when trying to find a way up Dhaulagiri in 1950.

The return trip from Larjung can be done in a day but you should make a very early start at around dawn. The route, shown on Map 7 (p149), can be tricky to follow at first but once you've reached the rocky outcrop, it's basically uphill all the way: a total altitude gain of about 1200m/4000ft.

Although you should feel nothing more than a little lightheadedness at this altitude you should read the information on AMS (p242) and don't try to spend the night up here with the yaks unless you, like them, are already acclimatised.

KHOBANG TO TUKUCHE   [MAP 8: p151]

Khobang (2560m/8399ft)

The trail through Khobang was once one long tunnel under the stone houses but this is rather less impressive now. High above the village is the Mahalaxmi Temple where the image of the goddess receives daily ablutions of milk mixed with water from the Kali Gandaki. It's difficult to find anyone to let you in if you wish to see the temple. Down by the river, however, the temple at the Makilakhang nunnery is usually open and interesting to look round. The nuns live in the small house beside it and will open the door if it's locked. Be sure to leave a donation if you visit. There are a couple of pleasant lodges in Khobang.

If the river is low, the trail to Tukuche is along the wide riverbed. Watch which way local people are going if you don't want to get your feet wet. You're now in an arid region that extends far north into Tibet. Each day pressure differences above the land to the north and to the south cause a fierce wind that begins sometimes as early as 8.30 am but usually not

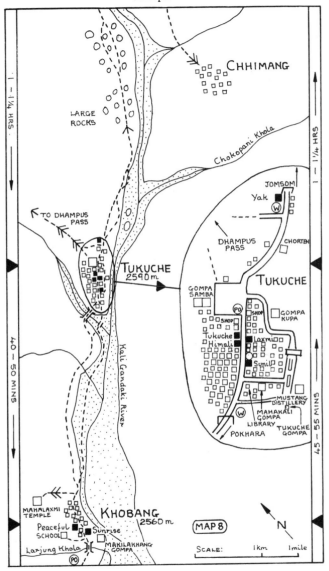

CHHIMANG

LARGE
ROCKS

Chokopani Khola

TO DHAMPUS
PASS

JOMSOM

Yak W

DHAMPUS
PASS

CHORTEN

TUKUCHE
2590 m

TUKUCHE

GOMPA
SAMBA

PO SHOP

SHOP GOMPA
KUPA

Tukuche
Himali

Laxmi

Sunil

Kali Gandaki River

MUSTANG
DISTILLERY

W

MAHAKALI
GOMPA

LIBRARY

POKHARA

TUKUCHE
GOMPA

MAHALAXMI
TEMPLE

KHOBANG
2560 m

MAP 8

N

Peaceful
SCHOOL

Sunrise

MAKILAKHANG
GOMPA

Larjung Khola

PO

SCALE: 1km 1mile

1 - 1¼ HRS

1 - 1¼ HRS

40 - 50 MINS

45 - 55 MINS

until around 10 am and it continues for much of the day. The wind blows up the valley from south to north so it's not really a problem if you're walking in this direction.

Tukuche/Tukche (2590m/8497ft)

When Professor Tucci stopped in Tukuche (pronounced 'Tugcha') in 1952 on his way to Lo Manthang, he noted huge warehouses filled with wool, salt and turquoise from Tibet and grain, rice, cloth, cigarettes and European goods which were bartered for the Tibetan supplies. By then the trade had, in fact, begun to wane since Indian salt had become available, popular not only because it was cheaper but also because it contained iodine. The diet of most people in Nepal had until then lacked this vital mineral and consequently many suffered from goitres.

When the Chinese invaded Tibet, trade declined further and some Thakalis moved out of Tukuche and the region to operate businesses in other parts of Nepal. Tourism has now brought some people back to the town.

The Thakalis

Wherever you're travelling in Nepal, you can almost always be sure of a warm welcome, a comfortable bed and good food at a Thakali inn. Known throughout the country as accomplished hoteliers and skilled traders, the Thakali people are of Tibetan origin but have their own language and customs. They're essentially Buddhists, although some have converted to Hinduism.

The Jomsom trek passes right through Thak Khola, the Thakali homeland which extends from just south of Jomsom down to Ghasa. Thak Khola is divided into two geographical areas: Panchagaon (the 'five villages' which comprise Marpha, Chhairo, Chhimang, Syang and Thimi) and Thakali Thasang (also known as Thak Satsae, the '700 houses', the southern region which extends from Tukuche to Ghasa).

The Thakalis who come from the southern region consider themselves to be the true Thakalis, since Tukuche, for years the dominant town in the area, lies within their borders. They refer to themselves as Tamang Thakalis and are divided into four clans, each with its own presiding animal deity and colour: Gauchan (elephant, red), Tulachan (dragon, blue/green), Sherchan (lioness, white) and Bhattachan (yak, black).

The people of Marpha (known as Mawatans) are also divided into four clans: Lalchan (meaning 'ruby'), Hirachan ('diamond'), Juharchan ('jewel') and Pannachan ('emerald') but they don't acknowledge any particular deity as their own.

The Thakalis are one of the richer groups of people in Nepal, having monopolised the trade route that follows the Kali Gandaki for several centuries. With the demise of this ancient route when the Chinese invaded Tibet, many Thakalis moved their businesses to other parts of the country.

Tourism and the development of new crops have given a significant boost to Thak Khola over the past 25 years. The traditional crops are buckwheat and millet but potatoes, barley, turnips and orchards of apple, peach and apricot trees have been established with considerable success, introduced by the experimental farm near Marpha. Tourism has further boosted Thak Khola and the accommodating Thakalis have converted their *bhattis*, which used to provide food and lodging for traders, into comfortable little trekking hotels.

Today the warehouses have crumbled away and the wind whistles through ruined buildings on the outskirts of the town. The grand facades of the houses that line the main street still give some indication of the former wealth of the inhabitants. Richest were the Sherchan clan, who held the monopoly on the salt trade. Their position was recognised by the government in the 19th century when the hereditary post of *subha* (tax collector) was granted to a member of their family. As well as having business interests in other parts of the country the family still operates the successful Mustang Distillery from their mansion to the south of the town.

Accommodation The most pleasant lodges in Tukuche are those in the centre: large houses formerly owned by rich merchants. They're built in the classic Thakali style, flat-roofed and around a courtyard to give protection from the wind. They all offer the traditional high standard of Thakali hospitality: extensive menus, hot showers, and tables with footwarmers beneath them. To the north of the town, in a building barely big enough to contain the stuffed yak that is its main feature, there's the **Yak Hotel**.

Other services There's a **post office** and several shops selling the powerful products of the Mustang Distillery.

Gompas When David Snellgrove (who wrote *Himalayan Pilgrimage* after research into Buddhism in this area) visited Tukuche in 1956 he remarked that this was the first town where he encountered hostile incomprehension to his questions. Most of these well-travelled traders wanted to have nothing to do with what they seemed to regard as a primitive religion. The lama of Gompa Samba had little interest in his calling but, like all Thakalis, was a skilled trader. 'How can I act as a lama if no one believes in me?', he complained while selling Snellgrove a toothbrush.

DS would no doubt be pleased to know that one monastery, **Gompa Kupa (Kyipar)**, is flourishing today, with a lama and 12 monks. It was relocated to its more central position in 1984. The wall-paintings in the temple are by Shashi Dhoj Tulachan and worth seeing. Visitors are welcome.

The other three temples are no longer operating as monasteries and are rather run down but they can be visited if you can find someone to let you in. **Gompa Samba** contains dusty statues and the best wall-paintings (depicting the sixteen arhats, Sakyamuni's disciples). The key is kept by the people in the house next door.

Near the Mustang Distillery, there's **Mahakali Gompa**, renamed after the Hindu goddess although it was originally dedicated to the three Buddhas of the past, present and future. Five minutes to the south of the town is the dilapidated **Rani Gompa**.

Mustang Distillery Kalpana Sherchan runs the distillery in her 200 year old family home and explains the distillation process to visitors. It was started by her husband who studied the process overseas, had all the equipment carried into Tukuche by porters and ponies and then promptly died. Mrs Sherchan 'cried for six months' and then decided she'd have to make a go of it so left Nepal to do the same course as her husband and has now turned his idea into a thriving business.

About 10,000 litres of alcohol are produced here annually, 80% of it being apple brandy. She also produces peach, orange and apricot brandy with most products in two strengths: 40% and 30%. They're all something of an acquired taste but certainly warm you up. A new line is apple cider, rather like the rough scrumpy you can buy on Devon farms.

The house itself is interesting, being over 200 years old and even has its own private temple in a room upstairs.

The distillery is closed between December and February.

TUKUCHE TO JOMSOM   [MAP 9: p155]

The trail north continues through a rocky area set about with sage and juniper bushes.

Chhairo
Off the main trail and across the bridge is an old gompa and this Tibetan refugee village. You'll probably have encountered some of the persuasive saleswomen from here already.

The **Sanga Choling Temple**, in the centre of the gompa, was built in the eighteenth century and still contains a three metre statue of Padmasambhava. In 1956, David Snellgrove reported that the temple was very well kept, tended by one lama, but was otherwise deserted. Unfortunately, in 1990 many of the smaller statues were stolen, no doubt to be sold to foreign collectors, a crime that is very much on the increase in Nepal. The gompa is kept locked most of the time now.

Marpha Horticultural Research Station
Also known as Marpha Farm, this research station was started in 1966 by Pasang Sherpa, who travelled with David Snellgrove in 1956, to introduce new strains of crops to the region. The results have been considerably successful and the apple, peach, plum, apricots and walnut trees that were first tried here now fill the orchards on both sides of the Thorung La.

You can look round the gardens and visit the distillery between 08.00 and 16.00, Sunday to Friday but they close for daal bhat between 11.00 and 12.00. The farm shop sells fruit, brandy, apple juice and excellent home-made jam.

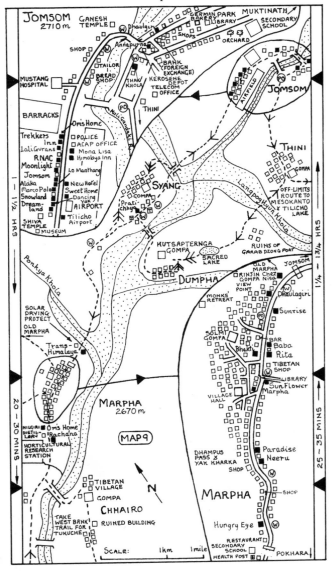

Continuing along the trail to Marpha another distillery, the Nilgiri, has set up in business. There are also a couple of lodges, including the upmarket **Om's Home**. (There are other Om's Homes, run by the same family, in Jomsom and Pokhara bazaar). This one not only has good food and comfortable lodgings but was the first building in the valley to sport a satellite dish on its roof.

Marpha (2670m/8760ft) [MAP 9: p155]

Trekkers, and everyone else who comes here, for that matter, eulogise over Marpha. It must be just about the cleanest, most efficiently run village in the country with excellent lodges and some of the most creative cuisine on the trek.

The long main street is paved with spotless flagstones and winds past dazzlingly white houses, each with little piles of firewood neatly stacked on its roof. No doubt the rather dictatorial town council, which is said to impose fines on villagers who do not keep the street outside their house clean or repaint their buildings annually, has something to do with the pristine state of Marpha.

Solmi/Tashi Lha K'an Gompa, in the centre of the village, supports a lama, twelve monks and seven trainees. Above the altar the three images are, from left to right, Amitabha ('Boundless Light'), Avalokitesvara ('Glancing Eye') and Padmasambhava (Guru Rinpoche). There are brightly coloured wall-paintings and, neatly stacked in racks, the 225 books of the Tenjur (the canonical commentary). The big prayer-wheel outside the temple is over 100 years old; it came from Tibet and was a present from the Dalai Lama. If the temple is closed, the caretaker, who lives in the house near the entrance, will let you in. On the cliff above the village is a small **temple** that is used for retreats.

Marpha has electricity linked to the 260kw micro-hydro scheme on Chokopani Khola that also serves Khobang, Tukuche and Jomsom. As well as a secondary school, the town now has a **library**, jointly funded by the village and a Canadian organisation. Any donations, whether in book or financial form would obviously be welcome to fill the shelves. If it's closed, enquire at Bhakti Guest House.

Accommodation Marpha's lodges seem to be of a uniformly high standard and the majority have not only solar-heated showers but also electric blenders and food-mixers. Check with other trekkers to find out whose cooking is the current favourite.

From south to north, there are a couple of very small, family-run places soon after you enter the villages. Further along the main street, **Neeru's** has a good reputation and specialities here include brown bread, potato cheese pizza and apple momos (that one trekker likened to a McDonald's apple pie, cinnamony and with a thin crispy coating of pastry). **Paradise**, nearby, provides stiff competition ('great apple crumble'). **Marpha Guest House** is run by a friendly family and across the street is the small but also friendly **Hotel Sun Flower**.

Rita Guest House has a pleasant courtyard and **Bhakti Guest House**, opposite, is an interesting place to stay. It's run by Bhakti Hirachan, a local teacher and social worker who is very well informed about the area. As well as standard 'apple-pie' cuisine, there's also good local food here. **Baba Lodge** is a friendly place and they also run the massage place next door.

The **New Dhaulagiri Lodge** ('Remember for comfortable cheap homely feeling') is a big place that's clean and well-run. **New Hotel Sunrise** and **Chez Nisa** are a little smaller but still very pleasant and run by friendly people.

For more local atmosphere than the rather Westernised lodges, appealing as they are, can offer, stop by for a glass of raksi in the bar opposite Baba Lodge. Sukuti (smoked meat) makes an excellent accompaniment.

Other services Marpha has a **post office** (mail goes via Jomsom), several provision shops, four Tibetan souvenir shops, a shoe repair centre and a massage parlour. There's a **health post** (open Sun to Fri, 10.00-14.00) just south of the village.

Just north of Marpha is the posh **Trans-Himalaya Hotel**, with double rooms with attached bathrooms and Western loos. The rooms even have phones so you can dial up room service! Near the hotel, a German-Nepali **solar drying project** was set up in 1994. It takes just one day to dry apples in the glass panels, and the results, of a much higher quality than the usual dried fruit available, are on sale in local shops.

Between Marpha and Jomsom, the trail passes below the village of **Syang** (2700m/8858ft), which has a new gompa, founded in1975, with a community of 35 monks and nuns.

Jomsom (2710m/8891ft) [MAP 9: p155]

There's no reason to stop in this modern town unless you're catching a flight or need to change some money. Since the early 1970s it's been the capital of Mustang district and it also houses the Royal Nepalese Army School of High Altitude Mountain Warfare.

The increase in the frequency of flights into Jomsom has brought more tourists to this area in the last three years or so. Hotel standards have risen dramatically and the best places now offer facilities that are more what you would expect in Pokhara than on a trek. In some you can drink shots of Johnnie Walker Black label as you watch the *Oprah Winfrey Show* on Star TV.

The **Mustang Eco Museum** has opened recently at the top of a discouragingly long flight of steps right at the southern end of the town. A cultural video show is promised, there are photographic displays of flora and fauna, and a library. There's also a traditional herbal medicine doctor who has a surgery here. The museum's opening hours are 10am to 4pm, Sunday to Friday; entry is Rs25 for foreigners.

Accommodation   The best lodges are along the street by the airport. **Om's Home** is an 'A' grade place with 'A' grade prices, Rs350 for a carpeted double room with attached tiled bathroom and flushing loo! With common bathroom their singles/doubles/triples cost Rs75/100/125. The **Trekkers' Inn** is also impressive but then most of the lodges here are of a high standard with varied menus, tables with footwarmers beneath them and hot showers, some of which are electrically heated.

Rather better value and run by an extremely friendly woman, the **Moonlight Guest House** is a great place to stay. The rooms are set around a sunny courtyard at the back.

On the south bank of the river the **Thak Khola** attracts custom through its claim that Jimi Hendrix slept here (in Room No 6, in October 1967) leaving his words: 'If I don't see you in this world, I'll see you in the next one. Don't be late', on the restaurant wall. Mick Jagger is also reported to have dropped by.

At the northern end of the town is a **German Bakery Coffee Shop** serving croissants, apple pie and coffee. There's a provisions' shop which also stocks books.

Flights   Several airlines have flights using Jomsom landing strip (which, incidentally, is owned by Marpha village). The fact that flights are dependent on perfect weather occasionally causes a backlog of stranded passengers, although the use of helicopters by some airlines has reduced the problem.

RNAC have daily flights to Pokhara (US$50, 25 minutes) at 07.10 and 08.30 with extra morning flights in the tourist season. Their ticket office, open only from 10.00 to 17.00 daily, is near Moonlight Lodge. Try to get a ticket at the airport if they're closed.

Everest Air (office at Om's Home, open 10.00 to 17.00 daily) have direct flights to Kathmandu (US$110, 45 mins) at 07.10 on Thursday and Sunday and at least one flight a day to Pokhara. **Nepal Airways** has an office outside the Trekkers' Inn. They plan two flights a day to Pokhara in the season and will use helicopters on some flights.

Walking times on trail maps
Note that on all the trail maps in this book the times shown alongside each map refer only to time spent actually walking.. Add 20-30% to allow for rest stops.

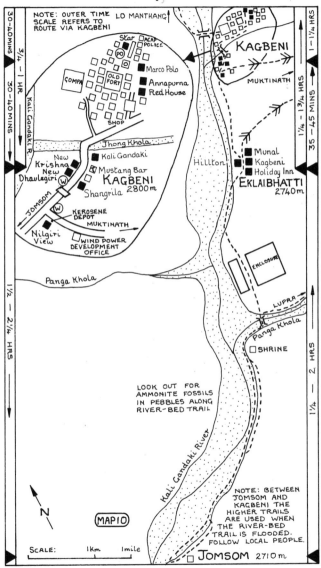

NOTE: OUTER TIME SCALE REFERS TO ROUTE VIA KAGBENI

LO MANTHANG

30-40 MINS
3/4 - 1 HR
30-40 MINS

Kali Gandaki R.

Star
ACAP POLICE
PO
Marco Polo
COMPA
OLD FORT
Annapurna
Red House
SHOP

KAGBENI

MUKTINATH

1 - 1¼ HRS

1¼ - 1¾ HRS

35 - 45 MINS

Jhong Khola
New Krishna
New Dhaulagiri
Kali Gandaki
Mustang Bar
KAGBENI 2800m
Shangrila
Jomsom
KEROSENE DEPOT
MUKTINATH
Nilgiri View
WIND POWER DEVELOPMENT OFFICE

Hilltop

Munal
Kagbeni
Holiday Inn
EKLAIBHATTI 2740m

Panga Khola

1½ - 2¼ HRS

ENCLOSURE

LUPRA

Panga Khola

SHRINE

1½ - 2 HRS

LOOK OUT FOR AMMONITE FOSSILS IN PEBBLES ALONG RIVER-BED TRAIL

Kali Gandaki River

N

MAP 10

SCALE: 1 Km   1 mile

NOTE: BETWEEN JOMSOM AND KAGBENI THE HIGHER TRAILS ARE USED WHEN THE RIVER-BED TRAIL IS FLOODED. FOLLOW LOCAL PEOPLE.

JOMSOM 2710m

Other services Most useful is the **bank** where the exchange counter is open daily (including Saturday) from 07.30 to 18.00. There's a **post office** and post restante seems to work here but allow about a month for an airmail letter from home. Nearby is a **telecom office** from where, currently, only telegrams can be sent but international phone calls may soon be possible. If you've got absolutely nothing better to do you could visit the **public youth library** and peruse their eclectic collection of books that includes *Elementary Hygiene*, *Lenin* and Barbara Cartland's *Love on the Run*.

Stool tests and X-rays are available at **Mustang Hospital**, where the clinic is open daily 09.00-13.00.

There are numerous shops for provisions in Jomsom and in some of the lodges you can buy interesting delicacies that have been left behind by mountaineering expeditions.

Side trip to Katsapternga Gompa (3000m/9840ft) Set on a high spur with superb views up and down the Kali Gandaki Valley this Kagyupa sect gompa is famous for its five 'Treasures of the Bodily Representation', a set of small terracotta images which came from the monastery of Samye, in central Tibet. Pilgrims come for the celebrations in the seventh month of the Tibetan calendar (August-September).

It's no longer a working gompa and it's kept locked most of the time but a lama sometimes comes up here from Thini in the early morning or evening. Even if it's closed it's a pleasant walk up past the beautiful sacred lake, beside which Padmasambhava is said to have left his footprints, and worth it just for the views.

If you can find someone to let you into the gompa you might be able to see a unique relic: one lama spent his whole life concentrating on the sound of the Tibetan letter 'a', the most basic vowel in any language and when he had died this letter was found imprinted on his skull, part of which is kept here.

JOMSOM TO KAGBENI   [MAP 10: p159]

Walking this section of the trail is an other-worldly experience. The landscape is barren, the sun is often hot and the powerful wind that blows from the south can almost blow you over. The Kali Gandaki river-bed is about a kilometre wide here but the water flows in several separate streams. Some parts of the trail are over the pebbles and rocks by the river, others high above the bank. Take your lead from local people and, if you have to ford a stream, take off your boots. Wet socks and boots are the surest way to get blisters.

(Opposite) Marpha, little more than an hour's walk from Jomsom, is one of the most attractive villages in the Kali Gandaki Valley and a popular place to stay. See p156.

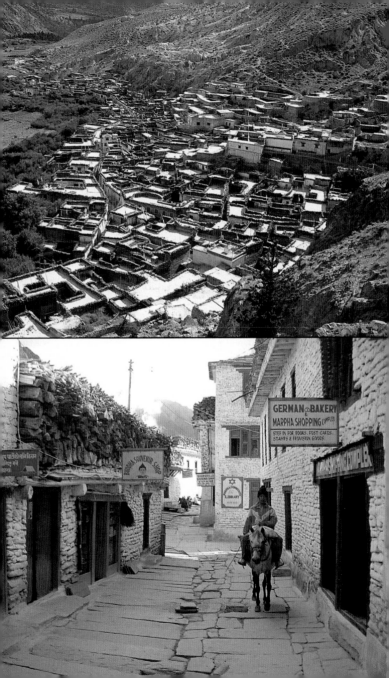

From Jomsom north to Muktinath is the region known as Baragaon ('the twelve villages'). The people here are not Thakalis but Towas, although some Thakalis may have moved here to operate hotels. Like the Thakalis they speak a language that is related to Tibetan.

Eklaibhatti/Eklebhatti (2740m/8989ft)
The name means 'one teashop' but there are now four lodges here. With the river relentlessly eroding away the edge of this settlement one wonders how long they will all be here. If you're not going to Kagbeni, take the direct trail to Muktinath up the hillside just after Eklaibhatti.

Kagbeni (2800m/9186ft)   [MAP 10: p159]
Kagbeni, a fascinating mediaeval rabbit-warren of crumbling mud-brick houses, stands in a little green oasis dominated by its red gompa. In the centre, the ruins of the old fort bear witness to the fact that this was once an important place, strategically placed at the junction of two valleys.

If it weren't for the ugly powerlines, all that remains of a badly-planned wind-power project that failed several years ago, you would have difficulty believing you're still in the 20th century. The dusty streets are narrow and from them little doorways give into stables below each house. Above some doors are curious fetishes, wooden crosses with wool woven round them, to ward off evil. Around the north and south gates (now within the village) you can see primitive male and female figures harking back to animist beliefs practised here long before the arrival of Buddhism in the 11th or 12th centuries.

Accommodation The most interesting place to stay is the **Red House Lodge**. Run by three jolly sisters, it's in one of the oldest houses in Kagbeni and even has a dusty private temple in one room. Accommodation is in a dormitory or in the small rooms on the roof, where there's a glassed-in dining room. The **Hotel Star** has also been recommended. The **Marco Polo** has a pleasant glassed-in sitting area. The **Shangrila** is a flashy new place that was recently building some rooms with attached bath.

All the lodges offer the local specialities which are Kagbeni bread (heavy buckwheat bread rolls) and *mithi* soup, made from spinach-like Swiss chard. At the **Mustang Bar** there's said to be live music some nights and free popcorn with drinks.

Other services The **post office** is beside the prayer-wheel wall in the north of Kagbeni. Nearby is the **police checkpoint** and the **ACAP information centre**, which has an interesting display of local handicrafts. This is as far up the Kali Gandaki as you can go without a special permit to the

---

(Opposite) Top: On the trail between Kagbeni and Jharkot. **Bottom:** Making momos for the Yartung festival in Muktinath.

North Mustang region (see p32). Beside the Nilgiri View is ACAP's **kerosene depot**. You can rent horses from Kagbeni to Muktinath (Rs600), Jomsom (Rs400) or Marpha (Rs600). You may be able to bargain these prices down a bit.

KAGBENI TO MUKTINATH   [MAP 11: p163]

From Kagbeni the trail climbs past the remains of the wind-power project to join the more direct route from Jomsom to Muktinath. You have now left the Kali Gandaki Valley and the worst of the wind that rushes daily up it.

The route bypasses the village of **Khingar (3200m/10,497ft)**, and there's a reasonable lodge by the trail here.

Jharkot (3550m/11,647ft)

Dominating a ridge on the eastern side of the valley, the mud-brick houses of Jharkot cluster round the ruins of the old fort. At the end of the ridge is Sakya Gompa. Some of the wall-paintings here have recently been restored and the temple can be visited. Beside it is a traditional medical centre, opened in 1991 with Japanese backing.

One of the most pleasant places to stay in the area is the **Himali Hotel**. An American guest suggested modifications to the traditional design of the building and large windows have been incorporated to trap the heat from the sunny courtyard outside. There's a solar-heated shower. The varied menu here includes cheese fried rice, yak chowmein and excellent apple fritters.

The **Hotel Sonam**, right by the trail, is also popular. It's run by a welcoming family and offers good hot showers and excellent food. At the **New Plaza** there are views from some of the rooms and a pleasant roof top restaurant said to serve 'the best cheese and potato momos in the country'!

Side trip to Dzong/Jhong Across the valley from Jharkot you can see the crumbling ruins of the fort of **Rab-rgyal-rtse** ('Peak of Supreme Victory'), in the village of Dzong. From here the chief controlled the six villages in the Muktinath Valley.

Dzong, which means 'fort' in Tibetan, makes an interesting side trip from Jharkot (1$^{1}/_{2}$-2 hours each way). It's also possible to walk there from Ranipauwa. Amongst the ruins of the fort there's now a school and the children will probably pester you for money.

The ancient **gompa** supports about 20 monks of the Sakya-pa sect, one of whom will open the temple if it's locked. Inside, statues of Sakyamuni and Lama Tenzing Repa gaze out from the altar upon wall-paintings darkened by time and the flames of yak-butter lamps.

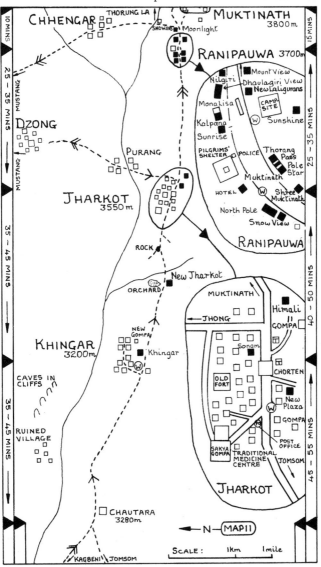

CHHENGAR
THORUNG LA
SHOWERS   Moonlight
MUKTINATH 3800m

10 MINS

25 - 35 MINS

MUSTANG

DZONG

MUSTANG

35 - 45 MINS

RANIPAUWA 3700m
Mount View
Nilgiri   Dhaulagiri View
New Laligurans
Monalisa
CAMP SITE
Kalpana   Sunshine
Sunrise
PILGRIMS' SHELTER   POLICE
Thorang Pass
Pole Star
Muktinath
HOTEL   Shree Muktinath
North Pole
Snow View
RANIPAUWA

PURANG

JHARKOT 3550m

ROCK

ORCHARD   New Jharkot

MUKTINATH
JHONG
Himali GOMPA
Sonam
OLD FORT
CHORTEN
New Plaza
GOMPA
SAKYA GOMPA
TRADITIONAL MEDICINE CENTRE
POST OFFICE
JOMSOM
JHARKOT

NEW GOMPA
Khingar

KHINGAR 3200m

CAVES IN CLIFFS

RUINED VILLAGE

15 MINS

25 - 35 MINS

40 - 50 MINS

45 - 55 MINS

35 - 45 MINS

CHAUTARA 3280m

◀ N   MAP 11

SCALE: 1km   1mile

KAGBENI   JOMSOM

Ranipauwa (3700m/12,139ft)

Although most people refer to this village as Muktinath, strictly speaking that name applies just to the pilgrimage centre above Ranipauwa. Since there are no lodges within the Muktinath temple complex, everyone stays here.

The most interesting building in this small village is the old pilgrim hostel, built around a large courtyard. The wooden floors in some of the bare dormitories shine from the bodies of the thousands of pilgrims who have slept here over the years. Far fewer pilgrims come now.

Electricity came to Ranipauwa in 1988, in a project arranged and paid for by the people themselves, with the technical help of the Nepali group Development Consulting Services and the British charity Intermediate Technology. Initially a 9kw generator was installed but this has now been uprated to 25kw. Some of the lodges have low-wattage cookers and a novel use for all the excess electricity generated during the day has been found: weary trekkers who have just staggered over the Thorung La can have hot showers in the bathroom built beside the power house. The showers are operated by tokens sold at the lodges and the money goes to fund the local primary school.

If you're in the area in August or early September, it's worth trying to be up here for the Muktinath Yartung, a harvest festival and horse race that draws people from all over Mustang. After a dignified procession headed by the Abbot of Jharkot up to the temples, wild horsemen thunder up and down Ranipauwa picking up money put down in their path.

Accommodation Food at the **Hotel North Pole** has such a good reputation that other lodges have a two-scale bed charge: the usual price if you eat in and a higher price if you eat at the North Pole. Compared to the lodges in Thak Khola accommodation in most of the places here is fairly basic. The **Dhaulagiri View** is also recommended and the **Shree Muktinath** is popular. There are views down the valley from some of the rooms at the **Hotel Moonlight**, just north of Ranipauwa. The new **Sunshine Lodge** appeals to the taller trekker: 'We have two meter bed. Feets hanging not outside', and lists such exotica as 'Kartoffelpuree mit 2 spiegelen' on the menu.

Other services Since most of the people who go missing in the Annapurna region do so on the Thorung La, it's vital to sign the book at the **police checkpoint** here.

Muktinath (3800m/12,467ft)

The walled temple complex of Muktinath has been attracting pilgrims, both Hindu and Buddhist, for centuries. For Hindus it's the next most holy place in Nepal after Pashupatinath. There's even a helipad here so that the king can visit.

Muktinath's fame rests mainly on a natural phenomenon that can be seen beneath the altar in the **Jwala Mai Temple**. A nun lifts the grubby curtain to reveal, deep within the cavity, a thin blue flame of natural gas burning from a hole that also emits a trickle of water. The Hindus believe that this miracle of lighting a fire upon water was an offering made by Brahma himself. The fact that this is now very much a Buddhist temple doesn't seem to worry Nepali Hindus with their mix-and-match approach to religion; if only Indian Hindus and Moslems could learn to do the same. This temple is at the extreme right of the temple complex as you approach it from Ranipauwa.

The Newar-style **Vishnu Temple** with its courtyard of 108 brass water spouts stands in the centre of the complex. To bathe under the freezing water here (all 108 spouts) is said to bring salvation to Hindus. You can get a blessing in the temple or, for US$20 (£13.30), you can have a tree planted in someone's memory in the Muktinath Darshan Memorial Garden. They say they'll send you a photo each year to show how it's doing.

Beyond the Vishnu Temple is the Buddhist **Marme Lhakhang** which has recently been gaudily restored. It stands by the sacred grove of poplars said to have sprouted from the walking sticks left here by the eighty-four Great Magicians on their way to Tibet.

In the **Gompa Sarwa**, just to the left of the temple complex entrance, there are three terracotta images, from left to right: Avalokitesvara, Sakyamuni and Padmasambhava. Also known as Guru Rinpoche, Padmasambhava was a Buddhist saint who passed through Muktinath in the 8th century. He left his footprints in a stone outside the temple enclosure, near the Gompa Sarwa.

When visiting the temples of Muktinath you should be modestly dressed, take your shoes off when going inside the temples and leave donations.

For a continuation of the route over the Thorung La, see p224.

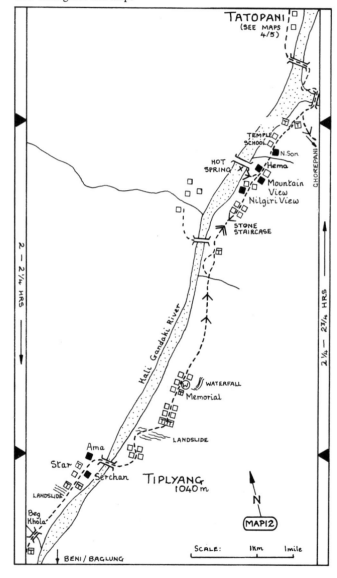

TATOPANI
(SEE MAPS
4/5)

TEMPLE
SCHOOL
N.Son

HOT
SPRING
Hema

Mountain
View

Nilgiri View

STONE
STAIRCASE

CHOREPANI

2½ — 2¾ HRS

2 — 2¼ HRS

Kali Gandaki River

WATERFALL
Memorial

LANDSLIDE

Ama

Star

Serchan

TIPLYANG
1040m

LANDSLIDE

Beg
Khola

N

MAP12

BENI / BAGLUNG

SCALE: 1Km   1mile

Tatopani to Pokhara via Baglung

If you don't fancy the climb back up to Ghorepani from the Kali Gandaki valley on the return trip to Pokhara, you can continue to follow the river downstream to join the new road at Baglung, or Beni if it's got that far. There seems to be some confusion over who's building the Beni-Baglung extension, His Majesty's Government or the World Food Programme. Work has begun on both projects, one on each side of the river!

Note that because this route is at low altitude it gets uncomfortably hot here between April and September. Although the route is not as busy with trekkers as the trail via Ghorepani, many more are now going this way and standards of accommodation have risen in recent years.

TATOPANI TO TIPLYANG   [MAP 12: p166]
Leaving Tatopani
From Tatopani cross the bridge to the east side of the Kali Gandaki and, shortly afterwards, the bridge over the Ghara Khola. Passing the trail up to Ghorepani, continue south along the Kali Gandaki. **Hema Guest House** is a reasonable place and there's a hot spring with a small pool by the river near here. Continuing south the trail rises and falls through small villages and in places is cut into the rock high above the river.

Tiplyang (1040m/3412ft) Cross the suspension bridge to reach this small village where there are some tea-houses, two basic lodges and a little shop. **Sherchan** has a fridge full of cold drinks. **Memorial** is a pleasant little tea-house near the stream.

From Tiplyang the trail follows the west bank of the river, through acres of marijuana. Landslides are frequent in this area. There are several tea-shops in the village of **Baisari** where you could get a meal.

TIPLYANG TO BENI   [MAP 13: p169]
Galeshor/Ranipauwa (1170m/3839ft) This is the largest village between Tatopani and Beni with a couple of good lodges, although Beni is under an hour's walk away. **Paradise Guest House** is the top place and it even boasts satellite TV.

Beni (830m/2723ft)
This bustling market town and administrative centre has three good lodges. The Thakali-run **Hotel Yeti** is the smartest place, relocated to an

impressive new concrete building such as you'd find in Kathmandu. It's still run by the same friendly people and in the restaurant there's an extensive menu and chocolate cake on request. Roast chicken and chips is Rs140. Rooms are Rs60/80 with common bath, Rs150 for a double with bath attached.

In the centre of town is the **Hotel Dolphin** (☎ 20107), similarly priced and also with a popular restaurant. **Namaste Lodge**, down by the river, is a friendly family-run place.

The town's other facilities include a large hospital, a French-run medical aid post beside the Hotel Yeti, numerous pharmacies, police station, cinema bank and a telephone office where you can make international phonecalls.

From Beni south there are trails on both sides of the river; the west bank trail is the quieter. **Phorse (825m/2707ft)** is by the suspension bridge on the east bank and there are some basic lodges here and in **Khaniyaghat (825m/2707ft)**. Just before Khaniyaghat is the UNICEF paper depot. Paper made locally from the bark of the daphne is collected here and sent to craft printers in Bhaktapur.

Continue through Khaniyaghat until you reach the collection of teahouses by the **road**. Buses coming down from Baglung pick up passengers for Pokhara (see below). If you want to be sure of a seat, however, you'll have to climb the hill to Baglung which sits 145m/476ft above the river.

BENI TO BAGLUNG   [MAP 14: p170]

Baglung (970m/3182ft)

As well as being the administrative headquarters of Baglung district, Baglung is famous for the sacred forest that lies at the southern end of this promontory, high above the river. The tall sal trees have been protected for hundreds of years and are all that is left of a large forest that once covered the whole area. There's a temple at the centre of forest.

Baglung is a large town with many shops and several places to stay, all in the Campus Rd area. They include the **New Gauchan Hotel** with rooms for Rs30/60, the **Hotel Jyoti** at Rs60/80 (common bath) and the **Hotel Hill View** with rooms with bath attached for Rs100/200.

The bus stand is in the south of the town. Buses leave Baglung hourly from 06.00 to 18.00 for the 74km-journey to Pokhara (Rs23, three hours). There are also slightly faster minibuses for Rs40. Taxis are sometimes available and their prices will depend on how keen they are to make the journey. They'll charge between Rs800 and Rs1200.

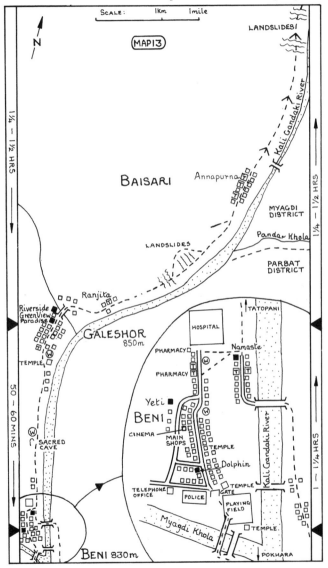

SCALE: 1Km   1mile

N

MAP13

LANDSLIDES!

Kali Gandaki River

BAISARI

Annapurna

MYAGDI
DISTRICT

Pandar Khola

LANDSLIDES

PARBAT
DISTRICT

1¼ — 1½ HRS

1¼ — 1½ HRS

Ranjita

Riverside
GreenView
Paradise

GALESHOR
850m

TEMPLE

HOSPITAL

TATOPANI

PHARMACY

Namaste

PHARMACY

Yeti

BENI

CINEMA

MAIN
SHOPS

TEMPLE

Dolphin

TELEPHONE
OFFICE

POLICE

TEMPLE
GATE

Kali Gandaki River

PLAYING
FIELD

TEMPLE

50 — 60 MINS

SACRED
CAVE

1 — 1¼ HRS

BENI 830m

Myagdi Khola

POKHARA

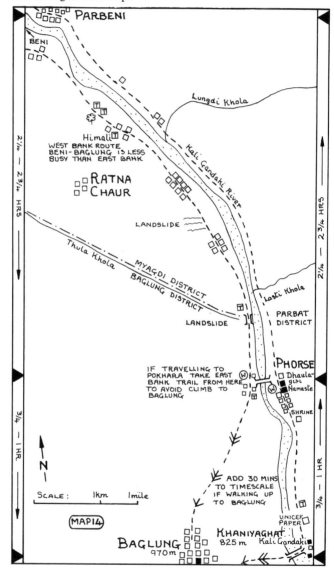

PARBENI

BENI

Lungdi Khola

Kali Gandaki River

Himali

WEST BANK ROUTE
BENI-BAGLUNG IS LESS
BUSY THAN EAST BANK

RATNA
CHAUR

LANDSLIDE

Thula Khola

MYAGDI DISTRICT
BAGLUNG DISTRICT

Lasti Khola

LANDSLIDE

PARBAT
DISTRICT

PHORSE

IF TRAVELLING TO
POKHARA TAKE EAST
BANK TRAIL FROM HERE
TO AVOID CLIMB TO
BAGLUNG

Dhaula-
giri
Namaste

SHRINE

N

ADD 30 MINS
TO TIMESCALE
IF WALKING UP
TO BAGLUNG

SCALE: 1km   1mile

UNICEF
PAPER

MAP14

BAGLUNG
970m

KHANIYAGHAT
825m   Kali Gandaki

2¼ — 2¾ HRS

2¾ HRS

2¼

3¼ — 1 HR

3¾ — 1 HR

Ghorepani to Ghandruk and Chomrong

This forest trail through the rhododendrons makes a convenient link between Ghorepani and the large Gurung town of Ghandruk, via Tadapani. From Tadapani you can descend to the Kimrong Khola and reach Chomrong, a village with excellent lodges and stunning views. Chomrong is also the starting point for the Annapurna Sanctuary trek.

You should be aware that the first part of this route can be very slippery if it has rained recently. During the monsoon the rhododendron forests are infested with leeches.

GHOREPANI TO DEURALI   [MAP 3: p139]

Leaving Ghorepani
From Lower Ghorepani a sign points to a trail that ascends steeply to a long and undulating ridge, climbing above 3000m before dropping to Deurali. It's a very pleasant walk and there are excellent views each side of the ridge. The rhododendrons here are spectacular in March and April when they are in flower.

Deurali (2987m/9800ft) is just a couple of teahouses by the junction with the path down to Chitre. The Hotel Excellent here doesn't exactly live up to its name and offers very basic accommodation.

DEURALI TO GHANDRUK & CHOMRONG   [MAP 15: p173]

From Deurali the trail descends quite steeply at times into the impressive river gorge to the village of **Banthanti**. The ethnic **Hotel Tranquility** or the slightly less basic **Annapurna Lodge** are probably the best places to stay here. You often see langur monkeys in the trees in this area. Crossing the wooden bridge east of the Annapurna Lodge, the trail climbs and passes a disused youth club before descending to a second bridge. From here it's an exhausting climb to Tadapani.

Tadapani (2595m/8514ft)
The name of this village means 'distant water' and Tadapani is not to be confused with Tatopani ('hot water'), in the Kali Gandaki Valley.

Most of the accommodation here is of a reasonable standard, although the area around Tadapani has been subject to much deforestation over the years. With this in mind, ACAP have requested that trekkers select lodges that have backboilers, or use kerosene rather than firewood.

Route to Ghandruk

From Tadapani this easy trail heads south to **Baisi Kharka** where there are a couple of small lodges. There's then a choice of routes. Take the left-hand trail for the lodges at the northern end of Ghandruk and descend to the main Ghandruk-Chomrong trail where you turn right. Alternatively, take the right-hand route from Baisi Kharka which brings you into Ghandruk at the top of the town. See p176 for more information on Ghandruk.

Routes to Chomrong

There are two routes between Tadapani and Chomrong across the Kimrong Khola.

Low route The more commonly followed route descends to Melaje. From here the trail drops steeply down through the terraced fields of maize and potatoes. The path is not always clear but you're aiming for the big suspension bridge over the Kimrong Khola. Just up from the bridge, the **Hotel Peaceful** is a pleasant place to stay and indeed peaceful. From this village you join the main Ghandruk-Chomrong trail that climbs, steeply at first, up the northern side of the valley to Daulu. Just around the corner you reach the first lodges of upper Chomrong (see p179).

High route The other route from Tadapani crosses the Kimrong Khola higher up the river. The first section, from Tadapani to Chiukle, is difficult to follow but this route makes an interesting alternative to the main trail. As it is longer, very few trekkers come this way. Leave Tadapani on the path that begins from the teashop near Hotel View Top. After a short distance, this trail veers to the north and comes out into a small clearing before dropping steeply through the rhododendrons. After another clearing you follow a wall, cross a stile and reach the Namaste teashop at Chisapani. The trail then drops steeply to **Chiukle**, where there's one

---

Route times

The following times refer to routes shown on the map opposite:

Deurali to Tadapani: $1^1/_2$-$2^1/_4$ hours
Tadapani to Deurali: 2-3 hours

Tadapani to Ghandruk: 2-$2^1/_2$ hours
Ghandruk to Tadapani: $2^1/_2$-$3^1/_4$ hours

Tadapani to Chomrong (or vice versa) via Chiukle: $3^1/_2$ -$4^1/_2$ hours

Tadapani to Chomrong (or vice versa) via Kimrong Khola: 3-4 hours

Ghandruk to Chomrong (or vice versa) via Kimrong Khola: 3-4 hours

Chomrong to Landruk via New Bridge: $2^1/_2$ -3 hours
Landruk to Chomrong via New Bridge: $3^1/_4$ -$4^1/_4$ hours

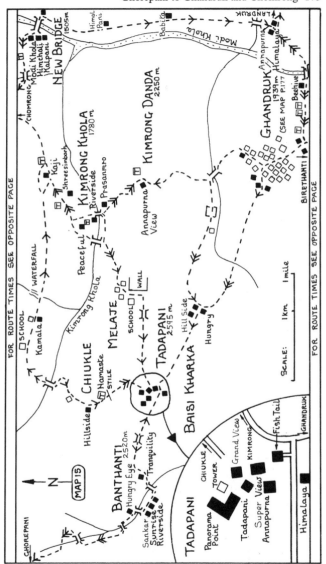

small lodge. A maze of small paths leads down through the terraced fields to the big suspension bridge, built in 1989, over the Kimrong Khola.

From the bridge, the trail climbs past the school and along the terraces to the little village of **Klisigo Chiukle** where the Kamala Lodge is run by a hospitable and friendly family. Ten minutes beyond is a series of waterfalls, a refreshingly cool spot. From here the trail climbs a little and contours along the terraces to join the main Ghandruk-Chomrong route (see p178).

Birethanti to Ghandruk and Chomrong

BIRETHANTI TO GHANDRUK [MAP 16: p175]

Leave Birethanti either by the path past the post office or along the path beside Laxmi Lodge. Both routes pass the school and follow the Modi Khola valley through fields. Twenty-five minutes beyond Birethanti you reach Ker & Downey's comfortable **Sanctuary Lodge**. It's set in a peaceful garden just above the river with views up the valley to Machhapuchhre. The bedrooms here even have attached bathrooms (with Western-style sit-down loos). When the lodge is not being used by their clients, rooms may be let to independent trekkers (see p30).

Less than ten minutes beyond the Sanctuary Lodge is **Chimrong**, where a trail leads over the bridge and up to Chandrakot. For Ghandruk, stay on this side and follow the river to **Syauli Bazaar** where there are several small places to stay. From here the path climbs steeply up to the village of **Kimche** where there are four lodges, all of them fairly basic.

The Gurungs

Forming the largest group in the Annapurna region, the Gurungs are a Tibeto-Burman people who were originally herders in western Tibet. Most Gurungs are now involved in agriculture, working the terraces that surround villages like Ghandruk but a large proportion of Gurung earnings comes from the few amongst them who are employed in Gurkha regiments abroad.

In the hills, Gurung men are easily recognisable by the bag they wear crisscrossed around their chest, and the *jama* (a type of kilt) held up by a large belt, sometimes with a military buckle. Women wear a sari-like *fariya* and often have a nosering and necklaces of turquoise and coral.

Although essentially Buddhist, some Gurungs are now Hindu but often both Hindu and Buddhist festivals are observed. 'The Gurungs are a very jolly tribe', say DB Shrestha and CB Singh in *Ethnic groups of Nepal and their Ways of Living*, 'They make merry on each and every occasion'. Certainly, their good humour and friendliness are immediately apparent to the foreign trekker.

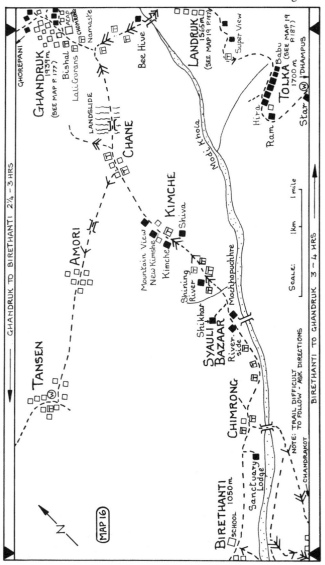

The path then levels out and in **Chane** meets the trail to Tirkhedunga ($3^{1}/_{2}$-$4^{1}/_{2}$ hours from here). In Chane there are a couple of teashops which, like most bhattis, also offer very basic accommodation. Few trekkers stay in these kinds of places now which is a shame since a night in a local inn can be an enjoyable and enlightening experience.

On the eastern edge of Chane a massive landslide during the 1995 monsoon wiped out the trail. If a path hasn't been forged across it you'll have to climb high. East of the landslide the path becomes a wide paved trail, well-kept and reminiscent of remaining parts of the Inca Trail that trekkers still follow on the way to Machu Pichu in Peru.

Ghandruk (1939m/6362ft)
This picturesque town of slate-roofed houses surrounded by terraced fields is a pleasant place to spend a night. The headquarters of the Annapurna Conservation Area Project are here (in the impressive white buildings at the lower end of the town) and many of the lodges have the more environmentally-friendly features that ACAP encourages: back-boilers, solar-panels etc.

Electricity recently arrived in Ghandruk, although its installation was not without problems. Again, ACAP's policy of not imposing new schemes upon the people but rather backing projects that the people wanted and were prepared to instigate themselves has proved best. When the pipe that supplied water to the generator burst, the people lobbied the Nepali company that supplied it and ensured that a replacement was quickly supplied. Each house has two 25w bulbs; lodges also have low-wattage cookers.

This is a largely Gurung town of about 7000 people. Traditionally, Gurungs are Buddhist but some, particularly those pursuing government positions, converted to Hinduism.

Accommodation Ghandruk has a large range of places to stay, more than sixteen lodges in all. The ones with the best views are at the top end of town but you could hardly complain about the views from any part of Ghandruk. For budget travellers, the accommodation that stands above all others is the **Trekkers Inn**, ACAP's Lodge of the Year in 1994. As well as fulfilling ACAP's criteria for minimising environmental damage, it is also a welcoming and friendly place, run efficiently by the indefatigable Jagan Gurung.

The **Milan**, **Sakura** and **SangriLa** have also been recommended. Recently opened, again with ACAP's endorsement, there's an environmentally-friendly campsite, the **Eco-Camping Place**.

The most expensive and most comfortable place is **Himalaya Lodge** (see p30) where trekkers can stay if it's not being used by a group.

ACAP headquarters It's well worth visiting the display here, which details ACAP's work in the area and has models of back-boilers and other energy-saving water heaters and cookers. There's an interesting 20-minute video which they show at 9.30 am, 12 noon and 3pm, or at other times for groups. They also sell ACAP T-shirts, post-cards, maps, stickers and posters.

For further information about ACAP see p81.

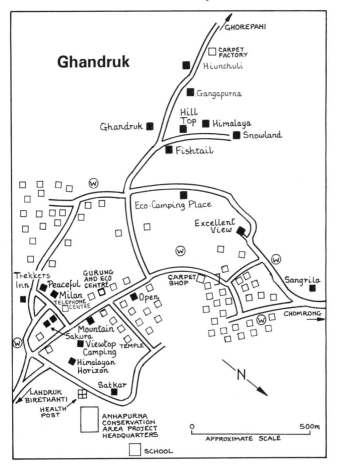

Other services Just beside the ACAP headquarters is a **health post** (open daily, 10.00-14.00). In an emergency, a message can be sent using ACAP's radio. The **post office** is in the same building as the well-advertised Sakura Lodge. At the top end of the town is a **carpet factory** that can be visited, and, should you decide that a carpet would make a useful addition to your trekking kit, you can buy one here or in the shop in the lower part of the town.

Not far from the Mountain Guest House is the **Gurung Museum,** set up by a local woman. There are displays of furnishings, dress and tools to describe the traditional Gurung way of life. Entrance is free but donations are requested.

Next door is the **Local Youth Eco-Trekking Centre** where guides and porters can be arranged (in advance via the operator at the telecom centre, if you wish). Nearby is the new **telecom centre** (☎ 061-29322); international calls from here cost the same as from Pokhara.

GHANDRUK TO CHOMRONG   [MAP 15: p173; MAP 17: p181]
Leaving Ghandruk
The main trail to Chomrong leaves Ghandruk on the northern side of the village, past Sangrila Guest House. About 15 minutes beyond you cross a bridge over a stream. The path to Baisi Kharka and Tadapani leaves the main trail just north of this stream.

Kimrong Danda (2250m/7382ft) For Chomrong, continue along the main trail which begins to climb towards the small pass you can see ahead, Kimrong Danda. You won't need any encouragement to stop for a drink here and there are two small teahouses, one of which also has basic accommodation.

Kimrong Khola (1780m/5840ft) Dropping steeply from Kimrong Danda, you can see the large suspension bridge across the Kimrong Khola from just above the Prasanmro Tea House. In the monsoon season this is the only crossing over the river, and it is reached by following the main trail until a stone wall appears on your left. Climbing over this wall, you follow a minor path to the bridge. When the river is low, you can cross on a few logs just below Riverside Lodge. In the village here, **Peaceful Lodge** is a pleasant place to stay.

Daulu/Taulung (2180m/7152ft) From Kimrong Khola the trail climbs very sharply to Kaji, passing the turn-off for the high route to Tadapani via Chiukle. Contouring across terraced fields you reach Daulu at the end of the ridge. There are several teahouses here, some also offering accommodation but Chomrong, with rather better lodges and stunning views of the Annapurnas, is only about twenty minutes beyond, following the trail round the ridge. A second trail (see p186) leads steeply downhill from Daulu to New Bridge, Landruk and on to Pokhara via Dhampus.

Chomrong (2170m/7119ft)   [MAP 17: p181]
From Chomrong you can at last see why Machhupuchhre got its name 'Fishtail Peak'. The views from here of the other peaks that surround the Annapurna Sanctuary are so impressive that you can't spend less than a night here. This is, in fact, an excellent place for a rest day since most of the lodges have sunny terraces, ideal for relaxing and taking in the scenery.

This is the start of the trek to the Annapurna Sanctuary, and if you're camping, fires are forbidden above Chomrong (although you shouldn't be making fires anywhere in the Annapurna region.)

Chomrong's original micro-hydro electricity supply was installed and paid for by a Japanese trekker, Katsuyuki Hayashi, in 1982. He was known locally as the Japanese Electricity Man but his schemes have recently come into conflict with ACAP and their plans. Some of the lodges are still without electricity.

Accommodation There's a large range of places to stay here. The newer lodges are high up the hill to make the most of the views. They're large wooden buildings, efficiently-run (solar-heated showers and back-boilers) and offering some of the best food on the trek.

The **Chomrong Guest House** is still setting the standards with good showers, comfortable rooms, and an unmatched reputation for delicious pizza. They produce up to 100 of them a day at the height of the season! The other lodges up here come pretty close, however, and both the **Moonlight** and **International** have been recommended as less-crowded alternatives.

Down in the main part of the village is the **Captain's Lodge**. Both the lodge and the crusty character who presides over it (and over the village) are Chomrong institutions and it can be fun to stay here. Dinner is a sit-down affair served at 6.30pm sharp, by candlelight. The Captain can't really be bothered with pizza but he'll knock one up for you if you insist. His pumpkin soup, on the other hand, is excellent and he prides himself on his hot chocolate pudding and his apple roll with its chocolate centre.

Other services In the lower part of the village the **kerosene depot** sells a range of provisions as well as fuel. Prices here for things like chocolate, beer, muesli, honey and biscuits are lower than in all the lodges apart from the Captain's (where you can also get delicious yak's cheese). You can rent camping gear from the Captain; his stocks include tents, stoves, sleeping-bags, down jackets, boots, gloves, hats and sunglasses. The Captain has been involved in many climbing expeditions and is probably the best person to contact in an emergency.

Chomrong to the Annapurna Sanctuary

The Annapurna Sanctuary trek

At the top of the trail that begins in Chomrong and follows the Modi Khola lies a natural amphitheatre known as the Annapurna Sanctuary. This little valley is as magical as the name suggests, with ten peaks of 6000-8000m (20,000-26,000ft) rising from it.

Annapurna Base Camp, or, more correctly, Annapurna South Base Camp since Herzog's camp for the original conquest of the peak (see p33) lies on its north side, is, at 4130m/13,550ft, the highest place here that offers accommodation. Although the route is for the most part uninhabited, groups of lodges have been set up along the way so that it is no longer necessary to camp.

Sections of this trek are subject to avalanches particularly in the spring. Although you won't be aware of the mountain, one part of the trail passes almost directly under Hiunchuli and there are annual avalanches and landslides in this area. You should check on conditions at the ACAP information booth in Khuldigar before leaving. If you're trekking outside the main seasons they can tell you which lodges are open. In January and February it may be impossible to reach the Sanctuary.

CHOMRONG TO DOVAN   [MAP 17: p181]

Leaving Chomrong

From the lower part of the village, you descend to the suspension bridge over the Chomro Khola and climb, steeply at first.

Passing through Tilche, represented on the trail by the Annapurna General Store, a stiff climb brings you to Bhanuwa, a perfect place to stop and admire the view back down the Modi Khola behind you. Continue climbing to the small settlement of **Sinuwa** which is the last village you go through.

The Fish Tail

Viewed from Pokhara, Machhapuchhre (6977m/22,942ft) is certainly striking but the feature that gave it its name can only be seen from the Modi Khola. From Chomrong the mountain is particularly impressive, and even more so from the Sanctuary.

A holy mountain to the Gurungs, no mountaineering expeditions have been allowed on Machhapuchhre since the 1957 expedition led by Colonel Jimmy Roberts reached a point 50m below the summit. It remains one of the few peaks in the country never to have been conquered.

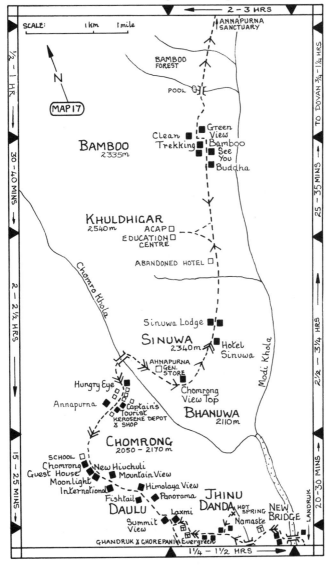

Khuldigar (2540m/8333ft) Passing the defunct Hotel Machhupuchhure, now operating as the Buddha Guest House at Bamboo, one soon
reaches Khuldigar and the last **checkpost** on the trail. There are no lodges
here but a small path leads up to ACAP's **Centre for Outdoor and
Conservation Education**, which is worth a short visit.

Bamboo (2335m/7660ft) The path from Khuldigar to Bamboo is
steeply downhill and you soon enter the damp bamboo forest from which
the collection of lodges takes its name. The **Buddha Guest House**,
despite its scruffy appearance, is warm, friendly and serves good food.

Dovan (2505m/8218ft) From Bamboo the trail climbs steadily, crossing first the Bamboo River and then several small streams, until eventually it reaches three lodges in a forest clearing at Dovan. **Tiptop Lodge**,
recently moved after years in isolation below Dovan, serves not only the
best food but is also run by probably the only woman in the whole valley.

DOVAN TO ANNAPURNA BASE CAMP   [MAP 18: p183]

The next stretch of forest from Dovan to Himalaya is the sacred home of
the deity Baraha Than. About half an hour from Dovan a **shrine** stands in
his honour, and it is traditional to leave flowers or strips of coloured cloth
here. It is also said that any eggs or meat carried north of here will anger
the deities and bring bad luck.

Next door to the shrine is a viewpoint of an impressive waterfall, said
to consist of up to seventy streams. From here the trail climbs high above
the river and there are fewer clumps of bamboo. You may find wild straw-
berries growing in this area.

Himalaya (2920m/9580ft) The small lodges here stand beside a little
stream. The **Hotel Himalaya** features 'Put it in the Pan' on the menu, a
tasty vegetarian mixture.

Hinku Cave (3170m/10,400ft) Forty minutes from Himalaya stands
the huge rock that forms Hinku Cave. A favourite camping shelter and
landmark for mountaineering expeditions, the tea-house here is, alas, no
more and the site has been abandoned. Nevertheless, it's still a pleasant
place to rest weary limbs and in the distance one can see the lodges of
Deurali about 40 minutes' away.

Deurali (3230m/10,597ft) The owner of the **Panorama Guest House**,
Om Prasad Gurung, built both the steps leading up to Deurali and the
Baraha Than shrine, and he is a good source of local information. It is
worth noting that with the demise of the village of Bagar, Deurali is the
last accommodation available before the sanctuary.

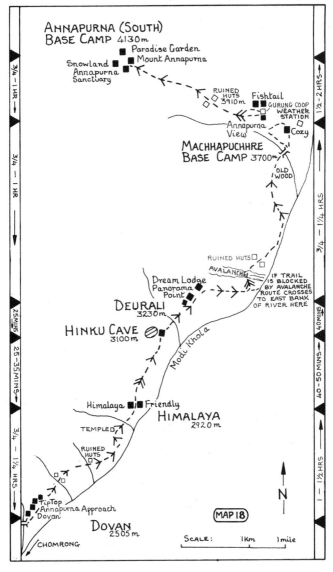

ANNAPURNA (SOUTH)
BASE CAMP 4130m
Paradise Garden
Mount Annapurna
Snowland
Annapurna
Sanctuary

RUINED
HUTS
3910m
Fishtail
GURUNG COOP
WEATHER
STATION
Annapurna
View
Cozy

MACHHAPUCHHRE
BASE CAMP 3700m

OLD
WOOD

RUINED HUTS
AVALANCHE
IF TRAIL
IS BLOCKED
BY AVALANCHE
ROUTE CROSSES
TO EAST BANK
OF RIVER HERE

Dream Lodge
Panorama
Point

DEURALI
3230m

HINKU CAVE
3100m

Modi Khola

Himalaya Friendly
HIMALAYA
2920m

TEMPLE

RUINED
HUTS

TipTop
Annapurna Approach
Dovan

DOVAN
2505m

CHOMRONG

MAP 18

N

SCALE: 1Km   1mile

3/4 – 1 HR
3/4 – 1 HR
25 MINS 25 – 35 MINS
3/4 – 1 1/4 HRS

1 1/2 – 2 HRS
3/4 – 1 1/4 HRS
40 MINS 40 – 50 MINS
1 – 1 1/2 HRS

Machhapuchhre Base Camp (3700m/12,139ft)

Leaving Deurali, the route passes the ruins of Bagar, as well as a couple of small avalanches. Crossing several streams, you climb again, passing through a gully beside a sparse wood: the remains of what was probably once a large forest. Amongst the rocks you may see marmots, which live in large underground colonies around here.

You now enter the sanctuary itself and it was at this eastern end of the valley that the base camp for the 1957 attempt on Machhapuchhre was established. You cross a stream on a small wooden bridge to a junction. The Machhapuchhre Cozy Guest House is still at the top of the steps, although ACAP, unhappy at its location on public land, are currently attempting to have it removed. Following instead the left-hand path you arrive at the other three lodges, including the **Gurung Cooperative**, probably the best place here with a nice warm kitchen/dining area and good food. If you're being badly affected by the altitude you should not press on to Annapurna Base Camp since it's 430m/1410ft higher and 1$^{1}/_{2}$ -2 hours further on.

Annapurna Base Camp (4130m/13,550ft)

The path up here is not particularly steep but if you're tired and unacclimatised the trek can seem relentless. If you've just spent the night at Machhapuchhre Base Camp and are well rested you'll probably find this stretch very pleasant, a gentle uphill stroll along the river, through tranquil meadows with many boulders to rest upon and gaze in awe at the surrounding peaks.

The four lodges stand on a level area that was the base camp for the 1970 Annapurna South Face expedition (see below). It's a chilly spot but if you're acclimatised it's worth spending the night here since you can be up to watch the sunrise over the peaks. You'll also be able to climb up one of the sides of the valley on hard snow (ie before it turns mushy and becomes difficult to walk on) for even better views. Whilst accommodation is inexpensive, expect to pay a lot more for your food up here – a pizza costs about Rs125. The **Hotel Snowland** and the **Annapurna Sanctuary Lodge** are both recommended as comfortable places to stay. Plans are afoot to build a special lodge exclusively for porters, which will be much cheaper than the other accommodation available.

Even if viewed from the terrace of one of the lodges, with a warming cup of tea in your hand, the panorama is magnificent. There are further treks from Base Camp, however, such as the trekking peak Tharpu Chuli (Tent Peak), which give even more glorious perspectives on the Sanctuary. Raju and Jagan Gurung at Snowland will be able to give details on these walks. You could easily spend several days up here exploring the different viewpoints around the sides of this truly spectacular valley.

CLIMBING ANNAPURNA I

The two most famous climbs on this 8091m/26,545ft peak (the world's tenth highest) are Maurice Herzog's original conquest with the French expedition in 1950 and Chris Bonington's South Face expedition in 1970.

The Conquest of Annapurna – 1950

When most modern mountaineering expeditions set out, their objectives are usually well defined, sometimes down to the exact route to be followed up a peak. In the light of this Maurice Herzog's 1950 expedition seems delightfully amateurish and their success all the more heroic. Their single objective was to be the first expedition to conquer a peak over 8000m yet not only were they unsure as to which 8000m peak it should be, Dhaulagiri or Annapurna, but the maps of the area were so inaccurate the first problem was simply to reach the mountains themselves. Only one team member had ever set eyes on the Himalaya before and not in this area since Nepal had only just opened its borders to climbing expeditions.

Being unable to find a viable route up Dhaulagiri they crossed the Kali Gandaki and pioneered a route up the north face of Annapurna I. On 3rd June 1950, Herzog and Louis Lachenal reached the summit and could look across the Annapurna Sanctuary to Machhapuchhre. They paid heavily for their victory with severe frostbite in the terrible conditions on the descent. Herzog was never to climb again, losing most of his fingers and toes. He returned to a career in politics in France where he was eventually made Minister of Sport.

Even if you're not particularly interested in climbing Herzog's account of the expedition, *The Conquest of Annapurna 1950*, is a gripping read and gives good descriptions of some of the villages in the region.

Annapurna, South Face – 1970

Looking up at the solid wall of rock and ice that forms the south face of Annapurna from the Sanctuary, it seems inconceivable (certainly as far as a non-climber is concerned) that anyone could find a way up it. Indeed, before 1970, nothing so steep and demanding had ever been attempted in the Himalaya.

A series of camps was established up the slope, the highest, Camp 6, at 7300m and pairs of climbers installed in each. With a copy of Chris Bonington's account of the expedition, Annapurna South Face , you can make out the exact route that was followed. As with the first attempt on Annapurna, the expedition became a race against the fast-approaching monsoon. On 27th May Don Whillans and Dougal Haston, having set out to establish a seventh camp, continued up to reach the summit and the point where, twenty years before, Herzog and Lachenal had first looked down into the Sanctuary. Although it was planned that most team members would have a chance to reach the summit, only these first two did. The expedition was not without its share of tragedy. On the descent one of the climbers, Ian Clough, was killed in an avalanche below Camp 2. He was buried just above Annapurna Base Camp.

Chomrong to Pokhara via Landruk

CHOMRONG TO NEW BRIDGE   [MAP 17: p181]
Leaving Chomrong
Follow the main trail out of Upper Chomrong and after about 20 minutes
you reach Summit View at **Daulu/Taulung**. A signpost there points the
way to Jhinu Danda, 45 minutes away down a steeply descending path
dotted with teahouses.

Jhinu Danda The hot spring near here makes this a popular place to
stop, although it's a 20 minute walk down to the river to reach the two
pools. In Jhinu Danda there are five lodges including **Namaste Lodge**,
the largest place and the only lodge here with a generator.

The main path continues down to a bridge, recently constructed by
ACAP, over the Samrong Khola. Passing terraced fields and the occasional teashop it drops steeply again, this time down to **New Bridge/
Nayapul/Himalpani**. There's nothing here other than the large suspension bridge over the Modi Khola and four lodges beside it. This is not a
bad place to spend the night, particularly if you're travelling in the opposite direction, as the climb up to Daula and Chomrong is best done in the
early part of the day, before it gets too hot.

NEW BRIDGE TO LANDRUK   [MAP15: p173]

The trail to Landruk continues through the trees along the river. Twenty
minutes beyond New Bridge is the rustic **Babita Lodge** and after fifteen
minutes the path begins to gain height, passing terraced rice fields.
Crossing a small suspension bridge it climbs to the first few lodges of
Landruk. From here one path leads steeply down to the river and the other
climbs to the main part of the village.

Landruk (1565m/5135ft)
This large Gurung village, directly across the valley from Ghandruk,
stretches 500m up the hillside. There are good views up the Modi Khola
to the Annapurnas from here. Many of the lodges are large impressive
affairs advertising hot-showers and roof-top dining. The **Maya Guest
House** is perhaps the biggest, and they do superb banana cake. The
Hungry Eye at the top of the hill is pleasantly situated and has a very
extensive menu. The **Moonlight**, whilst lacking the facilities of these
larger places, is cosy and extremely friendly.

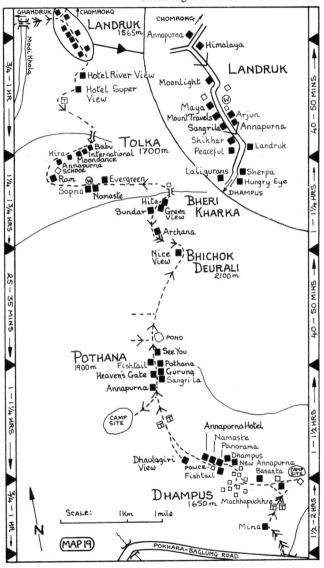

GHANDRUK   CHOMRONG
LANDRUK
1565m

CHOMRONG

Annapurna
Himalaya

LANDRUK

Hotel River View
Hotel Super View

Moonlight

Maya
Mount Travels
Sangrila
Shikhar
Peaceful

Arjun
Annapurna

Landruk

Babu
International
Moondance

Hira
Annapurna
SCHOOL
Ram
Sopna

TOLKA
1700m

Laligurans

Sherpa
Hungry Eye

DHAMPUS

Evergreen
Namaste

Hita
Sundar   Green View

BHERI KHARKA

Archana

Nice View

BHICHOK DEURALI
2100m

POND

See You

POTHANA
1900m

Fishtail
Heaven's Gate
Annapurna

Pothana
Gurung
Sangri La

CAMP SITE

Annapurna Hotel

Namaste
Panorama
Dhampus
New Annapurna
Basanta   CAMP SITE

Dhaulagiri View
POLICE
Fishtail

DHAMPUS
1650m   Machhapuchhre

Mina

SCALE: 1 Km   1 mile

N

MAP 19

POKHARA-BAGLUNG ROAD

Modi Khola

3/4 – 1 HR
1 1/4 – 1 3/4 HRS
25 – 35 MINS
1 – 1 1/4 HRS
3/4 – 1 HR

40 – 50 MINS
1 – 1 1/4 HRS
40 – 50 MINS
1 – 1 1/2 HRS
1 1/2 – 2 HRS

LANDRUK TO DHAMPUS   [MAP 19: p187]

Leaving Landruk   Between Landruk and the pass, Bhichok Deurali, the trail winds around two side valleys and climbs 550m/1804ft.

Tolka/Medigara (1700m/5577ft)   This village is nothing more than a collection of lodges built specifically for trekker-tourism. Most of the lodges have view-towers and/or roof-top dining, a good enough excuse to stop and admire the Annapurnas behind you. The first two, the **Babu** and the **International**, are particularly good. The path meanders through the village past the school (where you may be accosted for a donation), and a few minutes beyond is the highly recommended **Ram Lodge**, with a pleasant sitting area with an umbrella right by the path.

The trail continues on the level until reaching the remains of the old suspension bridge at **Bheri Kharka**, after which there's a stiff climb through the trees to the pass. There are numerous small lodges, many little more than teahouses; **Green View Guest House** and **Hita Guest House** are reasonable places to stay.

Bhichok Deurali (2100m/6890ft)   The tea-houses at this pass are the perfect excuse for a stop. There are views through the rhododendrons in several directions, and Dhaulagiri is visible from here. **Nice View Lodge** is appropriately named and it has a glassed in dining-area.

The path, now partly paved, descends gently from Bichok Deurali to Pothana and Dhampus. This amble through the forest is probably most welcome after your recent exertions. **Pothana (1900m/6236ft)** has more lodges for trekkers than houses for local people. Just past it is a small trail west leading up to a popular camping site known as Australia Field.

Dhampus (1650m/5413ft)
Tourists come up to Dhampus from Pokhara for the night to watch the sunrise over the mountains so there are several places to stay. Take particular care if you're camping as thieves operate at night here.

Just before the checkpost is the **Dhaulgiri View Hotel**, whose owner has cleverly redesigned the trail from Pothana so that most trekkers enter the village past his lodge. After the school the trail splits. Take the right-hand route via the **Basanta Lodge**, the top place to stay and part of the Ker & Downey group (see p30). When it's not being used by trekking groups independent trekkers can also stay here.

When leaving Dhampus for Pokhara, take the steep trail that begins opposite the Machhupuchhure Guest House. You can get taxis or buses to Pokhara from where the path meets the road. Taxi-drivers, however, know that in your relief at the thought of not having to use your legs for a change, you'll probably pay almost anything for the privilege of squeezing into their battered Corollas. Bargain hard.

Dumre to the Thorung La

Dumre (445m/1460ft)

Populated mainly by Newars, dirty dusty Dumre is nothing more than a junction town on the Prithvi Highway. Avoid staying here unless you arrive late. Trucks and buses (see below) can make the trip from here to Besisahar in around 4^1/$_2$hrs without breakdowns but since these are common it's likely to take much longer, often up to eight hours. Direct buses are now available from Kathmandu and although these are no more reliable than the services which start in Dumre, at least you won't have to fight for a seat. If you're walking, the first place with basic accommodation available is around 2^1/$_2$hrs along the road at Turture.

Accommodation There are quite a few places to choose from, though they're all very basic. The **Hotel Mustang** seems to be the place that's most popular with travellers. You'll get a reasonably clean double with fan for Rs60, and in the restaurant here daal bhat costs Rs30. The **Hotel Jomsom** is similar. The **Hotel New Manaslu** is run by very friendly people but rooms lack fans.

Other services The **bank** (sign board in Nepali only) is four doors east of the Hotel Mustang. Note that the only other banks this side of the Thorung La (ie until Jomsom) are in Besisahar and Chame. There's also a **post office**.

On foot or by public transport to Besisahar?

Buses have now joined the dilapidated collection of old Russian Gazs, Chinese Jeeps and Indian 4WD Shaktiman trucks that lurch up the rough track from Dumre to Besisahar.

How comfortable you are on this trip depends on how much space you have. You may get a seat on a bus but then have to share it with a farmer and his chickens. In a truck you probably won't get a seat, rather a perch on top of whatever's in the back, but if there's a fair amount of space it could be quite an comfy journey.

As far as the ride up to Besisahar goes, you'll either love it or hate it. One recent traveller claimed that it was like a marathon funfair ride, one of the highlights of his trip. A local VSO worker who made the journey frequently finally decided that the dangers and discomforts involved were not worth the saving of time when her truck overturned during the monsoon killing one passenger and injuring many others.

The road is no more than a very rough track in many places, treacherous after rains, and the vehicles are poorly maintained, operational brakes being a rare luxury on the trucks. Despite all this, most trekkers opt for them since the walk to Besisahar takes 8^1/$_2$-11hrs along the hot, dusty and uninteresting road.

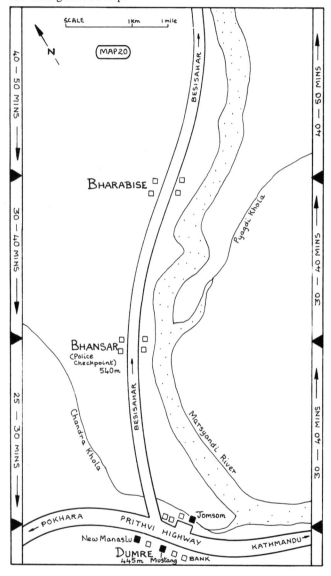

Getting away Buses, trucks and jeeps for Besisahar run from the centre of Dumre. There's no schedule, they go when there's absolutely no
possibility of cramming in another body. This is long after they're actually full so don't go for an empty vehicle or you're likely to have a long
wait. If you're coming from Kathmandu it's best to get a direct bus for
Besisahar so you won't have to scramble for a seat.

Operators have now got used to desperate foreigners paying higher
than normal fares; what you pay can vary enormously, from less than
Rs100 to as much as Rs250. Hold out for as low a price as possible or the
prices will rise even further. Drivers make a small charge for backpacks.

It's sometimes possible to get together with other travellers and rent a
whole jeep, rather than just a place in it. However you go, the ride is dusty
so ensure your belongings, especially cameras, are packed in plastic bags
and within sight as there have been some thefts.

There are frequent buses throughout the day to Pokhara (Rs25, $2^{3}/_{4}$
hours; Rs40, $2^{1}/_{2}$ express) and Kathmandu (Rs60, 5 hours) as well as to
many other places in Nepal.

DUMRE TO BESISAHAR   [MAPS 20-24]

First stop on the road north is at the police checkpoint in the Gurung settlement of **Bhansar (540m/1772ft)**, 15 mins by truck from Dumre. All
foreigners are required to fill in their names and passport and trekking
visa/permit numbers. If the police aren't about truck drivers don't bother
to stop.

Turture (540m/1772ft) This village has some very basic accommodation but, as with the other 'hotels' in villages between Dumre and
Besisahar, they're not representative of the kind of lodgings you can look
forward to further up the valley. The **Lamjung** is on the main road; the
Marsyangdi, Muktinath and **Shakti** are on the side road down to the
bridge.

Paundi (520m/1706ft) This settlement is situated where the Paundi
Khola joins the Marsyandi River. There are a number of teahouses here
including the **Hotel Shuraj & Lodge**, **Hotel Paundi & Lodge**, **Hotel
Himalaya & Lodge** and **Ashok Hotel** but as you will now have realised,
'hotel' is something of a misnomer. As in many parts of the Indian sub-
continent, it's come to mean a place to eat rather than sleep but you can
unroll your sleeping bag at most of these places.

There are several little shops, including one selling face masks against
the dust. It might be worth buying some fruit here as you won't see much,
other than apples in season, when you get up into the hills. There's a good
swimming place under the bridge.

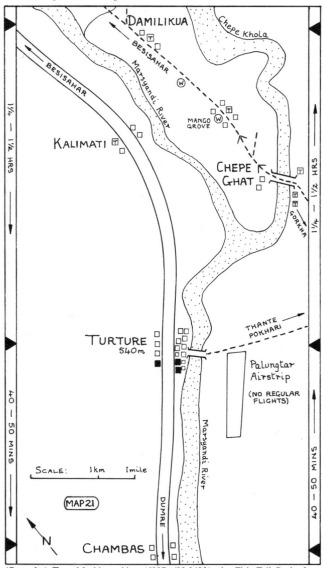

(Opposite) Top: Machhapuchhre (6997m/22,942ft), the Fish Tail Peak, from Chomrong. **Bottom:** The lodges of Annapurna Base Camp (4130m/13,550ft).

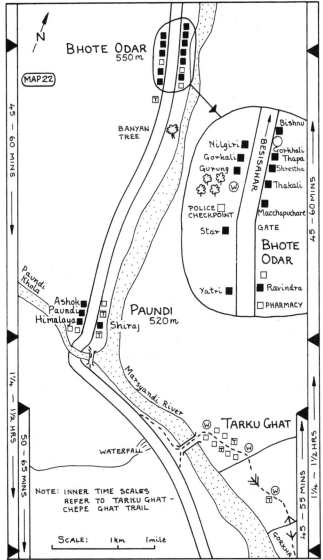

N

BHOTE ODAR
550 m

MAP 22

BANYAN
TREE

Bishnu

Nilgiri
Gorkali
Gurung

Gorkhali
Thapa

Shrestha

Thakali

BESISAHAR

POLICE
CHECKPOINT

Macchapuchare

GATE

Star

BHOTE
ODAR

Yatri

Ravindra

PHARMACY

Paundi
Khola

Ashok
Paundi
Himalaya

PAUNDI
520m

Shiraj

Marsyandi River

TARKU GHAT

WATERFALL

NOTE: INNER TIME SCALES
REFER TO TARKU GHAT -
CHEPE GHAT TRAIL

GORKHA

SCALE: 1km   1mile

45 - 60 MINS

1¼ - 1½ HRS

50 - 65 MINS

45 - 60 MINS

1¼ - 1½ HRS

1¼ - 55 MINS

45 - 55 MINS

(Opposite) Top: The village of Braga in the Manang Valley. **Bottom:** Traditional houses in the dry Manang Valley have flat roofs. (Photo: Henry Stedman).

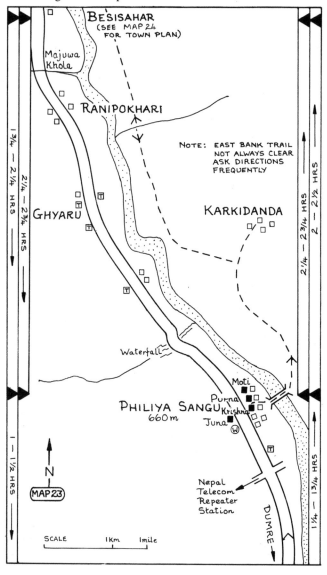

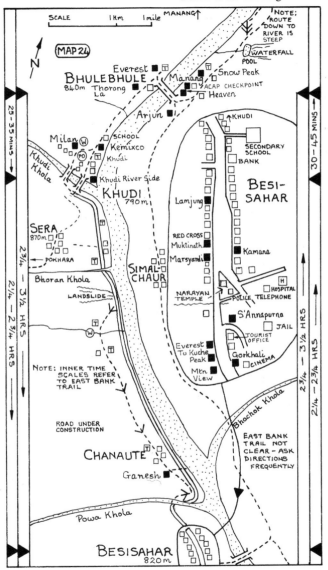

Bhoti Odar (550m/1804ft), or 'Botty Odour' as local VSO workers call it, is not as bad as the name would suggest. The accommodation is quite reasonable and the best available between Dumre and Besisahar.

The best places to stay in Bhote Odar are probably the **Ravindra Hotel & Lodge** and the **Thakali Hotel & Lodge** which boasts a 'love room'. This turns out to be nothing more than a double bed, although it's something of a novelty in the hills.

There's another **police checkpoint** here and a **pharmacy** to the south of the town.

Philiya Sangu/Phalesaagu/Phalenksanku (660m/2165ft)

The name that no-one knows how to spell is said to be derived from the English 'plank' and the Nepali *saaghu* meaning bridge. A substantial suspension bridge now crosses the Marsyandi here. There is basic accommodation in Philiya Sangu.

An **alternative route** crosses the river to follow a higher trail and you can rejoin the main route either at Besisahar or Bhulebhule (see p197). It's not an easy path to follow, however, so ask directions frequently.

On the **main route** following the road, you're now only 2-2¹/₂hrs from Besisahar on foot.

Besisahar (820m/2690ft)   [MAP 24: p195]

The booming capital of Lamjung District lies at the end of the road. It has been expanding rapidly since the road reached it and much of the new business is funded by Gurkhas retiring here on their British or Indian Army pensions.

Accommodation The best lodges are near the road-head in the southern part of town. The **Hotel Tukuche Peak** is a modern place, much like anything you'd find in Pokhara, but it does have a fridge full of cold beer (Rs80). It's currently the top place in town and the best place to eat. There are plans to relocate the hotel to a quieter site down the road opposite the bank in the north of town, about 1km from here.

The **Hotel Mountain View** is another place that gets good reports. The other hotels in Besisahar are rather more basic but this may change as the area is developing fast.

Services There's a **tourist information centre**, the second last **bank** up the valley (the last being in Chame), a **post office**, and a **hospital**. International phone-calls may be made at the **telecommunications centre**. There's also a cinema, and if you haven't seen a Hindi/Nepali movie yet this may be as good a place as any.

BESISAHAR TO BHULEBHULE   [MAP 24: p195]

The road north through Besisahar is being pushed through to Ngadi, for transport vehicles for the hydroelectric project in the area. So far only a rough track has been made as far as Khudi but since there are no bridges there are no vehicles.

Ten minutes' north of Besisahar the road drops down to cross the Powa Khola. Unless the water is very low and there are stepping stones, you'll need to shed boots and socks and wade across. If you're just starting your trek don't risk getting your boots wet or you'll be sure to get blisters. Across the river you can either follow the new road which is easier, or make a short but stiff climb to join the old trail.

Khudi (790m/2592ft)

The new bridge was completed several years ago in anticipation of the collapse of the more convenient but dilapidated eastern bridge which is not a great advertisement for the workmanship of John M Henderson & Co Ltd of Aberdeen.

This Gurung village, with its large government seed nursery, stands above the Khudi Kola. Accommodation is basic but the **Khudi River Side** is at least pleasantly situated as the name suggests.

There's a **post office** and just north of the secondary school is a small Hindu temple dedicated to Shiva.

• Route to Begnas Tal and Pokhara See p235.

Bhulebhule (840m/2756ft)

The trail crosses to the east bank of the river here. The name of this village is said to be onomatopoeic, referring to the sound of the water in the spring nearby. You should stop for a break here to admire the first good mountain views on this trek. You can see Himalchuli (7893m/25,896ft) and, to the left of it, Ngadi Chuli (7835m/25,705ft), also known as Peak 29 or Manaslu II.

ACAP has opened a **checkpoint** in Bhulebhule so you'll be asked to sign in as you pass.

Accommodation is better here than in Khudi but varies considerably between the lodges. The relocated **Thorong La Guest House** is the first place you get to and boasts not only the most comfortable rooms in town but also an almost bottomless reserve of cold beer (Rs90) in their kerosene-powered fridge. The **Manang Lodge** ('You can observe the well behaviour of Tibetan') is a very good place to stay. It's run by a charming family from Bagarchap. There's a rudimentary shower in the garden and they even have some rooms with double beds. The dining area overlooking the river is very pleasant, and specialities include tuna pizza as well as Tibetan food. The **Arjun Lodge** has also been recommended.

Five minutes north of the village is a fine waterfall and two **pools** for cooling off or washing. As this is also the village water supply you should take care not to pollute it.

BHULEBHULE TO THANIGAON   [MAP 25: p199]

Just south of **Taranche** you come to a stream. For the last few years, the villagers have been doing a good trade in helping trekkers across the sometimes slippery single plank on the bridge. When the water is above the stepping stones, the alternative is to wade across if the bridge hasn't been repaired.

Ngadi (930m/3051ft) is about 15 minutes beyond. Now they've paved over the drain that runs through the centre of the village this place is a lot cleaner and more pleasant to stay in. There are half a dozen lodges; the **Himalaya Lodge** is probably about the best place. Massages are available for aching limbs. As work on the hydroelectric project advances there's a chance that some of the lodges in Ngadi may have to be relocated.

Cross the big suspension bridge over the Ngadi Khola (also known as the Musi Khola) and skirt around the conical hill to begin the hot ascent to Bahundanda passing through terraced fields and the small settlement of **Lamtaka/Lampata (1150m/3773ft)**. The **Hotel Manaslu** is a reasonable place, 10-15 minutes below Bahundanda. Beside it is the **police checkpoint**.

Bahundanda (1310m/4298ft)
Whichever direction you're going, the teashops of Bahundanda are a welcome stop after the sweaty slog up to this ridge-top village. Bahundanda means 'Brahmin Hill'.

There are six places to stay here including the very pleasant **Hotel Mountain View**, up the 'Stair Way to Heaven'. It has an enthusiastic young owner and a good view. The restaurant is pure vegetarian but has a slick menu including exotic specialities like French fries with cheese and ketchup.

International calls are possible from the new **phone office**. It's in the shop by the steps to the Hotel Mountain View.

Dropping steeply, the trail continues through terraced rice fields. In about 1¼ hours you reach **Thanigaun** with its maize fields and guava and lemon trees.

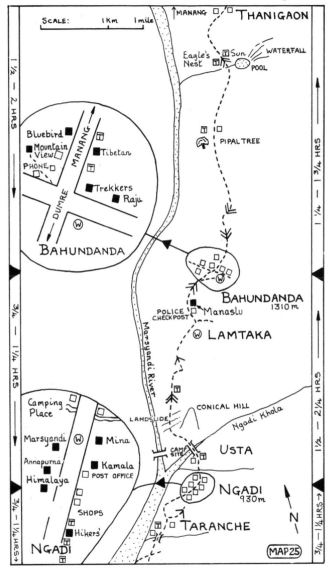

SCALE: 1 Km   1 mile

↑MANANG

THANIGAON

Eagle's Nest

Sun

WATERFALL

POOL

PIPAL TREE

1½ — 2 HRS

Bluebird

Mountain View

PHONE

Tibetan

MANANG

DUMRE

Trekkers

Raju

BAHUNDANDA

BAHUNDANDA 1310 m

POLICE CHECKPOST

Manaslu

LAMTAKA

Marsyandi River

1¼ — 1¾ HRS

¾ — 1¼ HRS

Camping Place

Marsyandi

Mina

Annapurna

Kamala

Himalaya

POST OFFICE

SHOPS

Hikers'

NGADI

LANDSLIDE

CONICAL HILL

Ngadi Khola

CAMP SITE

USTA

NGADI 930 m

TARANCHE

N

1½ — 2¼ HRS

¾ — 1¼ HRS →

MAP 25

SYANJE TO CHAMJE   [MAP 26: p201]

Syanje (1100m/3609ft)

The lodges in Syanje ('Sigh-ang-ee') lie across the big suspension bridge.
The **New Thakuri Guest House** has an attractive sitting area right above
the river. They serve good daal bhat as well as reasonable tourist food
(pizza, fried noodles with tuna, and vegetable momos).

Following the river and climbing gently you pass healthy marijuana
plants to reach the Tibetan-run **Hotel New Asia** in about 20 minutes.
Across the river are some hot springs, just some of the many that can be
found along this valley. Since most hot springs are close to the river
they're often submerged during the monsoon season.

It's the climb gets steeper you can see Jagat on the ridge above.

Jagat (1300m/4265ft)

The heavy boulders strewn about the lower part of this little settlement
give it a somewhat claustrophobic air. There's a good range of accommodation, however. At the northern end of Jagat, the **Sushma Guest
House** is very pleasant and the **Manaslu Lodge** also good. There are
some hot springs about 20 minutes away, down by the river.

Chamje (1430m/4692ft)

Just south of Chamje is the **Tibetan Lodge**, decorated with prayer flags.
It's now been going for 20 years and seems to get better every year. The
lodge is clean, comfortable and run by very friendly people. The other
places in Chamje can be less busy in the season, though, and the lodge-
owners are most welcoming.

Cross the long suspension bridge and climb through more fields of marijuana past the teahouse at Satele. The wide valley has now become a narrow gorge with the river thundering through it. There are steep drops
beside the path in some places.

It's a long hot climb up to the wide valley of Tal, a welcome sight just
around the corner from the little teahouse at the top. This is the district

---

One of the most popular songs in the country is the *Song of the Marsyandi* which is
frequently broadcast on Radio Nepal. Every Nepali knows not only the chorus
(below) but many of the verses and if you start them off they'll probably sing the
whole thing to you: *Paanko paat* (Pan leaf),
                        Maiya-lu-lai samjaanchhu (I remember my love),
                        Dinko rat (Night and day),
                        Marsyandi sa-la-la (The Marsyandi flows).
It's a great way to starting communicating and it puts everyone at their ease.
Tara Winterton (Nepal)

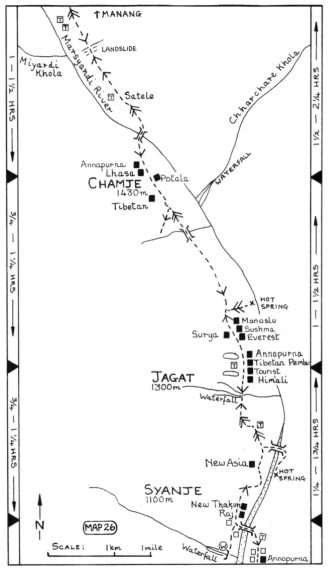

↑MANANG

Miyardi Khola

Marsyandi River

LANDSLIDE

Satele

Chharchare Khola

WATERFALL

Annapurna
Lhasa
CHAMJE
1430m
Pokala
Tibetan

HOT SPRING

Manaslu
Surya
Sushma
Everest

Annapurna
Tibetan Pembu
JAGAT
1300m
Tourist
Himali

Waterfall

New Asia

HOT SPRING

SYANJE
1100m
New Thakuri
Raj

N

MAP 26

Waterfall

Annapurna

SCALE: 1km   1mile

1 — 1½ HRS
¾ — 1¼ HRS
¾ — 1¼ HRS

1½ — 2¼ HRS
1 — 1½ HRS
1¼ — 1¾ HRS

border with Manang and it's not just an administrative boundary. From the point of view of culture, architecture and climate, the differences across from Lamjung district are striking: the people are Buddhists of Tibetan ancestry; mud and thatch houses give way to stone buildings with flat roofs; the rainfall is considerably lower in these northern regions and subtropical vegetation starts to give way to the firs and pine trees of the highlands.

TAL TO BAGARCHAP   [MAP 27: p203]

Tal (1700m/5577ft)

It's been said that this small town is reminiscent of the American Wild West and I guess you could imagine horses being tied up outside the shops and hotels along the wide dusty main drag. The name Tal means 'lake', since the whole of this wide valley was once a lake. Just north of the village is a spectacular **waterfall** that makes a refreshing but powerful shower.

It's well worth spending a night in Tal. There are several lodges including the atmospheric **Manaslu Guest House** run by a jolly Gurung woman. For years she's been dishing up her excellent and nutritious 'Potatoes, Beans, Veg, Pumpkin Special' (Rs40) with corn bread (Rs20). There's also Tibetan bread with cheese, and apple pie. Disregard the sign outside that promises, 'Fosters on tap'. The new **Paradise Guest House** is well-located near the waterfall at the northern end of Tal.

There's an **ACAP information centre**, a **kerosene depot**, and a surprisingly well-stocked **health post** (iodine, tiniba for giardia, paracetamol and penicillin). According to the health officer here the most common health problems in the area are worms, scabies and skin problems, toothache and conjunctivitis (caused by smoky houses). A **phone office** should be opening in Tal in 1996.

Opposite the Manaslu Guest House is a small **gift shop** whose owner will probably find you soon enough.

Leaving Tal you reach a **mani wall** in the middle of the path. You should always walk to the left of Buddhist shrines and monuments.

Gyasumdo
Although you're now in Manang District, this southern region, Gyasumdo, is culturally distinct from the area around Manang town. Manang District is an administrative unit, comprising three cultural groupings: Gyasumdo, Nyeshang (Manang Valley) and Narphu (in the east).

Gyasumdo means 'meeting-place of the three roads', since it is centred on Thonje. Three routes converge on Thonje: the route to Manang Valley, the route from Tal and the route to Tibet over the Gya La.

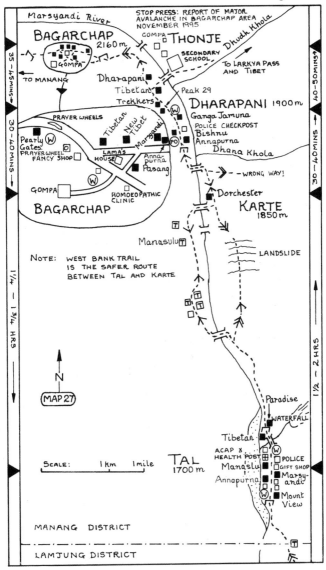

STOP PRESS: REPORT OF MAJOR
AVALANCHE IN BAGARCHAP AREA
NOVEMBER 1995

Marsyandi River

BAGARCHAP 2160 m

GOMPA

TO MANANG

GOMPA THONJE

Dhudh Khola

SECONDARY SCHOOL

TO LARKYA PASS AND TIBET

Dharapani

Tibetan
Trekkers

Peak 29

DHARAPANI 1900 m

Ganga Jamuna

POLICE CHECKPOST

Bishnu

Annapurna

Dhana Khola

PRAYER WHEELS

Pearly Gates

PRAYER WHEEL FANCY SHOP

Tibetan New Tibet

Marsyandi

LAMA'S HOUSE

Annapurna

Pasang

HOMOEOPATHIC CLINIC

GOMPA

BAGARCHAP

WRONG WAY!

Dorchester

KARTE 1850 m

Manasulu

LANDSLIDE

NOTE: WEST BANK TRAIL
IS THE SAFER ROUTE
BETWEEN TAL AND KARTE

N

MAP 27

SCALE: 1 km   1 mile

TAL 1700 m

Paradise

WATERFALL

Tibetan

ACAP &
HEALTH POST

Manaslu

Annapurna

POLICE

GIFT SHOP

Marsyandi

Mount View

MANANG DISTRICT

LAMJUNG DISTRICT

35 – 45 MINS →

30 – 40 MINS →

1¼ – 1¾ HRS

40 – 50 MINS?

30 – 40 MINS →

1½ – 2 HRS

Pass the fields of maize, barley and potatoes and the valley soon narrows again. Cross to the west bank of the river to avoid the landslide, then back again to Karte.

Karte (1850m/6070ft) This is really just one lodge, the **Dorchester**. The lodge owner has a leaflet giving the price of a night at the Dorchester as over £100 per person and a menu that promises whole Scottish lobster for £40 – from the London branch of this reputable chain, that is! This one's much cheaper, far better located and run by a friendly family.

Dharapani (1900m/6234ft) The village is approached through stone gateways, characteristic of all villages in Manang. Across the narrow gorge loom high cliffs. The Manaslu Circuit follows the valley opposite, across the bridge to Thonje and up the Dhudh Khola to the Larkya La (5210m/17,093ft). Tibet is beyond (about 50km from Thonje) over the Gya La, which is still used as a trading route although not as busy now as in 1950, when Tilman was here. He noted 'long strings' of dzos (cross-bred yaks) ferrying grain and rice up the valley and Tibetan salt down it.

You'll need to sign the register at the **police checkpoint**. Just north of the village are two new hotels, **Peak 29** and the **Trekkers' Hotel**, which both look good.

The route to Manang continues ahead. Up until now you've been travelling roughly north but the trail now swings due west.

Bagarchap (2160m/7087ft)

Surrounded by orchards of peach and apple trees, and with small streams running through it, this delightful village is a bit like Marpha in the Kali Gandaki Valley. Although only a short morning's walk from Tal, spending the night here is highly recommended (but see Stop Press below).

Water power is big in Bagarchap and whether it's to turn the flour mill, drive the prayer wheel or even flush the loo, water's been harnessed to do it. Whilst most of these are ecologically commendable, latrines built across streams pollute the Marsyandi.

Tibetan influences in the area are obvious: there are stone houses with firewood stacked on their flat roofs and above the village is the first *gompa* (Buddhist monastery and temple) you see on this trail. Known as **Diki Kalsang Gompa**, it was accidentally burnt down in December 1994 but has just been rebuilt.

Stop press
In November 1995 there were reports in the international press of a devastating landslide which hit Bagarchap flattening 17 houses and killing several people, some trekkers among them. It's difficult to say how much of the village will have been rebuilt by the time you read this or even whether it may have been relocated.

Accommodation There's good accommodation here. The **Tibetan** is a nice clean place with an excellent reputation, and the **Annapurna** and **Marsyandi** also look good. One tasty filling dish that seems to have been taken up by all the lodges in the area is 'hash brown and omlette and cheese in two chapattis'. Many of the lodges serve pizza and apple pie and the **Pearly Gates** has been promising 'heavenly food and lodging' for many years.

The **Pasang Guest House** is a homely place run by a very friendly and interesting family who speak excellent English. Their pumpkin soup is delicious. From the rooms upstairs views of Annapurna II and Lamjung can be seen.

A big **new hotel** is being built on the western edge of the village.

DANAGYU TO CHAME   [MAP 28: p206]

The route continues through **Danagyu (2300m/7546ft)** and forests of pine and fir. A considerable amount of work has gone into building this part of the trail. Previously, the only way into the Manang Valley from the south was over the 5785m/18,980ft Namun La along a now rarely-used route that runs from Khuldi to Danagyu.

Crossing a concrete bridge you pass a powerful waterfall, inhabited, according to local legend, by a water demon. Just after the steep stairway that follows the narrow gorge there's a junction for the alternative high route to Koto Qupar. Take the lower route via Latamrang which is easier to follow. Hung with lichen, the trees around this area include maple, oak and rhododendron. The most impressive rhododendron forests in the Annapurna region, however, are north of Pokhara around Ghorepani.

Latamrang (2400m/7874ft) There are a few small lodges here. The **Tatopani Lodge** is run by an ex-Gurkha. If the bridge across the river is not down you can reach the small hot spring on the other side.

The apple orchards of **Tanchok** (just a small tea-house) give way to impressive forests of pine, with some yew and larches dotted around. There have been several landslides in this area recently.

Koto Qupar (2600m/8530ft) The lodges are in two groups, some by the entrance gate and the others just before the **police checkpost** which guards two routes. The side trail across the bridge leads through the narrow Nar Valley to the two high altitude villages of Nar and Phu. This trail connects with a route that crosses into Tibet over the 6260m/20,538ft Lugu La Bhanjyang. The people of Nar-Phu are of Tibetan descent and although their remote region is administered as part of Manang district, their culture and language are unique. Sign the book at the checkpost and continue ahead for Manang.

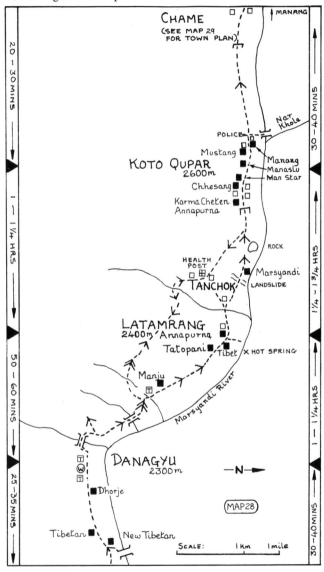

CHAME TO PISANG   [MAPS 29 & 30: p209, p211]

Chame (2670m/8760ft)

A large white gate with a corrugated iron roof marks the entrance to Chame ('Char-may'). It's the district headquarters of Manang and has all the trappings of an administrative centre, including electricity, a phone office and well-stocked shops.

Keep Chame Clean' says a notice but the place isn't exactly spotless; Tilman commented on its filthiness, passing through in 1950. For trekkers, Chame has just two attractions: the bank and the hot springs.

Accommodation The best place here is the **New Tibetan Hotel and Lodge**, away from the main part of the town in a wonderful riverside location, right by the hot springs. This makes it very crowded at the height of the season. The food is quite good though also quite expensive but the sunny terrace, with flowerbeds of pink and white cosmos, is a wonderful place for breakfast. Just beside the New Tibetan Hotel an even newer hotel should now be open, confusingly named the **Tibet Hotel**.

At the other end of town, the **Trekkers' Holiday Hotel** is clean, well run and popular.

Hot springs After a hard day's trekking there's nothing better than to soak your aching limbs in near boiling mineral water. A small pool has been built by the springs just accommodating two people in the shallow water. Take care not to pollute either the hot spring or the river with soap or shampoo; virtually impossible unless you borrow a bowl from your lodge. Don't skinny dip (wear a swimming costume) and don't soak your feet too long as it softens the skin and you'll be more susceptible to blisters.

Other services The **bank** is not the fastest of the subcontinent's financial institutions so allow up to an hour for a transaction. It's open Sunday to Thursday from 10.00 to 14.00 and on Friday from 10.00 to 12.00. When things are busy they may stay open a little longer. For travellers' cheques there's a service charge of Rs 30 and a commission of 0.5%. For cash there's a commission of 1% but no service charge. If you haven't brought your passport with you a trekking permit will suffice as ID.

There's also an efficiently-run **post office** and a **phone office** where international calls can be made. There's a good **health post** staffed by a doctor (most health posts are run by a health assistant) and basic medicines can be bought here. There are also a couple of **tailors**' where you can have trekking trousers made up, and several other well-stocked **shops**. You can even buy suncream and film here.

The town has a 45kW micro hydro-electric system, built in 1980, which operates between 18.00 and 23.00.

The trail to Manang continues along the river through **Keleku** to **Bhratang** (2850m/9350ft) which is surrounded by apple orchards and has a number of lodges. Here, as in other villages in the area, pine needles are strewn across the trail so that they are broken down into compost by the boots and hooves of passing traffic.

Across the river is **old Bhratang** which was a Tibetan refugee village. The people were mainly Khampas, notorious for being raiders and warriors, but they were resettled in the mid 1970s. Carved on a rock near the ruins of their village is a memorial to Japanese mountaineer, Akira Ochiai, who died near the Thorung La in 1979.

Between Bhratang and the bridge over the Marsyandi is an impressive section of the trail, blasted out of solid rock. As you approach this bridge **Paungda Danda**, a magnificent cliff of granite, looms up ahead like a gigantic wave. Across the suspension bridge you climb through the peaceful forest and in under an hour you emerge in the wide Manang Valley, another world indeed. There's been a lot of hotel building in recent years. You'll pass a new blue lodge in a peaceful spot near a pool.

Nyeshang

The area in Manang District that is known as Nyeshang extends up the Manang Valley from Pisang to Khangsar.

The main villages in Nyeshang are Manang, Braga and Ngawal, known as Manang-tsok-sum ('three communities'). In recent history, however, they don't appear to have had very close links, in spite of speaking the same language. David Snellgrove noted when he visited the area in 1956 that the people of Manang and Braga had only just made peace with each other after five years of war. Tilman remarked that Ngawal had close relations with Nar village, over a 5322m/17460ft pass in the culturally different Nar-phu region.

The people are of Tibetan origin but their language, Nyeshang, is not a Tibetan dialect. Whilst some can afford to travel, trade and run lodges for trekkers, most eke out a meagre living from buckwheat and potatoes, subsisting on a diet of buckwheat tsampa and Tibetan tea.

Tilman, among the first Western travellers in Nyeshang, was amazed when 'a man whom we attempted to photograph retorted by whipping out a camera himself' (*Nepal Himalaya*). Even in the 1950s, however, some of the men here were almost as well-travelled as the great mountaineer. From 1790, throughout the time when Nepal was operating a policy of isolationism, the people of Nyeshang were given special permission to travel abroad by the king. Snellgrove reported that some of the temples in the area were hung with Chinese silks from Singapore.

Contact with the world beyond Nyeshang seems to have had only negative effects upon the people. Snellgrove noted that they had lost their zeal for religion; the important gompa at Bodzo having been deserted and others very run down. The writings of Tilman, Snellgrove and Maurice Herzog are unanimous in branding the people as the least friendly, most parsimonious and amongst the dirtiest they met in their travels in this part of the Himalaya. Forty years on things seem to have greatly improved; lodge-owners are friendly and their kitchens, although unlikely to win any awards for cleanliness, are no worse than others this side of the Kali Gandaki.

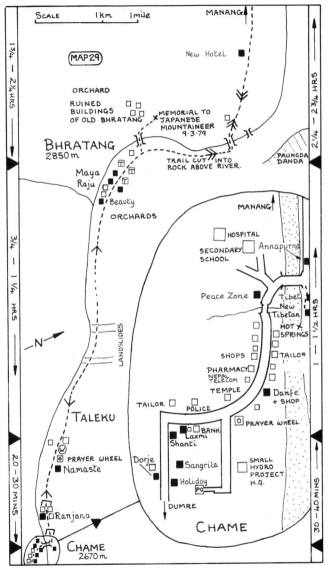

SCALE   1km   1mile

MAP 29

13/4 — 2½ HRS

MANANG

New Hotel

ORCHARD
RUINED
BUILDINGS
OF OLD BHRATANG

MEMORIAL TO
JAPANESE
MOUNTAINEER
9·3·79

BHRATANG
2850m

TRAIL CUT INTO
ROCK ABOVE RIVER.

PAUNGDA
DANDA

Maya
Raju

Beauty

ORCHARDS

MANANG

HOSPITAL

SECONDARY
SCHOOL

Annapurna

3/4 — 1¼ HRS

Peace Zone

Tibet
New
Tibetan

HOT
SPRINGS

LANDSLIDES

SHOPS

TAILOR

2¼ — 2¾ HRS

1 — 1½ HRS

—N—

PHARMACY
NEPAL
TELECOM

TEMPLE

Danfe
+ SHOP

TALEKU

TAILOR

POLICE

PRAYER WHEEL

PRAYER WHEEL

Namaste

Dorje

Laxmi
Shanti

BANK

SMALL
HYDRO
PROJECT
H.Q.

2.0 – 30 MINS

Sangrila

Holiday

PO

Ranjana

DUMRE

30 – 40 MINS

CHAME

CHAME
2670m

Pisang (3200-3300m/10,500-10,827ft)

There are numerous lodges strung out along the trail in **Lower Pisang**. First is the new swish **Swiss Hotel**, which does look a bit like an Alpine chalet. In Pisang, the **Hotel Maya** has had a good reputation for many years for producing excellent meals. Potatoes feature prominently on all menus in the Manang Valley. They're tasty local varieties that are delicious boiled in their skins.

Although the lodges in **Upper Pisang** are rather more basic than the ones below it's well worth spending the night up here and the climb is not as bad as it looks. The lodges are small, just a room or two in someone's house. Little has changed here in centuries and the place has a positively mediaeval atmosphere to it. Living quarters are upstairs in the houses, reached from the stables below by a ladder carved from a single tree trunk. The mountain scenery is superb. Across the valley Annapurna II looks close enough to touch. Pisang Peak rises behind you.

Watch out for flying arrows in the middle of the village. The area near the prayer wheel wall is used for archery practice, still a popular sport in many of these high villages. The **temple** above the village, containing a terracotta statue of Maitreya (the future Buddha), is not often used.

Low route or high route to Manang?

The quickest and easiest way to reach Manang is along the low route via Ongre. Walking fairly fast you could make the journey in under three hours along a trail that, apart from the climb to the viewpoint, is fairly level.

The extra effort and time involved in taking the high route is more than worthwhile: the views from this route are some of the best on the whole trek and combine with the altitude (you climb about 500m/1640ft above Lower Pisang) to really take your breath away. 'Climb high, sleep low' is part of the advice given to guard against altitude sickness (see p242) so taking the high route will help you acclimatise better than following the low one. The high route is also far more interesting, passing through the ancient villages of Ghyaru and Ngawal and past the ruins of an old fort.

PISANG TO MANANG – THE HIGH ROUTE   [MAPS 30-31]

From Upper Pisang the route roughly follows the contours of the land until you reach a wall of prayer wheels and mani stones.

The trail is not clear up to here and there may be more obvious goat tracks leading steeply upwards along the way, which you should avoid. There's an alternative path from just over the bridge from Lower Pisang which passes a small green lake and takes you through thin forest.

Ghyaru (3670m/12,041ft) From the mani wall you descend to cross the tributary and then take the trail leading steeply uphill. After the hard climb of about 350m/1148ft to Ghyaru you won't have any difficulty in stopping to admire the tremendous views from here. The tallest mountain,

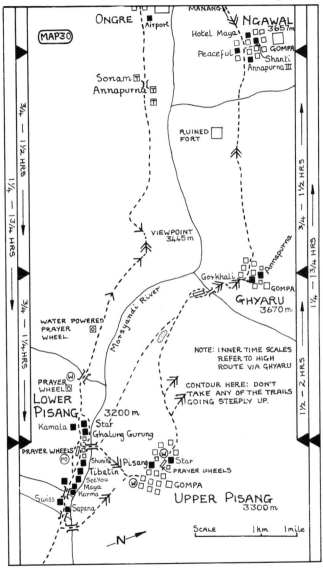

with the small pointed peak, is Annapurna II (7937m/26,040ft); you're looking at the impressive north face. To the left is Lamjung Himal (6931m/22,740ft) and to the right, above Manang, are Annapurna III (7555m/24,787ft) and Gangapurna (7455m/24,459ft). There's basic accommodation in Ghyaru which is lucky since you may be tempted to spend the rest of the day staring at the awe-inspiring scenery.

The temple is usually locked but the wall paintings are worth seeing if you can find someone to let you in. It was the only temple in the valley that the usually indefatigable Snellgrove was unable to gain access to during his Buddhist survey of the Manang Valley in 1956.

You're now above the tree-line and it can sometimes be windy and dusty up here. Five minutes outside Ghyaru you pass a white chorten containing a water-powered prayer wheel. There are also many mani walls on this route. The trail passes above the ruins of a fort and in 30 to 40 minutes after these you reach Ngawal.

Ngawal/Bangpa (3657m/11,998ft)
This is another mediaeval village like Ghyaru, with flat-roofed stone buildings and ladders to reach the living quarters above the stables. The views across the valley to the Annapurnas are as impressive as from Ghyaru. The trekking peaks, Chulu West (6419m/21,060ft) and Chulu East (6584m/21,601ft), rise to the north.

Snellgrove spent a few nights here in 1955. He was disappointed by the temple ('nothing but a few rough clay images') and not warmly disposed towards the locals, one of whom stole his torch, the first theft in several months of travel.

There's at least one basic place to stay but don't expect to have deep and meaningful conversations with the village people even if you speak Nepali. They speak Nyeshang and their English is limited to a cheerful 'Tea yes? Sleep yes?!'

From Ngawal the trail drops steeply, sometimes following the electricity wires and bypassing Paugba to join the lower Pisang-Manang route at **Mungji**.

PISANG TO MANANG – THE LOW ROUTE   [MAPS 30-31]

Follow the trail through Lower Pisang for the low route to Manang. It's a pleasant walk through the forest, climbing gently at first, with one steep section to reach the **viewpoint** on top of the spur. There are tall prayer flags and a small shrine here. Continue down to the wide level valley passing a number of teahouses. The **Sonam Hotel** has good vegetarian food and even a curio shop. The manager also dabbles in patent medicines prescribing dubious-looking powders as a cure-all.

Ongre/Humde (3330m/10,925ft)

This consists of **Manang airstrip** and a few houses and lodges in a small but spread-out settlement. One of the longest prayer wheel walls in the region, consisting of 266 wheels, runs through the centre of the village. At the western end of the airstrip is a **police checkpost**.

Except during the monsoon and when there's snow between December and February, Royal Nepal Airlines have flights between Pokhara and Manang airstrip for US$50 on Tuesday, Wednesday, Saturday and Sunday mornings. They have a **booking office** here. Note that these flights operate only when the flying conditions are good and so are liable to cancellation, like the Pokhara-Jomsom flights.

Continuing along the trail to Manang, you pass the **Nepal Mountaineering Association School**, founded in 1979 by Ales Kunaver, the Yugoslav alpinist, who died in 1984. Above it is the micro hydroelectric plant serving Ongre and Manang. Power demands are outstripping supply so electricity is switched between the two villages on alternate nights, when it's working at all, that is.

Crossing the Marsyandi just before Munji, you join the high trail from Ghyaru and Ngawal.

Braga/Drakar (3450m/11,319ft)

The flat-roofed houses of this photogenic village are built in steep tiers against the craggy cliffs that form a natural amphitheatre around the meadow below. Above them is the region's oldest and most interesting gompa, a complex of several buildings with the three-storeyed temple at the top.

There's only one lodge here, the comfortable **New Yak Hotel**, right by the trail and well run by a friendly lodge-owner. It's a good place to stay but since Manang is only about half an hour beyond most trekkers stay there and return to Braga the following day to see the gompa.

A sign on a building near the trail warns, 'Here siting, burn fire, cooking rice, dirty do is strictly prohibited'. The language may be quaint but the message is nonetheless important.

Braga Gompa Believed to be at least 500 years old, this gompa comprises three main buildings and belongs to the reformist Kagyupa sect of Tibetan Buddhism. Kagyu-pa was inspired by the monk Marpa who, in the 11th century, sought to make Tibetan Buddhism more spiritual.

The **main temple** is dark, mysterious and powerfully atmospheric. Come up here early in the morning or late in the afternoon when the monks are worshipping and the building is filled with the fragrance of burning juniper. You enter the main sanctuary past two prayer wheels and a dingy hall, leaving your boots outside. One of the main features of this temple is the hundred or so terracotta images that line the walls and include the 39 figures of the Kagyu-pa hierarchy including Marpa and Milarepa, his disciple. The altar is an amazing jumble of butter lamps, vases of plastic flowers, masks, tinsel and photos of the Dalai Lama. Leave a donation in the big brown safe, labelled 'Donttion Box'.

The three-storeyed temple is known as the **Chorten**. The middle room is entered round the back and contains a statue of Avalokitesvara. Believed to be saviour and protector from danger he's also the ultimate in altruism, having rejected the state of nirvana when he reached it because so few other mortals had attained that stage. Above this room is another small shrine with an image of Amitabha, ('Boundless Light'); you'll need a torch as it's very dark; below is a shrine with numerous wall paintings and a large statue of Maitreya, the future Buddha whose return to earth is expected around the year 3520 AD, 4000 years after the death of the last Buddha.

Between the Chorten and the main temple is another shrine, containing several images including Mahakala and Ma-ning.

Braga Gompa is open from 7 am to 10 am and 1 pm to 5 pm.

Bodzo Gompa is the most interesting of the other temples between Braga and Manang but you'll need to find someone to let you in. Perched on a rocky ridge it contains fine wall-paintings and was once the centre of a large community of monks.

Manang (3540m/11,614ft)
Most trekkers make this, the largest village in the valley, a base for at least a couple of nights, while they acclimatise (see p for some acclimatisation trips). The views of the Annapurnas, Gangapurna and the glacial lake below it are spectacular; even more so if you climb north above Manang. From left to right the peaks are Lamjung, Annapurna II, Annapurna IV, the false peak of Annapurna III and Gangapurna above the glacier.

The cost of a bed in and above Manang has now been pegged at Rs100 for a double room and Rs30 for a bed in a dorm, relatively high for trekking routes in Nepal. It is hoped that this doesn't encourage trekkers to hurry over the Thorung La before they are fully acclimatised. If you're travelling on a very tight budget spend a few nights in the villages of Ngawal and Ghyaru where a bed costs just a few rupees.

In Manang, the 200 or so flat-roofed houses are tightly packed together with prayer flags on long poles above them. Most of the lodges are beside fields to the south. There are several well-stocked shops (most attached to the lodges) and the wide range of goods on offer includes canned beer, cans of tuna, chocolate, cream crackers, woollen hats and gloves. You can pick up porters here, or even a horse to help you over the Thorung La – for around Rs1500!

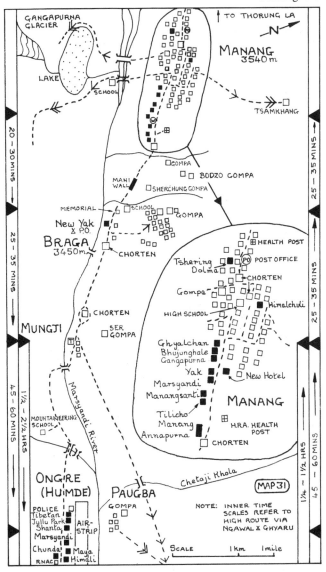

Acclimatisation trips around Manang

You must spend a minimum of two nights at around this altitude (3540m/11,614ft) in order to acclimatise before moving on to sleep safely at a higher altitude. Climbing high and sleeping low is the best advice so rather than sitting in a lodge in Manang eating apple pie, you should visit some of the following:

• **Braga Gompa** (see p213). You could also visit Bodzo Gompa, Sherchung Gompa and, above Mungji, Ser Gompa.

• **Tsamkhang** Halfway up the northern cliff that rises above Manang, in a cave, is a *tsamkhang* (hermitage) where a lama conducts a short puja on trekkers about to cross the Thorung La. He'll say a prayer for you and tie a piece of red ribbon around your neck for good luck. Blessing times are 10-11am and 4-6pm.

Even without the puja, the steep climb up here will help you to acclimatise and the views across the valley are stupendous. This tsamkhang is also known as Praban Gompa and Manang Vijek Gompa.

• **Gangapurna glacier** Across the river from Manang there are a couple of walks around the lake below this glacier.

• **Khangsar** A 1½-2 hour walk from Manang brings you to this undeveloped village surrounded by terraced fields. There are superb views up the Khangsar Khola to Tilicho Peak (7132m/23,399ft) and the Grande Barrière (so named by Herzog in 1950). There's a small plain temple in the village and beyond Khangsar is **Ta-hrap Gompa**, built by the lama of Braga several hundred years ago.

Side trip to Tilicho Lake

Maurice Herzog may have nipped up here from Manang alone with nothing more than a bar of chocolate but, having fallen in the river and spent the night in the open, he did almost die. You'll need a tent and supplies for the three-day return trip from Manang to this remote lake which lies at 4920m/16,142ft, below Tilicho Peak. It's a very tough climb over rough scree along a sometimes almost non-existent trail. A guide would be a good idea; ask in Khangsar. Buy supplies in Manang. In 1995 the trail to the lake was being improved and a lodge planned at the base of the first pass. If this has opened you could visit the lake as a side-trip without camping.

Routes Reach Khangsar in 1½-2 hours from Manang. There are two routes from here: the higher trail via the gompa from the far end of the village and the lower, easier route that descends to the river from the centre of the village. The lower route provides less acclimatisation and you should check with locals that the bridges are in place, and if not, you must take the high route.

The **lower route** follows the Khangsar Khola. Skirt around the lower part of the village and take the trail down to the river. Cross the river and follow it for 3-4 hours, then climb to join the higher trail, clearly visible above. Skirting round the ridge you come into an area of small streams and moraine debris. Eventually the well marked trail crosses a bridge and leads to a meadow which is the best place to camp. A lodge is under construction here.

The **higher route** follows the clear trail out of Khangsar, climbing as the valley narrows and then crossing large areas of scree. Watch out for falling rocks here. It's joined by the lower trail to reach the meadow: the first night's camp. Make an early start next day for the four hour climb. You begin by contouring round a couple of ridges before the hard climb up the moraine. After a series of zig-zags the route divides, although the cairned junction is easy to miss. Both trails are exposed but the path that continues straight up is the quicker if slightly higher route. From the small plateau at the top (5200m/17,060ft) there are views down to the lake. Herzog refers to it as the 'Great Ice Lake' since it was covered in a thick sheet of ice when he crossed it in May 1950.

It's possible to go down to the lake, over the Tilicho Pass (5099m/16,729ft; also known as Mesokanto Pass) and down to Thinigaun and Jomsom, along the route taken by Herzog. A high altitude army camp above Jomsom makes this route illegal, though, and, being difficult to follow, it could be very dangerous. It is, however, for trekking groups to obtain special permission for this crossing.

There's an **ACAP information centre** (a kerosene depot should be opening shortly) and a **post office** (open 10.00-16.00 Sunday to Thursday, 10.00-14.30 on Friday). Mail takes about seven days to reach Kathmandu. Testing the poste restante service here, I arrived to find my mail safely secured to the wall with nails.

Manang temple is in the centre of the town; the three presiding images in it are Padmasambhava ('Lotus Born'), Avalokitesvara ('Glancing Eye') and Amitabha ('Boundless Light'). Braga Gompa is, however, far more interesting and should not be missed. Nor, for your own safety, should you miss the daily lecture on AMS at the **Himalayan Rescue Association health post** (see below), if you didn't make it to one of their lectures in Kathmandu.

Accommodation Most trekkers go for the more luxurious lodge to the south of the main part of Manang. Most have large warm dining halls and varied menus including the usual trekking 'delicacies' such as chocolate cake, cinnamon rolls and apple pie. You should, however, try something of the local cuisine: buckwheat tsampa and Tibetan tea. Some lodges also make buckwheat bread; potato dishes are good, too and they all have their own specialities.

The **Yak Hotel**, open throughout the year, is very popular. The lodge has its own generator and shop. The kitchen turns out good food and excellent potato dishes; try the potato cheese balls (Rs30). The best food in Manang comes from the **Manangsangti Guest House** where Mavis Gurung, who comes from Calcutta, turns her hand to everything from Julienne salad to a curry and rice, all with excellent results.

HRA health post The Himalayan Rescue Association has done tremendous work in reducing the numbers of trekker-deaths from altitude sickness. During the trekking season this post is staffed by two foreign volunteer doctors. Their daily lectures, held each afternoon, on how to recognise the symptoms of altitude sickness and take appropriate action are both informative and entertaining. A Gamow Bag (see p243) is kept here for serious AMS cases. The general clinic is run for the benefit of the local people but the doctors are also happy to attend to foreigners for a small fee that goes towards running the HRA. They can do stool tests and sell basic medicines, including tiniba for giardia.

MANANG TO THORUNG LA [MAPS 32-33]

After spending a couple of nights at Manang (3540m/11,614ft) you should spend one more night between here and Thorung Phedi for acclimatisation.

Leaving Manang

Tengi (3650m/11,975ft) is reached in just half an hour. There are a couple of basic teahouses here. A hard climb follows to **Gunsang (3900m/12,795ft)** but the views back of Gangapurna and Annapurna III across the Manang Valley are a good enough excuse for frequent stops. In Gunsang there are three lodges some distance apart.

Beyond Gunsang you come to **Yak Kharka** which means 'yak pastures'. True to the name grazing yaks are to be seen around this area, and across the river on the mountainside. Take care in your efforts to photograph these shaggy creatures as they can be temperamental. There are several new lodges just north of here; the **Gangapurna** and **Thorung Peak** lodges look quite substantial.

Letdar (4200m/13,780ft)

Although under three hours from Thorung Phedi, this is the maximum altitude you should reach in one day from Manang. There's been considerable building activity here recently so the range of lodges should be better than the basic places that have been here for many years. ACAP has built a couple of latrines.

About an hour above Letdar is a new bridge over the Jhargeng Khola, at 4320m/14,173ft. The covered bridge that had been here for many years was swept away in 1991.

Thorung Phedi (4450m/14,600ft)

Literally 'the foot of the Thorung' this is just one very large lodge and a new smaller one below it. It's a bleak spot and can seem particularly grim if you're suffering from the altitude, as many people are. The place can get very busy, particularly if snow has closed the pass.

It's important to register at the **police checkpoint** on arrival. It's beside the Base Camp Lodge.

Thorung Base Camp Lodge, as the original hotel is now called, has undergone considerable improvements. In 1995 they were even building some rooms with attached bath (Rs350). All accommodation is expensive. A bed in one of the dorms is Rs60, doubles are Rs170 and triples are

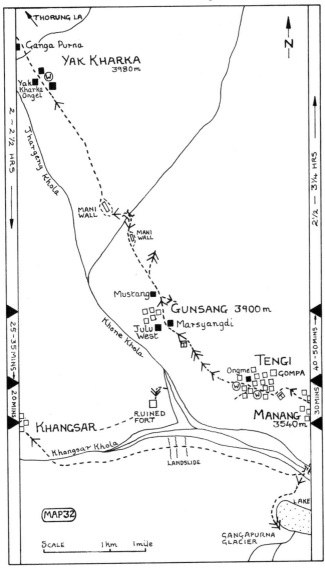

Rs240. Room heaters cost Rs60. Food is about 30% more expensive than in the best Manang lodges. Daal bhat is Rs70, porridge Rs45 and a Coke is Rs45, more than four times the price in Kathmandu or Pokhara. Everything does, of course, have to be lugged up here just for the benefit of the trekkers and they claim that their nearest source of firewood is Ongre, below Manang. The staff have a reputation for surly service, although I've always found them pleasant enough. The alternative is the smaller **Marsyandi Lodge** down by the river. Built around a small court-yard, it's not bad.

Most people have an early supper and retire to their sleeping bags to keep warm; it can be bitterly cold here.

Safety on the Thorung La

Although many thousands of people cross it each year, the Thorung La is a very high and potentially dangerous pass. Trek up here on a warm and sunny November day with many other trekkers for company and the route may seem innocent enough. If the weather turns or if there's snow on the ground the dangers of altitude are combined with exposure and can be lethal. Scarcely a year goes by without at least one fatality occurring here. Almost all of these could have been prevented.

For your own safety and for the safety of others, you must:

• **Be aware of the symptoms of altitude sickness** and know what to do about them (see p242). If you feel bad at Thorung Phedi, don't press on up but go down to Letdar or below for a night.

• **Don't attempt the pass in bad weather.** The route to the top is not a simple one; it meanders round valleys and over moraines, although it's clear enough when there's no snow. If conditions don't look good, take advice from the lodge-owner at Thorung Phedi before setting out.

• **Walk in a group of at least five people** and keep together even if the weather is good and you're all feeling fine when you set off. Rik Allen, whose grave you pass near the top of the Thorung La, was travelling with only two other people. When he and the other man developed serious AMS, their companion was only able to help one of them.

• **Be properly equipped for the cold** Ensure that everyone in your group (including your porters, if you have them) has proper footwear, warm hats, gloves and jackets. Although many trekkers now cross the pass in track shoes rather than boots, their chances of getting frostbite which could lead to the amputation of toes is significantly higher than those wearing boots, if the weather turns bad.

Leaving Phedi

You should aim to leave next morning at around 06.00, not much earlier as the steep track may be icy and dangerous in the dark. It'll probably take you around 4 hours to reach the top if the conditions are good and up to 4 1/2 hours to get from there to Muktinath. Allowing for stops totalling a couple of hours along the way, you should easily reach Muktinath by

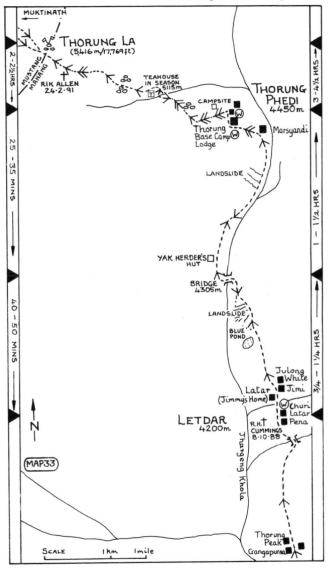

MAP33

SCALE   1 Km   1 mile

4.30pm. Make sure your water bottle is full and have as many cups of tea as you can manage before you leave. You'll acclimatise less well and feel more tired if you're dehydrated. Also, have sunscreen and a sunhat ready as it can be very hot on this exposed pass.

The route The trail begins with the ascent of the steep slope immediately behind the lodge. It's dishearteningly steep at first but becomes less so as you gain altitude. You pass many small cairns built by local travellers.

After about $1^1/4$ hours you cross a small valley, descending to the stream and climbing across the far slope. At 5115m/16,781ft, there's a little teashop open only during the season.

A seemingly never-ending series of false summits follow as the trail weaves through the stony moonscape. Tony and Jean Allen ask that passing trekkers check that the stones on their son's cairn are still in place. Marked with a headstone, it's in a gully just below the trail. Twenty minutes beyond is a large chorten and a short distance after this there are the prayer flags marking the top of the pass.

Thorung La (5416m/17,769ft)
It can be fairly breezy up here so most people stay just long enough to take the commemorative photograph of themselves on this elevated spot, one of the world's highest passes.

You're now standing on the equivalent of four Ben Nevises, $2^1/2$ Mt Kosciuskos, $1^1/2$ Mt Cooks and you're 938m/3077ft above the Matterhorn and 608m/1998ft higher than Mont Blanc! Unless you're a mountaineer you'll probably never reach as high an altitude in your life again.

Two peaks rise up from the saddle of the pass. To the north is Yakawa Kang (6482m/21,266ft) and to the south Khatung Kang (6488m/ 21,286ft). Far below you in the Kali Gandaki Valley you can just make out the fields of Kagbeni.

THORUNG LA TO MUKTINATH   [MAP 34: p223]

The descent
This can be very tough on the knees, although it's not steep at first. The views of the mountains lining the Kali Gandaki Valley are better from about halfway down this side than from the pass itself, particularly of Dhaulagiri (8167m/26,795ft), the world's seventh highest peak.

At about 4300m/14,108ft are the ruins of a yak herder's hut. It's now roofless but the walls offer some protection to campers. The trail continues steeply down from here, crossing a stream to another collection of huts. During the trekking season one of them, **Charbarbu**, is open as a lodge with basic accommodation. There's even a curio stall though most

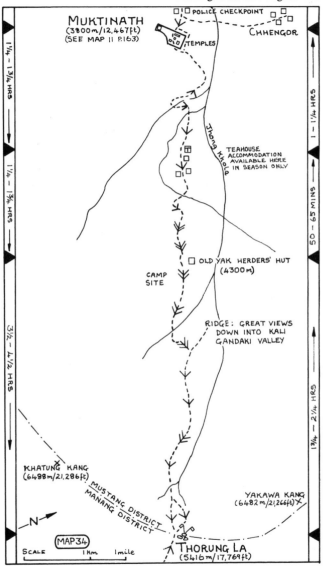

MUKTINATH
(3800m/12,467ft)
(SEE MAP 11 P.163)

POLICE CHECKPOINT

CHHENGOR

TEMPLES

Jhong Khola

TEAHOUSE
ACCOMMODATION
AVAILABLE HERE
IN SEASON ONLY

OLD YAK HERDERS' HUT
(4300m)

CAMP
SITE

RIDGE: GREAT VIEWS
DOWN INTO KALI
GANDAKI VALLEY

KHATUNG KANG
(6488m/21,286ft)

MUSTANG DISTRICT
MANANG DISTRICT

YAKAWA KANG
(6482m/21,266ft)

N

MAP 34

SCALE   1 Km   1 mile

THORUNG LA
(5416m/17,769ft)

1¼ – 1¾ HRS

1¼ – 1¾ HRS

3½ – 4½ HRS

1 – 1¼ HRS

50 – 65 MINS

1¾ – 2¼ HRS

people are more interested in resting their aching knees, attending to blisters and seeking liquid replenishment.

From here it's about an hour to the temples of **Muktinath**. The police checkpoint at **Ranipauwa** is a few minutes below where lodges and environmentally-friendly hot showers await you. Turn to p165 for the continuation of this trek.

▲ **Crossing the Thorung La in the opposite direction** Doing the Circuit in a clockwise direction is certainly harder but not impossible. Crossing this way in 1950, Tilman wrote, 'This climb of nearly 5,000ft nearly broke my heart', but then he was carrying a pack full of rocks, ammonites collected in Muktinath.

You can cut about 1½ hours off the climb by spending the night at **Charbarbu** (above) but it's open only during the trekking season. A very early start is essential and if you're setting out from Ranipauwa you should aim to leave soon after 4am. It can take up to eight hours to reach the top of the pass from Muktinath. Take note of the warnings for crossing the Thorung La on p220 and if you're feeling the effects of the altitude at all in Muktinath you must not attempt the crossing.

(Opposite) Top: Manang and the glacier below Gangapurna (7454m/24,455ft). **Bottom:** From the *tsamkhang* (hermitage) above Manang a lama dispenses blessings on travellers about to cross the Thorung La.

Gorkha to Besisahar

Few trekkers take this alternative route to Besisahar because it takes longer than the direct route from Dumre and because accommodation is only very basic. The route is through low-lying villages and rice fields and can be very hot early or late in the season and sweltering during the monsoon.

Meeting few other trekkers may, however, be an attraction, and you also avoid two-thirds of the dusty Dumre-Besisahar road. The spectacularly-situated fortified palace at Gorkha is well worth seeing. Including the bus trip from Kathmandu to Gorkha, this route will take three days, giving you time on the first afternoon to look round Gorkha.

Gorkha (1200m/3937ft)
Famous as the town from which the whole country was conquered in the 18th century, and also for giving its name to one of the world's most famous fighting forces (see p58), modern Gorkha looks just like any other bazaar in Nepal. But 250m/820ft above is an architectural gem, Gorkha Durbar, the fortified palace and temple of the kings of Gorkha. Originally built by Ram Shah in the early 17th century, it was expanded by Nepal's best-known king, Prithvi Narayan Shah, to commemorate his conquest and unification of the country in 1769.

You won't regret the half-hour slog up the hill to **Gorkha Durbar**. The views from the crenellated walls are superb and include Dhaulagiri and Manaslu to the north. In the western half of the palace is the Kali temple (so holy that only the King and the priests are allowed inside). The courtyard outside flows with the blood of sacrificed goats at Dasain (October) and Chaitra Dasain (late March). The palace living-quarters were in the eastern half of the complex. Guards forbid photography inside the main palace complex but you can take photos of the views and fine Newar carvings that decorate the eaves and windows.

Trails lead to the look-out posts of Upallokot and Tallokot. In the town is **Tallo Durbar**, an 18th century Newar-style building which is thought to have been used as the administrative headquarters. It's currently being restored and turned into a museum. The new statue of Prithvi Narayan Shah should now be in place in the park above the bus stand.

(Opposite) Top: From Thorung Phedi the trail up the Thorung La is not difficult to follow in good weather but if it snows or if the clouds come down conditions can become treacherous. (Photo James Powell). **Bottom:** Prayer flags and a cairn mark the Thorung La (5416m/17,769ft).

Accommodation The cleanest place to stay is the **Gorkha Lodging Centre**, in fact, just a few rooms that the pharmacy lets out. They charge Rs150 for a double or triple. The **Hotel Thakali** is a friendly place with doubles for Rs100; they do an excellent daal bhat here for Rs30. There's also good food at the **Rhododendron Hotel & Lodge**, and clean rooms for Rs100.

The **Hotel Gorkha Bisauni** is rather overpriced with attached doubles for Rs 300, Rs 200 without. There's also a dormitory for Rs 50 per bed. The hotel has a good restaurant, and you can make international calls from here.

The **Gorkha Hill Resort** (☎ 227929) is an upmarket hotel just off the road, 5km before you reach Gorkha. Rooms are US$30/40.

Other services The town is headquarters of Gorkha district and public services include a post office, bank, health post and a telecom office (open 07.00-19.00 daily) for international calls.

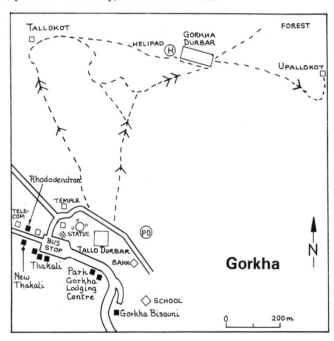

Buses Most buses leave early in the morning so you should check departure times the night before. There are several buses a day to Kathmandu (Rs50-75, six to seven hours) including a Sajha bus at 06.45 and 13.30 (tickets from the office beside Swagat Hotel). The bus to Pokhara (Rs45, five hours) leaves at 09.30 and there's sometimes a later bus, too. You can also get buses from here to Bhairawa/Sunauli (the border with Uttar Pradesh, India), Birgunj (the border with Bihar, India) and Bharatpur (on the Terai).

Get a direct bus if you want a seat. If you can't get a direct one you could take any bus from Gorkha to Anbu Khaireni (the junction with the Kathmandu-Pokhara road, 20km from Gorkha) and pick up another from there.

GORKHA TO CHEPE GHAT   [MAPS 35-36]

Allow ample time for the first section from Gorkha to Chorkate as the route down to the Daroundi Khola can be difficult to follow. Ask directions frequently. Do so, in fact, until you reach the Besisahar road, since you come to numerous tricky junctions along this route. A porter-guide as far as Chepe Ghat might be useful.

Leaving Gorkha
There are several trails down to the Daroundi Khola from Gorkha. For the most direct route, turn left before the temple and pass the barracks and the offices of the charity, Save the Children. The trail is fairly level to start with, then it loses height out of the town, eventually dropping steeply. Cross the Daroundi Khola on the big blue bridge at Jaleba. The alternative route to this will take you on a much longer jaunt to the north, crossing the river at Naya Sangu.

Chorkate is the first village you come to; nothing more than a couple of teashops. Cross the Busundi Khola a few minutes later and follow it upstream. After 20 minutes follow the left-hand valley and climb for a further 20 minutes to **Khoplang**, another small village. Descend and 30-40 minutes later you come to crossroads on a ridge. Continue ahead, not upwards to the left, and you reach the few houses that are **Putlikhet**.

Luitel Bhanjyang is on the crest of a low pass, though at 700m/2297ft it hardly deserves to be known as such. There's a teahouse and health post here. If you're feeling drained by the heat buy a packet of powdered glucose from the shop. Washed down with water it's a good source of instant energy.

Continue through rice fields. Beside the trail, you'll see the pink powder-puff flowers of the sensitive plant. Touch these small fern-like plants and the leaves instantly fold up.

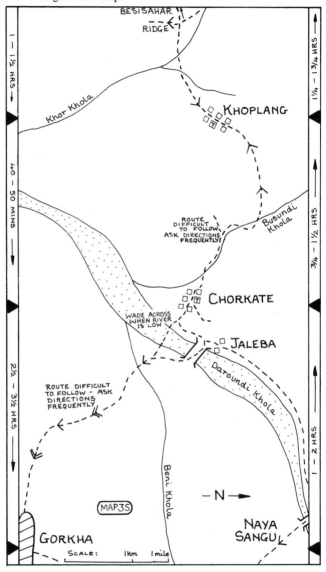

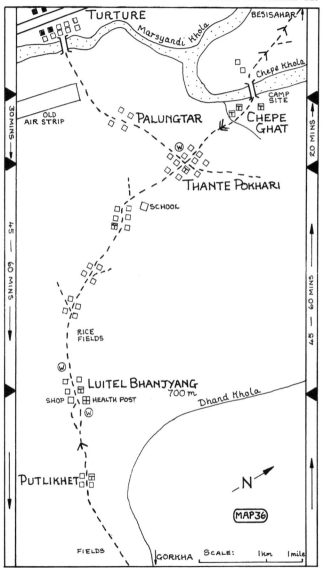

Thante Pokhari This is quite a large place with **post office** and bank but no exchange facilities. There's basic tea-house accommodation, although Chepe Ghat by the river is more pleasantly located. From here a path, passing the Palungtar airstrip that served Gorkha before the road reached it, leads you to Turture in about an hour. Turture is on the way to Besisahar but if you want to steer clear of the dusty road for as long as possible continue north through Chepe Ghat.

Chepe Ghat This small village is on the Chepe Khola, a tributary of the Marsyandi that forms the border between Gorkha and Lamjung districts. There are basic teahouses here where you can unroll your sleeping bag for the night and you can swim in the river by the bridge.

CHEPE GHAT TO TARKUGHAT   [MAPS 21-22: p192-3]

Ascend from Chepe Ghat and after 20 minutes you reach a small settlement amongst the mango groves. Continue along the level trail, high above the Chepe Khola, through the strung out village of **Damilikua**. After the village there are views down to the Marsyandi, the river you'll be following all the way to Manang. The trail drops steeply to the large village of **Tarku Ghat** where you cross the river to join the road to Besisahar. See p196 for the continuation of this route to Besisahar.

Pokhara to Khudi via Begnas Tal

Maps 37-41 This route is beginning to develop as an alternative to the not particularly pleasant Besisahar to Dumre road. The views are superb, excellent from the ridge between Nalma and Baglung Pani, but the climb up here is very tough – particularly if you're just starting your trek. The trail is not, however, always easy to find so you'll need to ask directions frequently or take a guide. Lodges are basic in comparison to those in the Kali Gandaki, and, since the first part of the trek is at low altitude, it can be very hot. The trek to Khudi will take 2-3 days, with the first night spent at Karputar and the second at Nalma or Baglung Pani. The best lodges on this trek are probably those at Nalma.

There are frequent buses for **Begnas Tal** from Pokhara. The route climbs above the lake, descends to just north of Rupa Tal and continues, sometimes following the new track, sometimes taking shortcuts. The first night is spent at **Karputar**, where the lodge by the bridge is reasonable. The route then follows the Midam Khola, climbs to **Nalma** and continues along the ridge to **Baglung Pani**. There's a steep climb down to the river which you follow past **Sera** to cross the Khudi Khola, joining the main trail up the Marsyandi at **Khudi** (see p197).

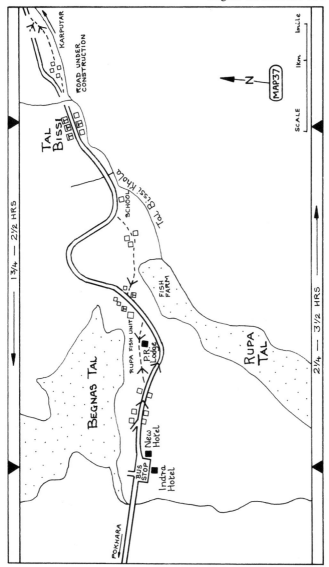

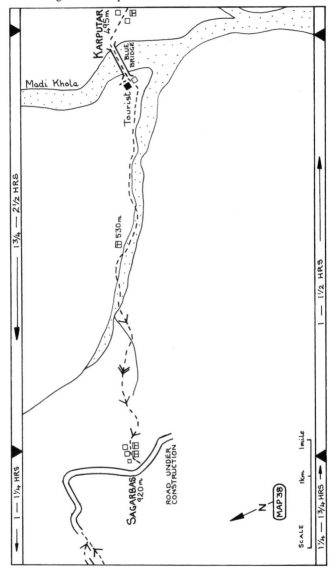

KARPUTAR 495 m.

BLUE BRIDGE

Madi Khola

Tourist

1¾ — 2½ HRS

⊞ 530 m.

1 — 1¼ HRS

1 — 1½ HRS

SAGARBAS 920 m.

ROAD UNDER CONSTRUCTION

N

MAP 38

SCALE 1km. 1mile

¼ — 1¾ HRS

1¼ HRS

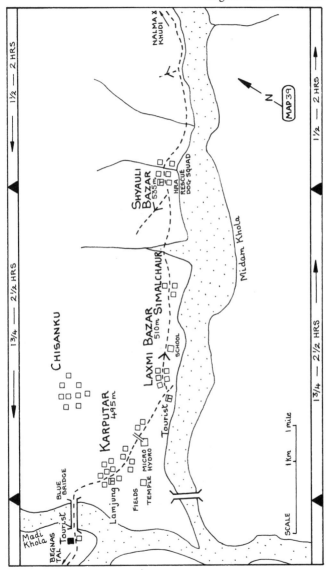

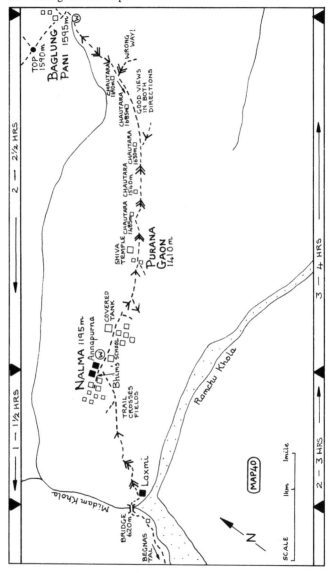

BAGLUNG PANI 1595m.
TOP 1590m.
WRONG WAY!
CHAUTARA 1140m.
CHAUTARA 1665m.
GOOD VIEWS IN BOTH DIRECTIONS
CHAUTARA 1630m.
CHAUTARA 1540m.
CHAUTARA 1485m.
SHIVA TEMPLE
PURANA GAON 1410m.
NALMA 1195m.
Annapurna
Bhlm5 SCHOOL
COVERED TANK
TRAIL CROSSES FIELDS
Laxmi
Midam Khola
BRIDGE 620m.
BEGNAS TAL
Ramchu Khola

1 — 1½ HRS   2 — 2½ HRS   3 — 4 HRS   2 — 3 HRS

MAP40

SCALE   1km   1mile

N

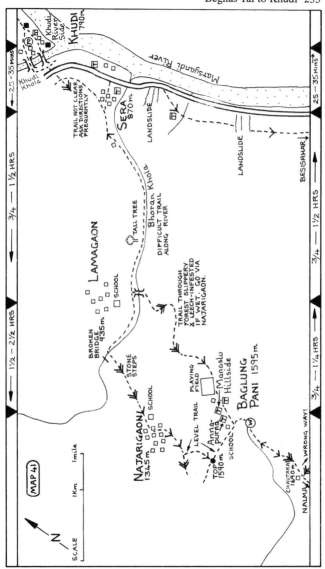

MAP 41

N

SCALE
1Km   1mile

KHUDI 790m
Khudi River Side
Khudi Khola

Marsyandi River

25 - 35 MINS
25 - 35 MINS

TRAIL NOT CLEAR, ASK DIRECTIONS FREQUENTLY

SERA 870m

LANDSLIDE

LANDSLIDE

LANDSLIDE

BESISAHAR

TALL TREE

Bhotan Khola

DIFFICULT TRAIL ALONG RIVER

3/4 — 1 1/2 HRS

LAMAGAON

SCHOOL

BROKEN BRIDGE 935m

STONE STEPS

TRAIL THROUGH FOREST, SLIPPERY & LEECH-INFESTED IF WET. GO VIA NAJARIGAON.

1 1/2 - 2 1/2 HRS

PLAYING FIELD

Manaslu Hillside

BAGLUNG PANI 1595m

SCHOOL

LEVEL TRAIL

NAJARIGAON 1345m

SCHOOL

Anna- purna

TOP 1510m

SCHOOL

3/4 — 1 1/4 HRS

CHAUTARA 1690m

NALMA — WRONG WAY!

3/4 — 1 1/2 HRS

APPENDIX A: NEPALESE EMBASSIES

Australia: Melbourne
Moncroft House
93 Rose St
Essendon, Vic 3040
(tel 09-337 0444)

Australia: Perth
Suite 2
16 Robinson St
Perth, WA 6009
(tel 386 2102)

Australia: Sydney
3rd Lvl, 441 Kent St
Sydney, NSW 2060
(tel 264 5909)

Belgium
21 Av. Champel B-1640
Rhode St Genese
(tel 02-358 5808)

Canada
Royal Bank Plaza
South Tower
Toronto
(tel 416-968 7252)

China
No 1 Sanleitaniliujie
(tel 532 1795)
Beijing
Norbulinka Rd 13
Lhasa, Tibet
(tel 36890)

Denmark
2 Teglgaardstraede
1452 Copenhagen
(tel 3124166)

Finland
Kaisaniemenkarul B a
00100 Helsinki
(tel 13 11 62 30)

France
45 bis rue des Acacais
75017 Paris
(tel 46 22 48 67)

Germany
Im Hag 15,
D-5300 Bonn
(tel 0228-343097)
Langerburgerstrasse
191, 8000 Munchen 21
(tel 089-570 4406)

India
1 Barakhamba Rd
New Delhi 110001
(tel 332 9969)

Italy
Piazzale Medaglia
d'Orro 20
Roma
(tel 06-348176)

Japan
14-9 Tokoroki
7-chome Setagaya-ku
Tokyo 158
(tel 3705 5558)

New Zealand
Lady Hillary
Hon Consul General
Auckland
(tel 09-520 3169)

Norway
Haakon VIIIs gt-5B
0116 Oslo
(tel 283 5510)

Sweden
Eriksbergsgatan 1A
S-11430 Stockholm
(tel 679 8039)

Switzerland
Asylstrasse 81
CH-8030 Zurich
(tel 475 993)

Thailand
189 Soi 71, Sukhumvit
Bangkok 10110
(tel 391 7240)

United Kingdom
12a Kensington
  Palace Gardens
London W8 4QU
(tel 0171-229 1594;
open 10.00-12.00,
Mon to Fri; a 30
day visa currently
costs £20)

USA: Atlanta
212 15th St NE
Atlanta GA 30309
(tel 404-892 8152)

USA: Chicago
1500 Lake Shore Dve
Chicago IL 60610
(tel 312-787 9199)

USA: Dallas
16250 Dallas Parkway
Suite 110, TX 75248
(tel 214-931 1212)

USA: Los Angeles
11661 San Vicente Blvd
Suite 510, CA 90049
(tel 310-420 4099)

USA: New York
247 W 87th St Apt 12G
NY 10024
(tel 212-874 2306)

USA: San Francisco
909 Montgomery St
CA 94133
(tel 415-434 1111)

USA: Tiffin
Heidelburg College
Tiffin OH 44883
(tel 419-448 2202)

USA: Washington
2131 Leroy Place
NW Washington
DC 20008
(tel 202-667 4550)

APPENDIX B: ITINERARIES

Suggested itineraries for the main treks in the region are given below to help you plan your trip. As has been stressed, a trek is not a route march to a rigid schedule; you should allow a few extra days so you can afford to be flexible.

These itineraries are based on a leisurely pace and to allow overnight stops in the more interesting villages. Walking more quickly you could easily reduce them by several days. See p242 for maximum recommended daily altitude gains.

Jomsom Trek

Day 01 Pokhara to Hille/Tirkhedunga (1540m)
02 Ghorepani (2750m)
03 Tatopani (1190m)
04 Ghasa/Kalopani (2010m/2530m)
05 Marpha (2670m)
06 Kagbeni (2800m)
07 Jharkot (3550m)
08 Muktinath (3800m)
09 Jomsom (2710m)
10 Tukuche/Khobang (2590m/2560m)
11 Kalopani/Ghasa (2530m/2010m)
12 Tatopani (1190m)
13 Ghorepani/Beni (2750m/830m)
14 Birethanti/Baglung (1050m/970m)
15 Pokhara (850m)

Annapurna Sanctuary

Day 01 Pokhara to Birethanti (1050m)
02 Ghandruk (1939m)
03 Chomrong (2050-2170m)
04 Bamboo (2400m)
05 Deurali (3200m)
06 Machhapuchhre Base Camp/Annapurna BC (3700m/4130m)
07 Dovan (2600m)
08 Chomrong (2050-2170m)
09 Landruk (1550m)
10 Dhampus/Pokhara (1650m/850m)

Annapurna Circuit

Day 01 Kathmandu - Dumre - Besisahar* (820m)
02 Bhulebhule/Ngadi (840m/930m)
03 Syanje (1100m)
04 Tal (1700m)
05 Bagarchap (2160m)
06 Chame (2670m)
07 Pisang (3200-3300m)
08 Manang (3540m)
09 Manang (3540m)
10 Letdar (4200m)
11 Thorung Phedi (4450m)
12 Muktinath (3800m)
13 Muktinath (3800m)
14-20 to Pokhara (see above)

* Add 2 days if walking from Dumre or Gorkha, add 3 days from Pokhara.

APPENDIX C: HEALTH

An illness may be caused by the planets. In such a case, it is useful to make a boat from the leaf of a sal tree and float it down the river. The boat should contain some barley, mas (black pulse), linseed and a lighted wick. If the boat is carried away by the current, rejoice, for the patient will soon recover. If it sinks or describes circles in the water, alas! there is little hope of recovery. **Kesar Lall** *Nepalese Customs and Manners*

REDUCING THE RISKS OF GETTING ILL

Trekkers, like other travellers in the Third World, seem to relish horror stories about the life-threatening diseases they might contract on the trail. Whilst Nepal does indeed have all the serious health problems of a very poor country, if you follow the guidelines below for reducing the risks the worst that you're likely to pick up is a mild bout of diarrhoea.

Before you arrive in Nepal
● Have all the required inoculations in good time (see p46).
● Check that your footwear is comfortable and will support your ankles. This is particularly important if you're doing a long trek such as the Annapurna Circuit.
● Ensure you're in good health at the start of your holiday. If you're tired and run-down at the beginning of your trek your resistance will be lowered.
● To reduce the effects of jet-lag, set your watch to Nepal time as soon as you board the plane, avoid alcohol but drink as much other liquid as possible, don't over-eat and try to get some sleep.

In Nepal
● Drink only purified water, bottled (Coke, Fanta etc) and hot drinks (tea, coffee, boiled milk, hot lemon).
● Eat only food that has just been cooked and is still hot or fruit you can peel yourself. And eat enough - as much carbohydrate and protein as you can manage. You'll burn it all off on the trail.
● Avoid ice-cream, salads and raw vegetables, and food from roadside stalls.
● If you're going to be trekking at altitude it is vital to follow the advice on acute mountain sickness (AMS or altitude sickness) given below.
● Take care of your feet, keeping them clean and dry. Stop and deal with a blister as soon as you feel it forming (see p243).
● Don't get knocked off the trail by a mule train or a yak. Stop on the mountain side of the path and let them pass.
● Slow down! Don't forget that this is a holiday not a competition to cover the routes faster than everyone else. Trekking before dawn (except where absolutely necessary) or after dark increases the risk of turning an ankle.
● In areas of increased natural danger (high passes, rarely-used routes) travel in a group of at least five people (see p220).

FIRST AID KIT

Some trekkers carry far too many pills and potions with them, including several potentially dangerous drugs they wouldn't know how to use if they got ill. Self-diagnosis can be very difficult and cases where trekkers have made themselves even more ill by taking the wrong drugs are not unknown. If you're trekking in a remote area a comprehensive medical kit could save a life. In the Annapurna region, however, there are health posts in many villages and they stock some medicines. For a basic first aid kit the following items should suffice:

- **Plasters/bandaids**
- **Moleskin** or **Second Skin** for treating blisters. In Britain Second Skin can usually be found at hiking/camping shops.
- **Bandage** for a sprained ankle or weak knee. An elasticated support (*Tubigrip*) may be useful if you are prone to knee or ankle problems.
- **Antiseptic cream** (eg *Savlon*)
- **Scissors/penknife**
- **Aspirin/paracetamol** for pain-relieving. Aspirin is also effective for reducing swelling.
- **Cough/throat lozenges** Sore throats are not uncommon. Lozenges containing anaesthetic (eg *Merocaine*) offer most relief.
- **Emergency Medical Kit** Also known as an 'Anti-Aids Kit', this contains sterilised syringes, needles and suture materials needed by a doctor in an emergency. They're now widely marketed in the West to travellers visiting Third World countries.
- **Oral rehydration solution** (*Dioralyte*) to replace salts and minerals lost through diarrhoea. *Jeevan Jal* is the Nepali equivalent.
- **Drugs** The two most useful drugs to take with you are all easily available in Nepal without a prescription. Buy six to eight tablets of **Tiniba** (also known as Tinidazole) for the treatment of giardia and either **Ciprofloxacin** (20 x 500mg) or **Norfloxacin** (12 x 400mg) as a general antibiotic.

HEALTH FACILITIES IN THE ANNAPURNA REGION

Along the main trails described in this book there are hospitals at Pokhara, Gorkha, Besisahar, Jomsom and Baglung as well as numerous small health posts in villages, as marked on the route maps.

During the main trekking season the Himalayan Rescue Associations operate a health post in Manang, staffed by Western volunteer doctors.

MOUNTAIN RESCUE

There are actually fewer emergency situations where a helicopter rescue is the best option than one might suppose. It can take many hours to reach a radio to get a message to the Royal Nepal Army who operate the rescue missions. The flight may be delayed if the weather is bad and will not even take off without an assurance of payment, since operational costs are more than US$600 per hour. Your embassy will usually be contacted and in turn will need to get in touch with your relatives. It is, therefore, vital to fill in a form giving trek details and the names of next of kin for your embassy in Kathmandu before you go trekking. The Himalayan Rescue Association (see p107) hold stocks of these forms.

If the patient could possibly be suffering from altitude sickness the most important thing is descent as fast as possible. Death could occur long before the arrival of the helicopter so carry the patient to a lower altitude without delay.

WATER PURIFICATION

The rule is simple: don't drink any liquid anywhere in Nepal that hasn't been purified. Beware also of innocent-looking streams high in the mountains since these may be polluted either by even higher human habitation or by animal faeces. Also be wary of restaurant signs that inform you that 'All Water is Filtered and Boiled'. If you haven't watched what you're about to drink being purified, don't drink it or even wash your teeth in it.

Staying healthy in Nepal is all about reducing the risks of getting ill. Using one of the methods below, it's not difficult to minimise the chances that you'll become ill from something you drink.

Boiling
Current research shows that water need be brought only to the boil (even at altitude) to kill the bugs in it. Given the shortage of firewood in the country and the large quantities of water that would need to be boiled up along the main routes to satisfy the needs of thirsty trekkers it's neither feasible nor ecologically sound to recommend this as a purification method. Tea, coffee, hot lemon and other drinks made from boiling water are, however, generally safe.

Filtering
You'll see large water filters in many of the hotels in Nepal and also in some of the lodges along the trails. These do nothing more than filter out some of the sediment in the water. They don't make it safe to drink. In some parts of the Annapurna region, however, the water has a high mica content so it's a good idea to fill your bottle from one of these filters before purifying it using one of the chemical methods described below.

A number of portable filters have come on the market over the last decade which also include a chemical purification stage in their filtration process. They may be effective but are expensive and heavy to carry.

Chemical purification
The most useful chemical for water purification is iodine. Chlorine based tablets (eg Puritabs), widely available in the West, are not recommended for use in Nepal unless combined with a fine filter since they're not effective against giardia and amoebic cysts.

Some people find the chemical taste of treated water reassuringly safe but if you don't like it, disguise it by adding vitamin C or fruit juice powders. These seem to be most refreshing when only small quantities are added.

● **Tincture of iodine** This is the method most widely used by trekkers for water purification. Since it's available in a range of concentrations you must know the strength in order to determine the quantity to use. Although it's available in Nepal, it's best to buy tincture of iodine in the West where you can be sure of the concentration. For a 2% solution, the dose is 5 drops per litre of clean water which must then stand for 20-30 minutes. If the water is cloudy double the dose. For a 10% solution use a fifth of the dose but wait for the same amount of time before drinking the water. You need a dropper to dispense the correct dose.

Wrap the bottle and dropper in more than one plastic bag. An iodine leak in the centre of a pack can be a very messy business.

● **Iodine tablets** There are a number of brands on the market in the West (eg Potable Aqua) but they're difficult to obtain in Nepal. One tablet purifies a litre of water in about ten minutes.

● **Iodine solution** Marketed as Polar Pure, iodine crystals are dissolved into a solution that is then added to your drinking water. Accidentally swallowing these crystals could kill you but a filter on the bottle prevents this happening.

DIARRHOEA
Diarrhoea seems to be one of the biggest fears amongst Westerners visiting a Third World country for the first time but it's important not to get things out of proportion. Few cases result in total loss of bowel control. If you get diarrhoea it will probably be several loose movements a day for just a few days.

Diarrhoea is caused by drinking or eating something contaminated by human faeces. The potential for contamination of this kind in a poor country like Nepal is great but you can significantly reduce the risk by ensuring that everything you drink is either boiled or purified and that all food is freshly cooked. Stick to fruit that can be peeled. Wash your hands frequently.

In their desire to regain control over their bowels Westerners are all too keen to take something. There are, however, several different causes for the intestinal infections that cause diarrhoea, making diagnosis difficult. Very often, the diarrhoea will clear up on its own in a few days. Avoid preparations like Imodium or Lomotil (except for long bus journeys) since these merely paralyse the bowel and are not a cure for the infection.

If the diarrhoea does not clear up by itself the most reliable method of diagnosis for its cause is a stool test. Since you may be several days' walk from a clinic you may need to do some self-diagnosis.

Dr David Schlim, the medical director of CIWEC clinic in Kathmandu, produces an excellent pamphlet (*Understanding Diarrhea in Travelers*) which is available at the clinic.

Bacterial diarrhoea
Also known as 'travellers' diarrhoea' (since it's the most common form of diarrhoea in travellers) this is caused by a change in diet. Even in the West your diet includes some bacteria but these are recognised by your body and so do not cause a reaction. Foreign bacteria may result in a bout of diarrhoea.

Symptoms Loose stools that may be frequent and watery, sometimes accompanied by vomiting, abdominal pain and fever. There may be some blood, pus or mucus in the stools.

Treatment Since it often goes away by itself, you should leave well alone for the first few days but drink plenty of fluids. It's most important not to become dehydrated. Oral Rehydration Solution (*Dialoryte/Jevan Jal* etc) can be useful; Coke or Pepsi (sugar-rich) are also good but get the fizz out first. If you feel you want to eat, stick to a plain diet (boiled rice or dry biscuits). If there is no improvement after five days, take 400mg Norfloxacin every 12 hours for three days.

Giardia
A single-celled parasite (*Giardia lamblia*), three times the size of the red blood cell, causes this unpleasant diarrhoeal disease. It's unpleasant not only for the sufferer but also for his or her companions since symptoms include 'rotten egg' burps and wind. Although other travellers may lead you to believe otherwise, it's not nearly as common as bacterial diarrhoea.

Symptoms As well as foul smelling burps and frequent wind, other uncomfortable symptoms include a gut that rumbles like an underloaded washing-machine producing only a few loose motions each day.

Treatment Take four 500mg Tiniba (a total of 2g) all at once. This single dose treatment is effective in 90% of cases. Don't mix this with alcohol.

Amoebic dysentery
There are several different species of amoeba that cause infection and symptoms but amoebic dysentery occurs rarely in trekkers.

Symptoms These vary from occasional loose stools and abdominal pain that occur in cycles (clearing up after a few days - then returning) to frequent and sometimes bloody diarrhoea. The result is weight loss and extreme fatigue.

Treatment Since the treatment involves a large dose of a powerful drug, it would be best to seek medical opinion and, if possible, a stool test rather than relying on self diagnosis. If it is established that you have amoebic dysentery, the treatment is 2g (4 x 500mg tablets) of Tiniba daily for three days.

ACUTE MOUNTAIN SICKNESS (AMS)

In the late 1960s and early 1970s, when trekkers in Nepal could be numbered in hundreds rather than in tens of thousands, about ten trekkers a year died from AMS in the country. Now that so much more is known about this sickness there are only one or two AMS-related deaths each year here. Given, however, that AMS is entirely preventable if certain precautions are taken, this is one or two lives lost unnecessarily.

The important thing to remember is that it is the speed of ascent not the altitude itself that causes AMS. The body takes several days to adapt to an increase in altitude. The higher you go above sea-level, the lower the barometric pressure, resulting in less oxygen reaching your lungs with each breath you take. At 2500m/8202ft it's about 25% lower but up to this altitude the effects of the altitude are rarely felt; at 5416m/17,769ft (the Thorung La, high point on the Annapurna Circuit trek) the pressure is almost 50% lower.

Prevention

● **Don't exceed the recommended rate of ascent** To prevent AMS you must not ascend too quickly since your body needs time to become accustomed to the thinner air. You should take two to three nights to reach 3000m or 10,000ft and spend the subsequent nights at about 300m or 1000ft above the previous night's altitude. After each 900m or 3000ft gain in altitude above 3000m or 10,000ft you should have a rest day and spend two nights (rather than one) at the same altitude.

It should be stressed that this is the absolute maximum rate of ascent and that even if you do not exceed it you may still get some symptoms of mild AMS since people adapt at different rates. Some doctors recommend taking three nights to reach 3000m or 10,000ft and then ascending 300m or 1000ft for only the first two days above 3000m or 10,000ft (ie to 3600m or 12,000ft) and thereafter only 150m or 500ft a day.

You should also be aware that being young and fit is no advantage against AMS. In fact, these people are probably more likely than older trekkers to get AMS symptoms since they are able to walk further and higher each day. Men and women are almost equally likely to get AMS.

● **Drink plenty of liquids** Try to drink at least four litres of liquid (water, tea, soup etc) per day at altitude. Passing large amounts of clear-coloured urine is a good sign that your body is adapting to the altitude. If your urine is dark yellow or orange coloured you are becoming dehydrated. Avoid alcohol at altitude.

● **Eat well** You should eat a diet that is rich in carbohydrates (potatoes, chapattis, pancakes, sugar etc). You may lose your appetite at altitude but it's important to try to eat even so; your body's energy consumption is probably far higher than usual.

● **Avoid over-exertion** Take the steep hills slowly at altitude, giving yourself adequate rest-breaks at frequent intervals.

● **Look out for symptoms of AMS** as listed below and take the required action. In Manang (on the Annapurna Circuit trek) there are afternoon lectures at the Himalayan Rescue Association Health Post which are worth attending.

If you feel ill, unless you know that whatever is causing your symptoms is definitely not AMS, the best advice is to assume that it is. The symptoms may be divided into two groups: mild/benign AMS and serious/malignant AMS. In both cases descent brings immediate relief of symptoms.

● **Using Diamox** There seems to be much debate in the medical profession over whether drugs like acetazolamide (Diamox) should be taken to prevent AMS. They are not effective in all cases but may be worth considering if you have had problems acclimatising in the past. Diamox is widely available in Nepal.

Symptoms & treatment

● **Mild/benign AMS - Don't go higher!** The symptoms of this primary stage of AMS are not dangerous in themselves but provide vital early warnings that must not be ignored. They include: **headache** (which may get worse during the night), **nausea** and **loss of appetite**, **difficulty in sleeping** (note that it could be dangerous to take sleeping-pills) and **light-headedness**.

If you experience any of these symptoms and they do not go away you should not go higher but spend a rest day at the altitude you've reached. If they get worse you should descend. This may not need to be all the way down to the previous lodge: only a few hundred metres lower may make all the difference.

● **Serious/malignant AMS - Descend immediately!** There are two types of serious AMS: high altitude cerebral oedema (swelling of the brain) and high altitude pulmonary oedema (where fluid builds up in the lungs). Both can be fatal.

Symptoms include extreme **tiredness**, **loss of co-ordination**, **delirium** and eventual **coma**, painful **headache**, frequent **vomiting**, **cyanosis** (blueness of the lips), **shortness of breath**, **coughing attacks** producing pink, brown or white sputum, **bubbling breath** or **rapid heartbeat at rest** (110 or more beats per minute).

Recognising the signs of serious AMS may be very difficult since your judgment can be affected. It's very important to let other people know how you feel and watch for symptoms of AMS in them. If you're travelling with porters this goes just as much for them as for your foreign companions. Don't think that they're 'naturally acclimatised' since some may have been recruited from the plains and have no experience of mountains.

Immediate descent to a lower altitude is of paramount importance. The patient may need to be carried by porters or on a horse or yak. If you're trekking with a group it's important that the interests of the patient are put above the group's schedule. There have been cases where AMS sufferers died being carried over high passes so as not to disrupt a group's schedule.

If you are trekking above Manang try to make for the Himalayan Rescue Association's Health Post in the town. As well as several drugs used in the treatment of AMS, they also have a Gamow Bag. Patients are zipped into this large air-proof bag and it is then inflated using a foot-pump. This increases the pressure inside the bag to simulate a lower altitude.

Visit the Himalayan Rescue Association in Kathmandu for further information about AMS.

CARE OF FEET, ANKLES & KNEES

A twisted ankle, swollen knee or a septic blister on your foot could ruin your trek so it's important to take care to avoid these.

Choose comfortable boots with good ankle support. This is particularly important if you're doing one of the longer treks. Avoid trekking in the dark and don't carry too heavy a load. Wash your feet and change your socks regularly. During lunch stops take off your boots and socks and let them dry in the sun. Attend to any blister as soon as you feel it developing.

Blisters

There are a number of different ways to treat blisters but prevention is far better than cure. Stop immediately you feel a 'hot spot' forming and cover it with a piece of moleskin or Second Skin. One trekker suggests using the membrane inside an egg-shell as an alternative form of Second Skin.

If a blister does form you can either burst it with a needle (sterilised in a flame) then apply a dressing or alternatively build a moleskin dressing around the unburst blister to protect it.

Sprains
You can lessen the risk of a sprained ankle by wearing boots which offer good ankle support and by watching where you walk. If you do sprain an ankle, cool it in a stream and keep it bandaged. If it's very painful you may need to stop for a few days and rest with your leg up and bandaged. Aspirin is helpful for reducing pain and swelling.

Knee problems
These are most common after long stretches of walking down-hill. It's important not to take long strides as you descend; small steps will lessen the jarring on the knee. It may be helpful to wear knee supports for long descents (eg Thorung La to Muktinath), especially if you have had problems with your knees before.

OTHER HEALTH PROBLEMS

Bedbugs and scabies
You'll probably only have problems with these night-time companions if you borrow quilts or blankets in the lodges. If you don't use a sheet-sleeping bag with a rented sleeping-bag there's a slight chance of scabies.

Bed-bugs may disturb your sleep and leave rows of itchy bites but they tend not to hitch a ride in your sleeping-bag when you leave since there's nowhere to hide. The tiny mites that cause scabies, however, are difficult to shake out of a sleeping-bag. They cause trails of little itchy red bites all over the body and you'll need to visit a health post for some scabies powder, wash all your clothes and air your sleeping-bag in the sun.

Boils
Staphylococcal skin infections cause painful pus-filled boils that may erupt on any part of the body. They're most common during the monsoon period and require antibiotic treatment. Visit a clinic in Kathmandu after your trek.

Constipation
Surprising as it may seem, constipation does affect some trekkers, although it's not nearly as common as diarrhoea.

The trekking diet can contain fairly large quantities of the roughage necessary to prevent constipation so more likely causes are dehydration (you can't drink too much) and psychological problems associated with the lack of Western plumbing!

The problem usually resolves itself without recourse to laxatives. If constipation occasionally troubles you, however, it might be helpful to bring laxatives with you. Some people recommend drinking several cups of coffee first thing in the morning to get the bowels moving.

Coughs and colds
These are common in Nepal and many trekkers succumb to them. Aspirin can be taken for a cold; lozenges containing anaesthetic are useful for a sore throat, as is gargling with warm salty water or TCP. Drink plenty.

A cough that produces mucus has one of a number of causes; most likely are the common cold or irritation of the bronchi by cold air which produces symptoms that are similar to flu. It could, however, point to AMS. A cough that produces thick green and yellow mucus could indicate bronchitis. If there is also chest pain (most severe when the patient breathes out), a high fever and blood-stained mucus, any of these could indicate pneumonia, requiring a course of antibiotics. Seek the advice of a doctor.

Exposure
Also known as hypothermia, this is caused by a combination of not wearing enough warm clothes against the cold, exhaustion, high altitude, dehydration and lack of food. Note that it does not need to be very cold for exposure to occur. Make sure everyone (porters included) is properly equipped.

Symptoms of exposure include a low body temperature (below 34.5°C or 94°F), poor co-ordination, exhaustion and shivering. As the condition deteriorates the shivering ceases, co-ordination gets worse making walking difficult and the patient may start hallucinating. The pulse then slows and unconsciousness and death follow shortly.

Treatment involves thoroughly warming the patient quickly. Find shelter as soon as possible. Put the patient into a sleeping-bag with hot water bottles (use your drinking water bottles). Another person should get into the sleeping-bag with the patient to warm him or her up.

Frostbite
The severe form of frostbite that affected Maurice Herzog on the 1950 Annapurna expedition (he lost all his fingers and toes) rarely happens to trekkers. You could, however, be affected if you get stuck or lost in the snow on a high pass such as the Thorung La. Ensure that all members of your party are properly kitted out with thick socks, boots, gloves and woolly hats.

The first stage of frostbite is known as 'frostnip'. The fingers or toes first become cold and painful, then numb and white. Heat them up on a warm part of the body (eg an armpit) until the colour comes back. In cases of severe frostbite the affected part of the body becomes frozen. Don't try to warm it up until you reach a lodge/camp. Immersion in warm water (40°C or 100°F) is the treatment. Medical help should then be sought.

Gynaecological problems
Periods may become irregular or even stop altogether but this should not cause concern. The menstrual cycle may be upset by travel and the strenuous exercise required on some treks.

If you have had a vaginal infection in the past it would be a good idea to bring a course of treatment in case it recurs.

Haemorrhoids
If you've suffered from these in the past bring the required ointments or suppositories with you since haemorrhoids can flare up on a trek, particularly if you get constipated.

Leeches
The fear of leeches amongst first-time trekkers seems to be out of all proportion to reality. They are not several inches long, they can't give you anaemia, Aids or any other disease. In the main trekking seasons you rarely see leeches.

They come out in force during the monsoon and are particularly numerous in the rhododendron forests around Ghorepani in the Annapurna region. They crawl up your boots and on to your feet and legs where they take their fill of blood before dropping off.

To remove a leech apply salt, iodine or a lighted cigarette.

Snowblindness
It's important to wear sunglasses when walking through snow to prevent this uncomfortable, though temporary, condition. Ensure everyone in your group,

including porters, has eye protection. The cure for snow-blindness is to keep the eyes closed, lying down in a dark room. Eye-drops and aspirin can be helpful.

If you lose your sunglasses a piece of cardboard with two narrow slits (just wide enough to see through) will protect your eyes.

Sunburn
Protect against sunburn by wearing a hat, sunglasses and a shirt with a collar that can be turned up. At altitude you'll also need sunscreen for your face.

AFTER YOUR TREK

Any leftover medicines and bandages that you may have will be welcomed at the Himalayan Rescue Association in Kathmandu. If they don't need them they can redistribute them to other charities in Nepal that do.

If you get ill after you've returned home it's vital to let your doctor know that you've been abroad. There have been cases where a serious illness picked up abroad has been misdiagnosed and wrongly treated leading to the death of the patient.

Note that if you've been taking anti-malarials it's most important to continue the course for four to six weeks after you leave a malarial region.

APPENDIX D: FLORA & FAUNA

The flora and fauna of the Annapurna region are particularly diverse, largely the result of wide variations in altitude and climate. An outline is given below; for more information consult the identification guides mentioned on p43.

FLORA

Sub-tropical plants are found at altitudes of around 1000m (eg Pokhara), where trees include the chestnut, schima, alder, chir pine and cotton tree.

In the temperate zone (2000-3000m) there are forests of broad-leafed trees such as rhododendron, conifers (spruce, silver fir, deodar, Himalayan cypress, hemlock) and a variety of oaks. In high damp areas bamboo is found.

Some conifers (silver fir, blue pine) grow also in the lower regions of the sub-alpine zone (3000-4200m). Birch and juniper are found in the upper regions. In the alpine zone (4200m and above) there is juniper and alpine grassland, with a wide diversity of flowers including primula, saxifrage, buttercups, gentian and edelweiss.

MAMMALS

Domestic animals you will see include water buffalo, mules and horses and, at higher elevations, yaks.

Although wild mammals are varied in this region, they are not frequently encountered by trekkers. You may, however, see the long-tailed grey langur (Hanuman monkey) and, on the route to the Sanctuary, the vole-like mouse hare (Royle's pika). You might catch a flash of the yellow-throated marten but you're unlikely to see the (nocturnal) red panda, the rare snow leopard and Himalayan musk deer. The barking call of the Indian muntjac (barking deer) is occasionally heard and the tahr (wild goat), goat-antelopes such as the goral and serow, and the bharal (blue sheep, main prey of the snow leopard) may sometimes be seen.

BIRDS

The avifauna of Nepal is extremely rich with more than 800 species having been recorded within the borders of this small country. In the Annapurna Conservation Area alone, 441 species have been identified. (See p13 for agencies that operate bird-watching treks here).

The following information was supplied by Simon Cohen (UK).

Trekkers can't fail to notice the wealth of birdlife in the Annapurna region. This account concentrates on the species that are easy to see and to identify. Although examined by habitat along the route to the Annapurna Sanctuary the information is transferable to corresponding areas within the region.

For a bird-watching trek, the size and weight of binoculars are important considerations; I'd recommend taking a good quality pair of 8x30 binoculars. Larger objective lenses make the binoculars too bulky, while higher magnifications with objective lenses below 40mm make them too dark. You'll also need a notebook and identification guide (see p43).

Pokhara and Phewa Tal
The numerous lodges and restaurants here have been built amongst pre-existing farms and many of the birds you see are typical of rural Nepal. Tree sparrow, jungle myna, pied bush-chat, magpie robin, red-vented bulbul and common swallow are all easy to spot around the town. The flowering trees and shrubs in the gardens of the lodges attract grey-headed myna, blue-throated barbet, warblers like the diminutive tailor bird and the golden oriole. In the surrounding farmland you may see black-headed shrike, black drogo and stone-chat.

The lake and its banks provide important habitat for a number of species. Most obvious are the white egrets that can be seen flying back and forth across the water, feeding in the shallows or roosting in the large trees along Lakeside. Three species are found: the cattle egret, the little egrets and the smaller, browner paddybird. Pied kingfisher are common but the shyer common kingfisher is generally seen only beside smaller streams. On the open water of the lake there are dabchick and coot.

Hillside villages
In Ghandruk, Chomrong and other hillside villages, the clusters of slate-roofed houses set amongst the terraced rice and corn fields offer a home to a similar range of birds as are found in the rural areas of Lakeside. Common myna, red-vented bulbul, dark grey bush-chat are numerous around the edges of the fields. Himalayan tree-pie, black-headed sibia and Himalayan greenfinch may be seen amongst the scrub around the paddies, while the streams attract grey wagtails and black redstarts. Overhead, Nepal house martins glide, catching insects to take back to their nests under the eaves of village houses.

Bamboo forest
Not generally good bird-watching country, bamboo forest is dense, dark and can be extremely wet. You tend to spend more time watching your feet than the birds and you'll certainly hear more than you see. The most likely birds that you'll come across are the noisy laughing thrushes; their cackling and squealing calls are most entertaining. The white-throated laughing thrush is the most common of the eleven species that occur in the Annapurna Conservation Area.

Mixed forest
The mixed forest in the region (between Chomrong and Ghorepani, for example) comprises a great variety of trees, with different areas dominated by rhododendron, oak, chestnut and sometimes deodar. The forest may appear devoid of birdlife but this can change within minutes as large mixed feeding flocks sweep

though the trees in 'bird waves', consisting mainly of warblers and tits. The more easily identified species are the black-faced warbler, grey-headed flycatcher, yellow-bellied fantail, as well as green-backed, coal and grey tits. You may also see the treecreeper, and the Darjeeling pied or golden-backed woodpeckers. With luck you may cross paths with two or three 'bird waves' in a day.

In winter the Himalayan monal (Danphe), the colourful pheasant that is Nepal's national bird, descends to the forests from its summer habitat above the treeline. Not often seen, the crimson horned pheasant (the satyr tragopan but confusingly called 'monal' in Nepali) is found as high as 3800m in summer but comes down to the rhododendron forests in winter.

Above the treeline
At altitude the forests begin to thin, giving way first to sparse birch woodland, then to dwarf willow and juniper scrub, and eventually to rough grassland. The birch and scrub (eg above Hinko Cave) attracts flocks of black tits as well as mixed flocks of red-headed bullfinch, Himalayan greenfinch and rosefinch. Their place is taken by blue-fronted redstart, Northern wren and Tickell's leaf warbler as the birch disappears, leaving thick growths of willow and juniper.

By around 3500m or 11,500ft, the higher altitude species like the plain mountain finch join the rosefinches and wrens amongst the dense scrub (below the Machhapuchhre weather station, for example). Above 4000m or 13,000ft (eg around Annapurna Base Camp) only the hardiest species remain: the plain mountain finch, pipit, blue-fronted redstart and hill pigeon. In autumn trekkers may find the very tame Alpine accentor around Base Camp. Another winter visitor, although much more elusive, is the wallcreeper which may be seen on the steep rock faces above the glaciers.

Rivers
Wider, slower rivers The slower stretches of these rivers (eg near Birethanti) provide pools that are attractive to the common kingfisher; the brown dipper and little forktail are also seen. By the rivers, the alluvial grasslands often grazed by mules and buffalo are good for pied and grey wagtails, and whistling thrush.

Wooded gorges Where the streams pass through the jungle they often cut deep, narrow gorges (eg between Banthanti and Deurali). The brown dipper and little forktail are still present, the latter being particularly fond of these heavily wooded areas. Another bird characteristic of these shady ravines is the plumbeous redstart. Except in areas of densest cover riverchats abound along the streams and in many dry areas higher up. The riverchat is probably the one bird that every trekker will spot: its brilliant plumage of white cap, red belly, black face and wings, and its constantly wagged tail make it easy to recognise.

Mountain streams above the treeline In summer the brown dipper and grey wagtail move up here to feed and breed, descending to lower, less exposed areas by October. The plumbeous redstart and whistling thrush may venture up here but this is really the domain of the riverchat, which can also be found in the dry ravines running up from the streams.

Vultures and eagles
Seeing a large bird of prey cruising high over a village or circling a distant peak, most trekkers assume it to be an eagle; in fact, most will be vultures. At lower levels around the villages you may see white-backed, long-billed and Egyptian vultures. As you go higher you enter the realm of the larger king (black) and Himalayan griffon vultures and the bone-eating lammergeyer (bearded vulture).

Eagles do occur in the Sanctuary. The largest of them is the golden eagle, which hunts across huge territories amongst the highest peaks. The black eagle is easier to spot, above the forest canopy in the valleys. The crested serpent eagle can be observed hunting snakes, lizards and small mammals around the villages.

APPENDIX E: NEPALI WORDS & PHRASES

Derived from Sanskrit, Nepali shares numerous words with Hindi and is also written in the Devanagari script. For many of the people to whom you speak, Nepali will, in fact, be their second language and everyone used to dealing with foreigners can speak some English. It is, however, really worth making the effort to learn even a few Nepali phrases since this will affect positively the attitude of the local people towards you and you'll be made all the more welcome.

Learning more of the language will greatly increase your understanding of the region and its people. What follows is no more than a few basic phrases. It could be complemented by a phrasebook: Lonely Planet Publications produce a useful pocket size *Nepal Phrasebook*. The language section in Stephen Bezruchka's *A Guide to Trekking in Nepal* is good and available on cassette. In London, South Chelsea College (4 Tunstall Rd, SW9 8BZ) runs a language programme in association with Universal Language Institute in Kathmandu (tel 418599).

Nepali includes several sounds not used in English. The transliterations given below are therefore only approximate but should be understood since pronunciation varies across the country.

Namasté
Probably the first word learnt by the newly-arrived foreigner in Nepal is this greeting, which is spoken with the hands together as if praying. Its meaning encompasses 'hello' and 'goodbye' as well as 'good morning', 'good afternoon' or 'good evening'. *Namaskar* is the more polite form.

General words

How are you?	*Bhaat khanu-boyo?* (Have you eaten your daal bhat?)
Fine thanks	*Khai-é* (I have eaten)
Please give me	*..... di-nus*
Do you speak English?	*Angrayzi bolnoo-hoon-cha?*
yes/no	(see below)
thank you	*dhan-yabad* (not often used)
excuse me (sorry)	*maf-garnus*
good/bad	*ramro/neramro*
cheap/expensive	*susto/mahongo*
Just a minute!	*Ek-chin!*
Brother/sister	*Dai/didi* (used to address anyone of your own age)
Good night	*sooba-ratry*

Questions and answers
To ask a question, end the phrase with a rising tone. An affirmative answer is given by restating the question without the rising tone. 'No' is translated as *chaina* (there isn't/aren't any) or *hoi-na* (it isn't/they aren't).

What's your name?	*Topaiko* (to adult)/*timro* (child) *nam ke ho?*		
My name is	*Mero nam ..... ho.*		
Where are you from?	*Topaiko/timro dess kay ho?*		
Britain/USA/Canada	*Belaiyot/Amerika/Canada*		
Australia/New Zealand	*Australia/New Zealand*		
Where are you going?	*Kaha jané?*		
I'm going to	*..... jané*		
Are you married?	*Bebah bo sokyo?*		
Have you any children?	*chora chori chon?*	boy/girl	*chora/chori*
How old are you?	*Koti borsa ko boyo?*	What is this?	*Yo kay ho?*

Directions

Ask directions frequently and avoid questions that require only 'yes' or 'no' as a reply; Nepalis are naturally polite and may not wish to disappoint you with a negative answer to your question.

Which path goes to ....?	........*janay bahto kun ho?*
Where is ...?	.....*kaha cho*
lodge/hotel	*bhatti*
shop	*possol*
latrine	*charpi*
What is this village called?	*Yo gaon ko nam kay ho?*
left/right	*baiya/daiya*
straight ahead	*seeda jannus*
steep uphill/downhill	*bhiralo matti/tollo*
far away	*tadah*
near	*nodjik*

Numerals/time

1 *ek*; 2 *du-i*; 3 *tin*; 4 *charr*; 5 *panch*; 6 *chho*; 7 *saat*; 8 *aatt*; 9 *nau*; 10 *dos*; 11 *eghaara*; 12 *baahra*; 13 *tehra*; 14 *chaudha*; 15 *pondhra*; 16 *sora*; 17 *sotra*; 18 *ottahra*; 19 *unnice*; 20 *beece*; 25 *pochis* 30 *teece*; 40 *chaalis*; 50 *pachaas*; 60 *saati*; 70 *sottorri*; 80 *ossi*; 90 *nobbi*; 100 *say*; 200 *du-i say*; 300 *tin-say*; 400 *charr say*; 500 *panch say* ; 600 *chho say*; 700 *saat say*; 800 *aatt say*; 900 *nau say*; 1000 *hozhar*

How much/many?	*koti?*
What time is it?	*koti bozhay?*
It's three o'clock	*tin bozhyo*
hours/minutes	*ghanta/minoot*
today	*ajo*
yesterday	*hidjo*
tomorrow	*bohli*
day after tomorrow	*parsi*

Food and drink

Restaurant/inn	*bhatti*	cheese	*cheese*
Please give me...	......*di-nus*	boiled egg	*phul*
mineral water	*khanni-panni*	omelette	*unda*
tea	*chiya*	salt	*noon*
coffee	*coffee*	spicy hot	*piro*
milk	*dood*	no chillis	*korsani chaina*
boiled milk	*oomaleko-dood*	sugar	*chinni*
beer	*beer*		
rice spirit	*ruxi*		
Cheers!	*khannus!*		

chicken	*kookhura-ko massu*
buffalo	*rango-ko massu*
pork	*sungur-ko massu*
rice	*bhaat*
lentils	*daal*
vegetables (cooked)	*takari*
potatoes	*aloo*
bread	*roti*
It tastes good	*Ekdum meeto*

APPENDIX F: GLOSSARY

beni	rivers' confluence
bhatti	teahouse, basic hotel
bhotia	mountain people originally from Tibet
Brahmin	member of the Hindu high priest caste
chang	home-brewed beer made from barley or rice
charpi	latrine
chautara	rest platform/seat beside the trail
chorten	Tibetan word for *stupa*
daal bhat	lentils and rice: the Nepali staple dish
deorali	pass
doko	conical basket used by porters
Ganesh	Hindu god with the head of an elephant
goan	village
gompa	Tibetan Buddhist monastery
goth	herder's shelter
Hanuman	Hindu monkey god
jhankri	faith healer
kharka	grazing pasture
khola	stream or river
khukri	curved knife, symbol of the Gurkhas
kosi	river
kot	fort
la	pass
lakh	100,000
lali gurans	rhododendron
lama	Tibetan Buddhist priest
mandir	temple
mani	prayer
mani stone	stones engraved with mantras
mantra	Buddhist prayer incantation
momo	small Tibetan steamed dumpling
pipal	tree (*Ficus religiosa*), Buddha's 'Bo/Bodhi' tree
pul	bridge
puja	act of worship
rakshi	local spirit made from rice or millet
Rinpoche	'Precious Jewel', title given to high lama
sadhu	Hindu ascetic
shaligram	ammonite fossils found in pebbles in Kali Gandaki
sherpa	assistant on organised trek
sirdar	trek leader
stupa	hemispherical Buddhist monument
suntala	mandarin orange
tal	lake
Tara	Buddhist goddess
thangka	Tibetan religious painting
tika	holy mark placed on forehead
tola	unit of weight equal to approximately 11.5g
topi	Nepali cap
tsampa	roasted barley flour

Other guides from Trailblazer Publications

Trekking in the Everest Region (Jamie McGuinness)
The first title in the Nepal Trekking Guides series covers the most famous trekking route in the country. It is, however, through a very fragile environment and this guide shows how to tread lightly and minimise your impact on the trek to Gorak Shep and Everest Base Camp.

Written by an experienced trek leader and climber, the book includes detailed background information on preparing for your trek, getting to Nepal, hotels and restaurants in Kathmandu and protecting your health. There's a fully comprehensive route guide based on 30 detailed maps with inset plans of major villages and information about where to sleep and eat along the way.
ISBN 1-873756-08-9 256pp (+16pp in colour)   Fully revised new edition £8.95

Silk Route by Rail (Dominic Streatfeild-James)
Traversing some of the most inaccessible lands on earth, the Silk Route stretched some 5000 miles west from the ancient Chinese capital, Chang'an (Xi'an), all the way to the Roman Empire. In 1992 a passenger service was inaugurated on the recently-built rail link between Alma Ata (Almati) in Kazakhstan and Urumqi in north-west China. It is, therefore, now possible to travel by rail between Moscow and Beijing on a new route via the cities of the Silk Route. Shortlisted for the Thomas Cook Travel & Guide Book Awards 1994.
ISBN 1-873756-03-8 320pp (+16pp in colour)   £9.95

Trans-Siberian Handbook (Bryn Thomas)
The first edition of this guide to the world's longest rail journey was shortlisted for the Thomas Cook Travel & Guide Book Awards. This comprehensive third edition is packed with practical information on planning your trip and booking tickets from Europe or North America. There's information on major towns, a kilometre-by-kilometre route guide and a full history of Siberia and the railway.
ISBN 1-873756-04-6 320pp (+16pp in colour)   £9.95

Siberian BAM Railway Guide (Athol Yates)
The 2100-mile Baikal Amur Mainline (BAM) Railway traverses north-east Siberia and is sometimes known as the 'Second Trans-Siberian'. This practical guide tells you how to be amongst the first foreign travellers to visit this fascinating new travel destination. Numerous black and white photographs and 30 maps.
ISBN 1-873756-06-2 366pp   £12.95

Trans-Canada Rail Guide (Melissa Graham)
A comprehensive guide to the world's most scenic rail ride, this book has practical information for all budgets. There's a mile-by-mile route guide to what to see along the way, and city guides to Halifax, Quebec City, Montreal, Toronto, Winnipeg, Edmonton and Vancouver. Includes the Hudson Bay trip.
ISBN 1-873756-05-4 224pp (+16pp in colour)   £9.95

In preparation: **Trekking in Langtang, Helambu and Gosainkund**
                Trekking in Ladakh

_____**Route guides for the adventurous traveller**_____

INDEX